GHOSTS OF
NEW YORK CITY

THERESE LANIGAN-SCHMIDT

Schiffer Publishing Ltd

4880 Lower Valley Road, Atglen, PA 19310 USA

Dedication

For Glenn, who does not [yet] believe in ghosts but believes in me, and Jade, our little girl, who lets me share her bedroom so I can write, and for being so understanding with all the baby-sitting so I could get my book done.

Copyright © 2003 by Therese Lanigan-Schmidt
Library of Congress Control Number: 2003105261

Designed by Bonnie M. Hensley
Cover design by Bruce Waters
Type set in A Charming Font Superexpanded/Lydian BT

ISBN: 0-7643-1714-8
Printed in China

Published by Schiffer Publishing Ltd.
4880 Lower Valley Road
Atglen, PA 19310
Phone: (610) 593-1777; Fax: (610) 593-2002; E-mail: Info@schifferbooks.com
Please visit our web site catalog at www.schifferbooks.com
We are always looking for people to write books on new and related subjects. If you have an idea for a book, please contact us at the above address.

This book may be purchased from the publisher. Include $3.95 for shipping.
Please try your bookstore first. You may write for a free catalog.

In Europe, Schiffer books are distributed by
Bushwood Books
6 Marksbury Avenue
Kew Gardens
Surrey TW9 4JF England
Phone: 44 (0) 20 8392 8585; Fax: 44 (0) 20 8392 9876; E-mail: Bushwd@aol.com
Free postage in the UK. Europe: air mail at cost.

Contents

Acknowledgements

Thanks to: The Parapsychology Foundation, New York City; Joana McMahon, Parapsychological Consultation Service, Inc., Short Hills, New Jersey; Brooklyn Public Library, Periodicals and Reference Departments, Grand Army Plaza; New York City Public Library; South Street Seaport Museum, Herman Melville Library, Norman Brouwer, Curator; Works Progress Administration, Writer's Project, Library of Congress, Washington, D.C.; Vivian Schafer, Prospect Park Alliance; Florence and Murray Forman; Jeff Forman; Ed Gersowitz; Jeff Tauscher; Peter Salzman; Chris Woodyard; Arthur Marks; Val Ginter; Owen Young, Computer Dogs; Raul Guevarez; the New York City Police Department; Nick Dowen, Richmondtown Restoration; the United States Post Office; Barbara Cary; Maria Reyes-Robertson; Joyce Gold History Tours; Eugenie Martin, Roosevelt Island Research; Katie Cain; Wendy Kelly; Louisa Ruby; Nina Kaufman, Esq.; and Lindy McCord, my editor.

Introduction

I love New York City, its history, people and energy and have always been interested in/ scared of ghosts. From my early days watching *Chiller Theatre* with my father to graduating to horror movies such as *The Haunting* and *Carnival of Souls*, I have enjoyed a good old fashioned horror story, the kind that make the hair on your arms stand straight up and your eyes water from fear. Couple that with my thirty plus years of living in Brooklyn, mix it with a love of history, and the result is this book.

My first experience with a New York City haunting occurred at the former 80 Jefferson Street, a three hundred year old building next to a Consolidated Edison generating plant located by the Brooklyn Bridge waterfront off of East Broadway. The building no longer exists, giving way to high rises when it was torn down in the 1980s. But when it existed, an upper floor had more than its share of ghostly activity.

On a visit to my friend's family who lived at 80 Jefferson Street, I noted that a white dog ran by my feet. I remarked to the family that I did not know they had a dog. They said no, they did not.

Their son, a serious architectural student studying building restoration, used to keep an old-fashioned school bell by his bed. He had been awakened so often by footsteps in the night that he took to ringing the bell wildly, announcing:

"I need my sleep. I have to get to school in the morning!"

Before the family moved in, the building had been unoccupied for hundreds of years. It was said that, with its close proximity to the waterfront, the building had been used as both a brothel and saloon, a common practice in those days, seeing more than its share of violence at regular intervals.

An auditory haunting I experienced took place at Kane Street, in the Cobble Hill section of Brooklyn where I used to live. I passed an iron fence in front of old carriage house, circa 1850s, now a residence.

I heard an otherworldly sigh or talking, as though from a child, but certainly not a visible child.

My interest in ghost history of New York City began with a haunted walking tour of Greenwich Village sponsored by Sidewalks of New York. I started collecting newspaper stories of hauntings, up until recently relegated to the Halloween issues, as opposed to the turn of the century papers when ghost sightings were reported in the newspapers alongside the rest of the news.

Given New York City's history, legends and quirks, *Ghosts of New York City* was a book "dying" to be written by someone with (once) good enough eyes to scan one hundred year old newspapers on microfilm, or 150 year old books not on microfilm, courtesy of the Herman Melville Library, a little known gold mine, curated by Norman Brouwer, who maintains a grand collection of New York City folklore and maritime books.

Research was laborious but fascinating. Photographing the sites of the hauntings in the five boroughs of New York City – Manhattan, the Bronx, Brooklyn, Queens, and Staten Island – involved all mass transit: subways, busses, ferries, and most of all, walking. Keeping up with New York's geographics was always a challenge. For instance, Brooklyn and Queens were once part of Long Island until their separate incorporations in the late 1800s. So, stories listed for say, Maspeth, Long Island, actually take place in Maspeth, Queens.

Probably the most fun was visiting the many sites. I had never been to Van Cortlandt Park in the Bronx and enjoyed my visit to the Van Cortlandt Manor House, even if it was on the last stop on the #1 train.

Whether it be a seventeenth century Jewish cemetery on the Lower East Side; Richmondtown Restoration, the Staten Island recreation of an eighteenth century village; or Tottenville in Staten Island, the last stop on their subway, where the scent of the sea fills the air, New York City is always a great town to explore. Many sites I could walk to from my home in Park Slope, including those in Carroll Gardens, Brooklyn Heights, Ft. Greene, Clinton Hill, and Green-Wood Cemetery.

I have taken literary license to include certain stories that do not specifically identify the exact location of the haunting, such as in the case of Henry Ward Beecher, because I feel that they still have enough pertinence due to their historical or architectural importance. The same applies to the haunting of sites that no longer exist, such as the old Metropolitan Opera House, which have a chapter devoted to them ("Ghosts without a Home").

Then there is the New York City subway system. While the subway's parent company, the Metropolitan Transportation Authority is close mouthed about hauntings, there are "ghost stations," stops no longer used, that glitter out of the darkness with ancient graffiti as you pass through the tunnels. As such, I have taken literary license with the stories in the underground world of the New York City subway system.

Blue Guide New York is a wonderful resource guide for the City of New York, providing much of the background information for the historical/architectural significance for many of the sites.

If you have a story to add, please contact me through the publisher. And if you plan to visit any of the sites mentioned in *Ghosts of New York City*, please, many are private homes and/or historic sites, so be sure to show proper respect. (In the case of historic sites, please visit often, as they need our financial support – now more than ever.)

Rock Kenyon, who leads a popular tour of haunted spots in New York City for the Discovery Center, an adult-education program in Manhattan, stated in a *New York Times* article:

"I think there are more ghosts in this City than almost anywhere else...more people were attached to this City in life."

—Therese Lanigan-Schmidt
March, 2003

The World Trade Center Disaster

On September 11, 2001, two planes highjacked by terrorists smashed into both the North and South Towers of the World Trade Center. Both towers subsequently collapsed, taking thousands to their deaths (at last count, almost 3,000). As of this writing, the final designs have been approved for the new building of the World Trade Center that would also commemorate not only those who could not escape the World Trade Center, but also numerous rescue workers – police, emergency medical personnel, and especially the New York City fireman – who lost 342 of their men, alone.

The downtown business district of Manhattan lost six buildings, and seventeen were damaged. The Greek Orthodox Church that stood proudly in front of the towers is no more, and Trinity Church, closed for toxic cleanup, has since reopened.

I have visited the former World Trade Center site three times, as close as you were allowed. Once I paid a visit in my capacity as a writer, another time to visit my ophthalmologist on Broadway and the last to view the lights put up in commemoration of the six-month anniversary of the destruction of the towers.

It was a horrific site. In the years to come, when the new towers are erected, the mass graveyard that essentially exists at "Ground Zero" now will yield myriad ghost stories. But this is premature to speculate about at this time, out of respect for the families and friends of those who perished in that ghastly attack.

I only hope an adequate memorial is erected to commemorate the second greatest loss of life ever witnessed on American soil (following the Battle of Antietam of the Civil War).

Many of the sites in the beginning of my book were directly affected by the disaster. It remains to be seen how the destruction of the World Trade Center and the loss of all those innocent people affects the supernatural – and natural – life of the City of New York.

Chapter I

The Statue of Liberty National Monument

Statue of Liberty. Photo: Giselle Ruiz

We begin with the Statue of Liberty, the first electrically lit lighthouse in the United States (serving as such until 1903). For many immigrants, the Statue of Liberty was their first sight of America. Originally the Statue sat on what was called Bedloe's ("Bedlow's") Island, later re-named Liberty Island. A gift from France sculpted by Frederic-Auguste Bartholdi, the Statue of Liberty was dedicated in 1886.

Four years after the erection of the Statue, the island was considered a location for a planned immigration station which was eventually placed on nearby Ellis Island.

Before the Revolutionary War, the original Bedloe's Island was used as a quarantine station for smallpox. In 1800, the government acquired it to build an 11-point, star-shaped military installation called Fort Wood, named after a hero of the War of 1812. The pedestal of the Statue is framed by and the statue rises above the filled-in walls of the old fort.

According to the book, *Ghostly Beacons: Haunted Lighthouses of North America*, the phan-toms of Bedloe's Island are said to roam around those ancient walls — a Fort Wood sergeant named Gibbs and a recruit named Carpenter.

Sgt. Gibbs was assigned to Fort Wood in 1825. Every year into his duty there, he and Pvt. Carpenter sought to find the treasure which was said to be buried somewhere around the Fort — by Captain Kidd.

Pirate William Kidd left treasures, corpses, and ghosts everywhere. Kidd spent about four years living in New York City, and even had a pew reserved for him at Trinity Church. There is evidence that some of his ill-gotten wealth was secreted in or around the harbor. For nearly two centuries after Kidd's execution in 1701, a story was told on Bedloe's Island that indirectly involved Captain Kidd and the ghosts he was said to have left behind.

Gibbs and Carpenter began their quest with a visit to a psychic in New York who told them to look for a large, flat rock on the island, wait for the full moon, and employ a witch hazel divining rod to pinpoint the treasure. One such night, the soldiers ventured from their barracks to come upon the biggest, flattest rock they had discovered on the island.

Sgt. Gibbs walked slowly upon the pebbly beach, divining rod in hand. Suddenly, the branch dipped. The treasure was beneath his feet. It was an easy dig into the sand and stones. A few feet down, more substantial ground was reached, and about five feet under, the shovel clunked on something solid.

To their astonishment, they gazed upon a chest. So as not to arouse the suspicions on the sentries posted along the walks of Fort Hood, they kept their excitement to themselves. As they prepared to bring the box up, the two men were shaken to their very souls by a brilliant flash, a powerful pressure, and a frightening figure.

It was, they later claimed, the ghost of a dead pirate risen from its grave next to the treasure chest. Legend has it that pirate captains always killed one or two crewmen and dumped their bodies in the same cavity as a treasure chest so the ghosts of the deceased seaman would forever guard the booty.

Gibbs and Carpenter's shrieks at the sighting of the unearthly ghost-guardian caught the attention of the fort's sentries, who hurried to the beach and the would-be treasure hunters. The sentries found Gibbs in a pool of water, knocked unconscious. Carpenter was captured as he ran from the hole he had helped dig.

Because they were beyond the walls of the fort without permission, they were turned over to the sergeant-at-arms. They told him their story of how a demonic figure rose from the soil, breathed sulfuric fumes, and glided along the ground in a menacing fashion. Both swore it was the specter of a dead pirate, disturbed by their digging and hell-bent on protecting the treasure.

Although their individual descriptions of the figure were different, each man was more than willing to sign an affidavit attesting to their experience of seeing the ghost of the pirate forever protecting his treasure chest.

Chapter II

The South Street Seaport & Lower Manhattan

From the early days of colonization, New York City's maritime trade was concentrated on the East River, which was not as subject to ice, flooding, and the typical westerly winds than the Hudson River. In the early nineteenth century, Fulton Street was a leading thoroughfare to the Fulton Ferry which crossed to Brooklyn starting in 1816. After the Civil War, steamships surpassed the clippers in supremacy and the deep-water docks of the Hudson River were in demand.

In the mid-1960s, preservationists started the necessary steps toward rescuing the old seaport, chartering the South Street Seaport Museum in 1967 and obtaining the historic buildings and ships. As of this printing, there is a massive refurbishment taking place to the many properties now held by the South Street Seaport Museum.

Lower Manhattan is the oldest section of the City of New York.

A *Woodstock Times* newspaper article related the Legend of the Storm Ship.

In 1624, the Dutch ship *Nieu Nederlandt* deposited eight men on what is now called Governors Island. Under the auspices of the Dutch West India Company, these men were joined in 1625 by six families who transported them and their essentials for sustenance farming.

They relocated to the south shore of Manhattan, where they constructed primitive huts and a fort to defend themselves from the Indians, who, originally cordial, grew unfriendly, due to the broken treaties, etc., that followed.

Battery Park is so named for a row of cannons that defended that original fort and stood near the present sidewalk west of the Custom House.

In the days when New York was a huddle of houses on the point currently known as the Battery, and contact with the old world was semi-yearly by means of the ships that voyaged the world and made occasional stops at the Battery, the Legend of the Storm Ship first came into New York lore.

The Legend of the Storm Ship made its appearance almost four hundred years ago. It caused the entire town one evening to be put into great commotion by the fact that a ship was coming up the bay.

When Henry Hudson first set sail upon the Osage (Hudson) River, his crewmen, fed up with his fruitless search for the new world, reportedly mutinied, forced Hudson into a small boat with meager supplies and set him adrift.

There are those who say the ghost ship, or Flying Dutchman, that appears in the wake of severe weather, is actually manned by Hudson, doomed to forever wander the waters of New York, hoping to drop anchor, but fated to never be able to do so.

Ballads of Old New York further illustrates the tale of the Flying Dutchman in *The Storm Ship*, which I quote in part:

> "...The clouds roll black where her helmsman steers;
> The silent shapes on her main-deck's height
> Are of Hudson old and his mutineers...
> Up Hudson's glamour-haunted stream...
> New horror froze the cutthroat band;
> For, as the phantom closer came,
> Her ghostly captain waved his hand...

The Former U.S. Custom House

Former U.S. Custom House.

Located south of Bowling Green at the beginning of Broadway, what was the U.S. Custom House is situated on what many believe is the likely site of New York's first permanent European settlement and fort.

Herman Melville, author of *Moby Dick* and other great works, worked as a customs inspector twenty years when his books were out of print and he could no longer get an advance on his work.

After the U.S. Custom Service moved to the World Trade Center, the building became home to the Museum of the American Indian.

Ghosts have been spotted around the old United States Custom House.

New York City Ghost Stories tells us about the ghost of a young native girl and other ghosts, in the area around the Custom House.

Where Broadway begins its seventeen miles through Manhattan is where the ghost of a young native girl killed by Dutch soldiers stationed at the seventeenth century fort has been sighted.

By the bronze bull sculpture that exemplifies what some consider the best of Wall Street, the most unusual specter of Edward Hyde, a.k.a. Viscount Cornbury, has been sighted. A cousin and look-alike of Queen Anne, Hyde was governor of the then British colony on Manhattan from 1702-1708 and loved dressing in the latest women's fashions.

A "filmy figure matching his description" has been sighted at the former Custom House and nearby Bowling Greene Park (where it is said that Peter Minuit paid $24 in beads to the natives for Manhattan Island). The Park was where the Dutch conducted marching drills, the British soldiers played "bowls" (similar to bowling) during the Revolutionary War, and where one of the three Croton fountains was installed in 1842 to provide New Yorkers with fresh water, always a problem in the early days of New York City.

Broadway, Maiden Lane to Little Greene Street

Maiden Lane was named by the Dutch for a footpath traveled by local girls en route to the brook where they washed their laundry.

In the early 1700s, City limits were south of today's Wall Street area and surrounded by woods, according to a *New York Daily News* article. In 1711, a slave market was set up at the foot of Wall Street. The average price for a slave was $150, and it was not until 1841 that slavery ceased as a practice in the City of New York. The first slave revolt in the English colonies of the New World took place in that general area and was later referred to as the "Great Negro Plot of 1741."

Twenty-three slaves, outfitted with an array of swords, knives, clubs, hatchets, and muskets, and sick of the inhumane treatment by their "masters," decided on a plan to kill all white men in New York City and capture the City.

Cuffee, a slave to Vantilburgh, set fire to his master's outhouse. As citizens rushed to put out the blaze, Cuffee and his associates fired upon them. Eight whites were killed, all in the Maiden Lane area. The slaves escaped into the woods.

A squadron of soldiers was dispatched and sealed off the area. At dawn, a search commenced for the escaped slaves. Six conspirators committed suicide rather than be apprehended, and the remaining twenty-seven, including followers, went on trial and were convicted. Twenty-one were sentenced to die. Most were hung or burned at the stake, others horribly tortured.

This suffering and violent death might account for the following story of "George Ship's Ghost." Could one of the uprisers of the "Great Negro Plot of 1741" forever be trying to escape, even after death?

The "Oswego Market" or "Old Swago Market" was built by monies raised by lottery. The "Market" stood at the corner of Broadway, running down Maiden Lane to Little Greene Street on the south side and a wide carriage-way on the north side.

One of the butchers, George Ship, was an exceptional businessman. In spite of being unable to read or write and having no formal education, he successfully ran a large business.

According to *The Market Book: Containing a Historical Account of the Public Markets in the Cities of New York, Boston, Philadelphia, and Brooklyn with a brief description of every Article of Human Food sold therein,* in about 1802, an alert watchman with a belief in the supernatural had sometimes observed, after midnight, a quick-footed, mysterious specter that did not make a sound, who materialized as a horse and rider, virtually soaring over the ground. At every leap, sparks would be seen at both ends of this extraordinary vision, passing down Elizabeth Street and vanishing before the then Bull's Head [stock]yards.

In this area were also the homes and slaughter-houses of the butchers of the Old Swago Market. Some of the watchman's butcher friends proposed seizing or halting the apparition by setting up a blockade across the street where it had been observed. They collected old carts, boxes, and timber, and constructed a barricade tall enough to stop "Old Nick" (as the ghost was called), if he again ventured onto that route.

Soon enough but later than customary, the crashing heels and streaks were made out and observed, and the regal horse dashed down the haunted street. Numerous observers beheld this frightening spectacle.

Just prior to reaching the blockade, the stead and driver made an abrupt turn to the left into Bowery Lane, down Bayard Street and swiftly vanished into her stable.

Captain Kidd

We have already mentioned Captain Kidd in regard to the buried treasure of Liberty Island. But that is not the only reference to the spirit of Captain Kidd in New York City ghost lore.

In the early 1700s, according to a *New York Times* article, John Adams maintained that:

> "New Yorkers were the rudest people he'd ever met and bemoaned the good old days when gentlemen still lived in Manhattan."

Captain Kidd, a British gentlemen who resided on Wall Street prior to becoming a pirate, accumulated a fortune in gold and jewels by pillaging all the vessels he encountered. After his hanging death in London, Wall Street con men sold shares in a search for Kidd's hidden wealth.

Apparently, Kidd, ever after death, took umbrage with that.

At a downtown meeting of investors, his apparition materialized and rendered sightless all those in attendance. To this day on Halloween, Captain Kidd's "bluish form can be seen at night in the streets of Lower Manhattan, winding through manholes and keyholes, looking to blind anyone still in pursuit of his hidden treasure." [6-14]

Chapter III

The Court District

Centre Street Lower Broadway

...The Hessian...
strolled through the fields to the Collect...
A lake that was loved by the angler...
But shunned after twilight, for monsters unnamed
Arose from the depths of its bottomless caves.

As Friedrich glanced out...
...He spied in the thicket...
A form, worn and wasted and lean as a file...

And, girding the big-hilted sword to his waist,
He splashed in the lake with a curse in his throat...

Fright-stricken, the Hessian surged forward – in vain!
The Fiend of the Collect has come for his toll!

...A huge scaly arm strained his thews, hold on fold,
He screamed in his madness; remorseless as Hate
A great, evil claw gripped his throat in its hold.

The bubbles rose, sobbing, then ceased and were still;
The ripple was hushed on the shell-littered shore;
...And field, camp, and prison knew Friedrich no more!
"The Fate of The Hessian"
A *Legend of the Collect Pond*

Where the City Prison – the Tombs – the third jail located here whose name is derived in part due to its purpose and look, now snarls out upon Center Street, an enchanting pond once beckoned both anglers and swimmers in summer and skaters in winter. Called by the Dutch "Kalch Hoeck" due to the great number of shells that lined its shores, the English later named it "the Fresh Water of Collect Pond."

The "Collect," as it was later shortened, was the site of Robert Fulton's launching of the model of his first steamboat.

Initially a place of sheer enjoyment, the City gained title to the "Collect" in 1791. By 1807, cartloads of filth and rubbish were being thrown into the pond. The once shining pond evolved into a sickening, smelly pool. Eventually the mounting garbage formed a foul-smelling island some fifteen feet above the water. In 1809, Canal Street was laid out and a sewer built beneath to drain the springs which formerly fed the pond.

By 1811, the pond had disappeared forever. Or so it was thought.

By the early 1800s, the infamous "Five Points District" was born atop the covered, but still festering, Collect Pond. The book *Five Points* quoted an 1873 *Frank Leslie's Illustrated Newspaper*, stating that Five Points was, "bounded by Canal Street, the Bowery, Chatham and Pearl, and Center Streets, forming a truncated triangle about one mile square."

The Five Points, as it was then known, was so squalid that it nauseated even the most hardened-to-odors New Yorkers. The mostly wooden houses were dilapidated and stuffed with people in windowless basements or pushed into back buildings quickly built in unlit rear yards by greedy landlords.

Interestingly enough, this area, once the scene of so much suffering, squalor and crime, is now the site of Foley Square, where many of the major courthouses of the City of New York are located.

It is in this area that noted parapsychologist, Hans Holzer, detailed "the Lady from Long Island" in *The Spirits of '76*.

Maurice O. ran a workshop set in a loft on the second story of a house on lower Broadway. Holzer learned of the story by the man's nephew, a Long Island teacher, in 1971.

When Holzer and psychic Ingrid Beckman met Mr. O., Holzer explained that he needed Beckman to see if she could gather something from "the atmosphere" of his loft. While Ingrid was in the rear of the loft, Holzer asked Mr. O. to tell him what happened to him there. But first, Mr. O. gave some background to his circumstances.

Mr. O. lived in the neighborhood for fifty-five years and recalled, as a young boy, that a different structure stood on the same location. The original building was red brick with few windows. In 1920, the old building was replaced by the factory loft, but the same foundations were used.

Mr. O. maintained and repaired high-speed sewing machines from throughout the United States. Usually he did the work himself. For a time, his brother Frank helped out.

The many odd sounds he repeatedly heard in the loft did not concern him, including heavy footfalls going up and down the stairs when he was the only one there.

But still he wanted to know their cause.

Around 4 P.M. one Saturday, as he was ready to clean up and close for the night, Mr. O. walked back into the shop. Suddenly, a weighty iron saw soared up on its own and crashed to the floor, cracking in two.

Mr. O. gathered the remains and said aloud:

"Ghost, come here. I am not afraid of you; I want to talk to you."

There was no reply.

Often he would see the outdoor latch to his loft move up and down, as if someone were trying to come in. Upon investigation, no one was there. Often, he would make out footfalls in the loft upstairs. When he investigated, the third-floor loft was bolted and no one was about.

Once, when alone in the building and having to use the men's room in the hall, he was locked out, in spite of leaving the door open. With the assistance of a friend, he broke the door open.

The loft was empty which completely unnerved Mr. O.

He saw shadows somewhat in the form of humans, gray in color, that would bounce up and down in the back of his workshop and were of a banana shape.

Strangely, in the first eight years Mr. O. worked in the loft, (having been across the street for forty years prior), he had no visitations. It was only in the last two years that the hauntings began.

Mr. O. heard stories of peculiar happenings in the structure. A prior owner of the building also had a music store where he spent Saturday nights in his shop with friends, listening to music.

One night, about midnight, goods began to fly off the shelves, soaring through the air, and the whole building vibrated as if there had been an earthquake.

While this took place, the people in the store heard a great sound from above. They became terrified and notified the police. But in spite of the many radio cars that answered, they could find nothing amiss. Soon after, the owner sold the building and relocated to California.

The day after Thanksgiving 1971, Maurice was alone in the loft, working on orders he had to complete. Because it was still a holiday, the building was silent.

A woman walked into his office. He did not hear his heavy door slam which it customarily did when someone came in. As such, he was puzzled as to how she had gotten into the building and his office.

She was attired in an old-fashioned stylish dress, white gloves, and a bonnet. Her cologne was of a pleasing scent.

But what was this woman doing there?

Maurice inquired what business she had of him. But he grew scared when he saw that her face looked like a skeleton encased in skin instead of "a flesh-and-blood person." She looked to be extremely white and made no reply. He again demanded what her business was.

She ultimately said, in a distant but distinct, very American voice:

"...I used to live in this building."

She walked to the window and indicated the street.

"I used to play over there...My father and mother had a corn farm where the Federal Building is now, downtown...The headquarters of the British Army used to be across the street."

Mr. O. was too disconcerted to speculate how this woman standing before him could recall where the headquarters of the British Army stood, which had departed New York City almost two hundred years prior.

Maurice eventually gathered the nerve to inquire as to where she was going. That caused the woman to grow unhappy, even distressed.

"I'm leaving to visit relatives on Long Island...[i]n the cemetery. My relatives, my friends, my father and mother."

Maurice grew more anxious. He pretended he had business in the rear of the shop and began to back away from the counter.

"I'm going to visit you again," the lady said and smiled.

For roughly one minute, Mr. O. occupied himself in the rear of the workshop, then returned to the office.

The woman had vanished. The door was shut. No one could have departed without his hearing it. Mr. O. immediately opened the door and looked around but there was no one there.

Maurice inspected his door and the door downstairs but neither had been opened. He resumed work, and in spite of still being shaken, stayed until five o'clock.

When he was ready to leave and put the keys into the door, he smelled the same perfume again that the mysterious woman had worn. She has returned, he thought. But when he looked, there was no one about. He fast bolted the door and flew downstairs.

O.'s nephew, also a researcher, noted that in regard to the mysterious woman stating that British headquarters were located across the street during the Revolution, they were indeed across the street from the same building his uncle occupied.

Trance medium Ingrid Beckman sensed that the location had seen much tumult, that there was a man ensconced there who was menacing, very dangerous, and that someone might have been hurt there in about 1945. She felt that at that time, it was a successful location, an active site. It was part home, part business. Prior to that, a family resided there that might have been "foreigners."

Beckman felt that the man was murdered. He had come here and invested his savings and wished to build up a family enterprise. A woman connected with the story is attired in a long dress, below the knees. She may have been a child there, what befell her father might have occurred at that site and she lived for years there.

Holzer asked if the woman had any reason to stay at this location.

Ingrid ventured:

"Maybe she doesn't understand why all this has happened, and she can't accept it yet. Perhaps she has lost a loved one."

Washington Square Arch.

Chapter IV

Greenwich Village

"The Village" (as it is often referred to), was originally an Indian colony, Sapokanican, located in the approximate locality of today's "Village" when Washington Square was marshland intersected by Minetta Brook. The Indians were driven out and their land broken up into large farms.

In 1644, a group of southern freed slaves made their homes in what would become the Village and lived there for two hundred years, according to a *New York Times* article. Slowly, they began to move uptown, especially after the Draft Riots in 1863, when mostly Irish immigrants attacked blacks, falsely thinking they were exempt from Civil War duty.

Under British rule, the area was called Greenwich (Green Village), its name first showing up in the 1713 city records. Early colonists, such as the De Lanceys, Lispenards, and Van Cortlandts, controlled the country fields until the 1790s.

The City grew north due to epidemics of yellow fever and other diseases. Washington Square Park itself was once the ground for burying victims of epidemics, and "the hanging tree" still stands today, used to execute convicted prisoners when public executions were still the norm and the public clambered to be a witness to such events.

After the great land monopolies were divided up, the Village started to evolve, in the beginning of the twentieth century, into what we know today. Due to "its historic charm," the nonchalance and social acceptance of its "foreign" inhabitants who clung to the religious teachings of Roman Catholicism, and the political ways of the Democratic Party machine (Tammany Hall), the Village was a refuge for the left-wing and artistic fringes of American life.

It was a cheap and free way of life, as opposed to the grinding social rules of the late-Victorian era. Max Eastman began *The Masses* in 1910, a left-wing publication that was silenced in 1918 due to its avowed resistance to the First World War. Clubs such as the "A" and Liberal Clubs were platforms for then explosive issues such as a woman's right to vote, birth control, anarchy and free love, years before the "free love" 1960s.

Greenwich Village writers included Theodore Dreiser, Sherwood Anderson, Marianne Moore, John Do Passos, and poets e.e. cummings and Hart Crane.

When Seventh Avenue South was cut through south of Greenwich Avenue and West 11th Street in 1919, and the Independent (IND) subway merged with what was the Interborough Rapid Transit (IRT), connecting the Village with the rest of the City in the 1930s, what many considered the heyday of the Village was over, until the beatniks and hippies put their own stamp on the Village in the 1950s and 1960s.

There are many ghost stories in the Village.

33 Bleecker Street at Mott Street

33 Bleecker Street. *Courtesy of Candice Kugel, Treasurer, 33 Bleecker St. Corp.*

A Moravian burying ground was located at Mott Street and used during the Revolution.

Herman Melville, already mentioned, lived most of his life in New York City. In 1824, the Melvill (as it was then spelled) family rented a new house at Bleecker Street at the corner of Mott Street.

The following year, when Herman was six years old, a curious occurrence took place. He was attempting to crawl up the chimney as he had seen a chimney sweep do a few days prior. His mother pulled him out of the chimney by his legs and promptly sent him to bed as punishment, in spite of it being only 2 P.M. on June 21st, the summer solstice, the longest day in the year.

After bemoaning his fate, young Melvill fitfully, finally, fell into a disturbed sleep.

In both *Moby Dick* and *The Melville Log*, Melville related what happened next:

> "…[A]nd slowly waking from it…[i]nstantly I felt a shock…a supernatural hand seemed placed in mine…[f]or what seemed ages…I lay there, frozen with the most awful fears, not daring to drag away my hand…

> "[I]n the morning, I shudderingly remembered it all, and for days and weeks and months afterwards I lost myself in confounding attempts to explain the mystery."

33 Bleecker Street has been updated since the 1824 building Melville wrote about and the circa 1900 structure now houses a cooperative apartment building.

Fire Patrol No. 2
84 West 3rd Street

Fire Patrol No. 2. *Courtesy of Raymond A. Carroll, Chief, Fire Patrol.*

The Fire Patrol is an unusual department, created and financed by the New York Board of Fire Underwriters, according to "The Fireman's Legs and Other Ghost Stories." Fire patrolmen wear the essential apparel of fire fighters, but safeguard property which may be threatened by a fire. There are three Fire Patrol stations in the City of New York.

The National Directory of Haunted Places tells us that the 1906 firehouse is home to the phantom of a middle-aged fireman.

He has been spotted wearing an old-fashioned helmet and a double-breasted red shirt and seen in an attic store room, on the stairs, and in a basement coal bin. His presence had been heard, felt and seen on the top floor, but has never been hateful or menacing.

In the 1930s, a clairvoyant stated the ghost's name to be "Schwartz." Patrolman Schwartz was extremely depressed after discovering that his wife was having an affair. As a result, he hung himself from a rafter on the fourth floor.

In 1991, a fireman was awakened at 2:30 A.M. by the specter of the dead fireman, leaning over his bed, staring down at him. The patrolman broke out in a cold sweat, hollered, jumped out of bed and began throwing blows and yelling at the ghost.

Patrolman Bill Tobin related that one day he was sitting at the watch booth in the northeast corner of the Fire Station and heard someone coming down the stairs. He assumed it was his relief. But when Tobin looked over, he saw a partial form from its shoes to about its waist and that was all. He gazed at it for a few seconds and the phone rang. The apparition disappeared.

The call was from a senior patrolman who was puzzled as to why Tobin had left his post and wandered upstairs. Tobin replied to the captain that he did not leave his post nor had he been upstairs, to which the officer responded that he clearly saw a fire patrolman stroll through the bunk room.

Tobin's father told him about the specter when Bill was young, hoping to be just like his dad in the fire patrolman service.

The fourth floor is thought to be the center of the spectral activity which is used as a workout room for the patrolmen and a storage area where there was a metal-wheeled oak dolly in the back.

Tobin related that once he was on the fourth floor, and had to go downstairs. Suddenly the patrolmen heard a "grinding sound" from the fourth floor although there was no one there.

When Tobin later inspected the upper floor, he found that the 150-pound dolly had moved completely across the room, near the front windows, seemingly on its own volition.

Tobin has also heard a rap which he believed came from former Patrolman Schwartz. At night, he and others have heard Schwartz' footfalls. Many patrolmen have had their hands rapped lightly as they make their way down the spiral staircase to answer a call. Some feel it is heartening to get the tap.

Patrolman Manny has met the ghost of Schwartz in the basement of Fire Patrol No. 2.

The station kitchen was once located in the cellar by the old coal bin which was filled with very old "black diamonds." Near the bin, Manny turned and saw the shape of a man coming out of the coal chute, which was impossible – the chute was too narrow to accommodate a man's body. Still, there was no one else there, and no other entrances or exits.

Patrolman Wade McQueen encountered the ghost of Schwartz upstairs when he felt something whisk past him. McQueen turned and beheld a form in blue that disappeared.

Others like Pete Domanski, Jon Ielpi, and Bill Galloway have had their experiences with the specter of Patrolman Schwartz. Their superiors are uncertain, but do allow that these men are reliable, and that Schwartz was part of Patrol No. 2 for more than fifty years.

A *New York Times* F.Y.I. column tells us that a clairvoyant was called in to "read" Patrol No. 2 and spent much time alone upstairs. She described the phantom as about forty years of age, with graying hair and moustache, and attired in the complete fire fighting uniform of the 1920s or 1930s.

After the psychic came down to report on what she picked up, she proceeded immediately to a kitchen wall at the back of the truck room. On the wall hung an undated, nameless, old group photograph of the Fire Patrol in full dress.

She indicated, without hesitation, one patrolman in the photo and said:

"There's your ghost."

It was Patrolman Schwartz.

174 Thompson Street
6th Floor
Between Bleecker and Houston Streets

Tina Skinner faxed this story to me about 174 Thompson Street.

DeBorah Goletz was feeling lonely after her roommate moved elsewhere, so she got a puppy for companionship. At night, she would corral the pup in the living room, her own bedroom being too tiny for a puppy to scamper about in. Alone in the living room, the pup would whimper.

But then he stopped whining.

"I would hear this young girl's laugh, like giggling," Goletz related. "And the puppy would never whine when she was giggling. Like she was playing with him."

One night before retiring, Goletz was relaxing in a living room chair. She glanced directly toward the bathroom door, less than twelve feet away. On the door hook, instead of her striking pink satin bathrobe, there was an orange and white striped terry cloth robe.

Goletz rose, walked over to the robe and it inexplicably turned back into her pink robe. She summoned up all her courage and said aloud:

"I know you're here. Speak to me."

The ghost simply laughed.

That so unnerved Goletz she said:

"Never mind, I can't handle this. Don't speak to me."

And so, the giggling phantom was silent.

Goletz, crazy with fear, phoned her boyfriend and told him to come over for she did not want to be alone.

Afterwards, Goletz spoke to neighbors, an elderly Italian couple. She asked if anything out of the ordinary had happened in the building and the couple said yes – a young woman had died.

To this day, Goletz firmly believes she shared an apartment with a spectral presence.

> "...[T]here was some kind of spirit...she played with my puppy...[and]kept him calm."

Goletz left the apartment a few months after and always regretted not pursuing her opportunity at communicating with another sphere.

12 Gay Street

12 Gay Street. *Courtesy of Dennis and Barbara Flanagan.*

Scottish weavers lived on Gay Street in the middle of the nineteenth century. Later, until the 1920s, Gay Street was the hub of the Village's African-American community, in addition to being servants' quarters. And, in the wild days of Prohibition, it featured the Pirate's Den, a speakeasy where waiters were said to never give change. And you knew better than to ask for it.

Gay Street has quite a theatrical history. In the 1930s, a writer from Ohio, Ruth McKenney, had a basement apartment at #14 with her sister, Eileen. McKenney transformed Eileen's zany antics on Gay Street into the 1938 best seller, My Sister Eileen, which later became a Broadway play, a movie and the Leonard Bernstein musical, "Wonderful Town."

But days prior to the opening of My Sister Eileen on Broadway in 1940, Eileen and her husband, novelist Nathaniel West, were killed in a car accident in Hollywood.

Mayor Jimmy Walker (called "Beau James" because of his jazzy dress) ran the City in the late 1920s and early 1930s. With high-living a greater priority than mayoring, Walker would often be found in this small house along with Betty Compson (Violet Halling), an actress who lived there. Walker, after being booted out of office due to scandal, divorced his wife and married Compson in 1936.

Boisterous parties took place at 12 Gay Street in the midst of Prohibition. The basement was filled with plenty of booze, due to its being the site of The Pirate's Den, a walled-up bathtub later found for the making of bathtub gin.

Personalities of all kinds encompass the ghosts of Gay Street, including a gent dressed to the nines, a tormented foreign diplomat, and a young woman from the 1930s, whose energy was picked up by a clairvoyant.

Former residents of this building, according to a New York Daily News article, have seen a shadowy figure moving up and down the stairways. Once, witnesses met the ghost of a man in a black suit standing on the steps in front of the building. The specter smiled politely and vanished. The spirit of a man in top-hat and tails has been sighted inside the house.

This three story building is also called the "Puppeteer's Theater" because of the artist who resided there in the 1970s and gave puppet shows in the basement. Howdy Doody was born here, creation of puppeteer Frank Paris of "Paris Puppets."

Paris and his puppeteer partner, T.E. Lewis, saw three specters, including a man in a black cape, vest, and top hat. Paris also noted the aroma of violets and frying onions when no one else was in the house. (To this day, present owners Dennis and Barbara Flanigan have also detected the odor of frying onions.) The very distinct din of footfalls up and down the stairs was customary, as was a pounding on the parlor walls.

Many of their houseguests often griped of rowdy shouts from people on the floor above them, a floor Paris always told his guests was without any living souls. Sometimes, the noise of shuffling feet on the steps was followed by the sighting of dimly distinct figures.

Another psychic, as reported in a New York Times article, felt an adolescent ghost who spent much of its time on the main staircase from the first floor. The specter of a young woman, attired in what psychics said was a "summery, 1960s style clothing," walks the sidewalk in front of the house and around the corner to Christopher Street and back.

Hans Holzer, in an article in the New York Daily News Magazine, stated that when medium Betty Ritter came to gather psychic feelings, she had an immediate image of a gambling den, and people smoking opium at 12 Gay Street.

14 West 10th Street
Between Fifth and Sixth Avenues
(The Mark Twain House)

West 10th Street between Fifth and Sixth Avenues is considered one of the loveliest blocks in the City, according to a *New York Times* article. The houses run the gamut from Greek Revival to the sumptuous Italianate, from rent-controlled apartments to town house owners.

The girl who would become Emily Post lived at #12 and #18 was once inhabited by the family of sugar refiner Moses Lazarus. His daughter, Emma, and her family lived there in 1883 when she created the poem, "The New Colossus," the inscription at the Statue of Liberty base.

With such abundant architectural beauty and flourishing creativity, it is rather strange that one of the most infamously haunted apartment buildings in the City is on West 10th Street.

"Murder apartments," sites where murder has taken place, are strangely in huge demand in New York City. So enthusiastic are some to bask in the public light that they in fact opt to reside in a house that was the sight of a horrific murder or suicide.

There is a line in the movie, *The Haunting*, that some houses are born bad. That, according to *the Bible*, they are "leprus or the House of Hades."

Built in 1855, what is referred to as the Mark Twain House was occupied by Twain and his wife during the winter of 1900-01 when the house was a mansion. Twain had to give up the house because his wife could not keep up with the housekeeping. But some thought the real reason was that she had a nervous breakdown there as a result of a malevolent spirit in residence.

A *New York Times* articles relate that, in 1974, actress and psychic Jan Bryant Bartell stated, in *Spindrift: Spray From a Psychic Sea*, that twenty-two lives were lost at 14 West 10th Street, her dog went insane at the site in the 1960s, and that she saw Twain's specter in the stairwell. A mother and daughter who rented the ground floor apartment in the 1930s witnessed seeing an elderly gent with white hair in the living room one night. When the unnerved mother inquired as to whom he was, the man responded:

"My name is Clemens, and I had a problem here I gotta settle" and vanished.

"It's very spooky," related Marilyn Stults, partner in Street Smarts N.Y., walking tours that includes 14 West 10th Street. "There just seems to be something evil there. I wish somebody would have a séance there; it's never been done."

In 1987, Joel Steinberg resided there with Hedda Nussbaum. On November 2, 1987, in Mark Twain's old rooms, Steinberg was charged with the beating death of his six-year-old adopted daughter, Lisa Steinberg. He is still serving time for that horrific crime, said to have been caused in part by his drug addiction. Another adopted child was removed from their custody. (When I took the haunted Sidewalks tour, I had an uneasy, unwelcome feeling about the building and its location).

West Village
West Street

Titanic Memorial.

Titanic Memorial (Plaque).

The *Titanic* Memorial, put up in 1913 at the once Seamen's Church Institute structure on South Street near Jeannette Park, is located in the triangle created by the converging of Water and Fulton Streets.

It is sad that with the great loss of life from the sinking of the *Titanic*, the memorial is the only notice given to the *Titanic* in the City of New York. But when the *Titanic* was launched, it was considered "unsinkable" which many believe brought about its downfall.

Stories abound as to the reasons why the *Titanic* went down. Yes, the iceberg. But, in the realm of the supernatural, it has been suggested that due to the great haste in building her, a workman who perished while she was under construction was left within her great hold, and that she was forever cursed as a result.

There are also theories that her demise was due to hundreds of years of injustices done to Irish Catholics, still to this day not allowed to labor in the great shipyards of Belfast where the *Titanic* was built.

In any event, the *Titanic* was due to dock in New York, which it never did. A former hotel off West Street in the Village, once the Great Eastern, then the Christopher Hotel, was a single-room-occupancy hotel that lodged the poor, along with Jerome A. Johnson, who shot reputed mobster Joe Colombo at the 1971 Columbus Day rally. Later called the River Hotel in 1984, it was refurbished and fleetingly opened as a commercial hotel with a glassed-in French restaurant at the top, and was later turned into an AIDS hospice.

Sidewalks of New York walking tour tells us that many of the drowned passengers of the *Titanic* are seen walking the great stairs of the hospice, futilely attempting to check into the hotel that was to be the landing point after their historic voyage of the "unsinkable" *Titanic*.

11 Bank Street

At one time, Bank Street was a major financial hub. In 1798, the Wall Street Bank of New York created a branch bank on a Greenwich Village lane with no name to be used in case of emergencies (the downtown branch was threatened with quarantine for yellow fever). During the smallpox epidemic of 1822, other banks were created for similar reasons.

In 1957, Hans Holzer investigated this private house that belonged to Dr. Harvey S., an engineer, and his wife, an artist and Osage Indian. Holzer wrote about the house, built in 1832, in *America's Haunted Houses: Public and Private*.

Looking into the history of their home, the S.'s discovered that, before they bought the house, a Mrs. M. operated the building as a nineteen-room boarding house.

After the S.'s bought the structure, emptied the building of tenants and renovated, the entire downstairs was transformed into one long living room. The back door of this room opened onto a small garden, and a narrow flight of stairs rose to the second floor.

Sometimes the S.'s thought they heard a woman's footfalls on the stairs which often walked the upper floors, creating a noise like a "light hammering." Oddly, the din was heard more often in daylight hours than at night (something most ghosts are not prone to do). The S.'s were never fearful when they heard the sounds. When they would try to determine their source, they always came up blank.

In January of that year, they timed the sounds and discovered that the spectral noises kept up all day. The S.'s would often race upstairs to catch the invader, only to come across vacant rooms and hallways.

An English carpenter, Arthur B. (nicknamed Brodie), also heard footfalls. The S.'s maid, Sadie, heard the sounds too. Initially frightened, she became used to the noises as part of the house's make-up.

One February morning, Arthur was hammering at the ceiling in a top floor room, atop a stepladder that enabled him to almost reach the ceiling. Instantly, plaster and dust rained down on his head and something weighty fell to the floor.

Mrs. S., on the first floor, heard the crash. But before she could look into the reason for the thunderous sound, Brodie came to her door and announced:

"It's me, Ma'am. I'm leaving the job! I've found the body!"

Brodie thought he was being funny. What he did discover was a black painted metal receptacle about twice the size of a coffee can sporting a faded label that read:

"The last remains of Elizabeth Bullock, deceased. Cremated January 21, 1931. The United States Crematory Company, Ltd., Middle Village, Queens, New York."

On top of the container was the number – 37251. Strangely, the ceiling where the container was hidden was from roughly 1880, years prior to Elizabeth Bullock's death.

In the crematory's records, Bullock's address was entered as 113 Perry Street. Dr. S. visited Charles Dominick, the undertaker who took care of Bullock's remains. At that time, Dominick's business was located on West 11th Street, not far from Bank Street.

Dominick related what happened to Elizabeth Bullock.

Bullock was a frail woman. One day, she crossed Hudson Street, a few blocks from the S's home. A car at full speed did not see her and ran her down. She was carried to a nearby drugstore and while bystanders called for an ambulance, she died.

Curiously, when Dr. S. checked the records, he learned that Bullock never lived at 11 Bank Street. But her ashes were discovered there.

The S's grew frightened. They thought it wise to look into why the ashes of a woman killed crossing in front of Bank Street were hidden in their house. Did her unsettled ghost insist on being interred in the ground?

Upon the owners' request, Holzer organized a séance with the assistance of medium Ethel Johnson Meyers. On July 17, 1957, they attempted to contact the unsettled spirit of Elizabeth Bullock.

In trance, Meyers learned through Bullock that she wed out of her religion, a great violation of family customs at that time. Her husband, at her death, had pilfered her ashes and hid them in a nearby house. When renovations were made to the house, Bullock's ashes were secreted away in the hope that no one would find them.

Holzer inquired of the spirit what she wished to have done with the ashes.

Bullock insisted that her remains be interred with her own family. While her mother never got over Bullock's wedding outside Roman Catholicism, being entombed in a Presbyterian cemetery to appease her late husband was not an alternative either, because it might distress her family.

The answer came from the then owners of the house.

A plain grave was made for Bullock in their backyard, with an unadorned non-denomination cross above it.

The ghost of Elizabeth Bullock's was finally appeased.

35 Charles Street

The New York Daily News ran an article about the haunting of 35 Charles Street.

In a back apartment, there was once an actor who could not keep a girlfriend. Each time he brought a woman to this apartment, she would mysteriously weep.

Upon investigation, it was learned that the spirit of a girl named Mary Boyd once lived there, explained Sam Stafford of Sidewalks of New York. "She died unhappily there," Stafford reported. The actor finally had to move.

A former tenant had hung himself in that back apartment and a woman in that same apartment had been found dead of natural causes.

Could that have been Mary Boyd?

Robert Kohler, a forty-year tenant of the building, reported in a telephone conversation that he senses a presence in his apartment that he speaks to. The presence means no harm and gives Kohler solace, but sometimes it proves mischievous, misplacing personal items of Kohler's that he never again finds.

Kohler wonders if it might be the spirit of his grandmother, who sadly died, like so many women did at one time, giving birth to his mother.

Commerce Street

Originally called Cherry Lane, Commerce Street was so named due to the swift appearance of several downtown businesses due to the 1822 smallpox epidemic.

One October, Mrs. M.N. signed a lease for an old house on Commerce Street, a lovely small white house with three floors and a basement, and five steps up from the street, protected by a wrought iron railing.

According to Hans Holzer's Best True Ghost Stories, Mrs. N. adored the house. At that time, she was in the midst of a "personal crisis." As a result, a circle of friends, much younger than she, moved in.

Prior to moving, Mrs. N. met a neighbor who was surprised she leased this house. The neighbor said:

"...[W]hy are you moving in there? Don't you know that place is haunted?"

Mrs. N. and her friends scoffed at the notion for none believed in ghosts.

A few days before the furniture was moved in, Mrs. N. and her roommates met in the stark living room, made a fire in the fireplace, and sanctified the house with prayers. They were adherents of the Baha'i religion and thought this was the ideal means to establish a compatible environment in what was to be their home.

They were in the empty living room for maybe an hour, praying and speculating on their future, when instantly there was a rap at the door. Dick, one of those closest to the door, answered the knock but there was no one there. It was a luminous, moonlit evening and the street was empty.

Fifteen minutes passed and someone knocked again. Still there was no one at the door. The knocking was heard once more that night. In spite of the knocking, they moved in.

Almost immediately, they heard the footfalls of an unseen person.

The first time they heard the steps, they were at dinner in the basement dining room. The locked front door opened and closed by itself, footsteps went into the living room, circled the room, stopping sometimes, and then repeated the pattern. Dick ran upstairs to investigate and discovered no one was about. Still, they felt no fear and thought their spirit benevolent.

From that time on, the footsteps of a ghost were part of their lives. They were heard going up and downstairs, lurking in the living room but never entering any of the bedrooms. Sometimes, they heard the opening of the front door, followed by a loud slamming, but there was never anyone there.

One night, they invited a party of Baha'i Youth to stay with them. As a result, Mrs. N. had to sleep on the couch in the basement dining room.

Although she never saw anything, fright hung about her "like a thick fog." The next morning, Mrs. N. questioned Kay (who customarily slept on the basement couch) as to whether or not she had ever experienced a similar ordeal. She replied she had not.

Kay, however, a few days later, related an odd dream she had while on that couch.

She woke as the area-way door opened. Frightened, she sat up in bed and saw a group of Indians floating through the door, traveling along the dining room, drifting through the kitchen and exiting out the back door, "where she could make out their feet quietly upon the dead leaves." They paid no heed to her and "were in full war paint" [many of today's New York City streets were originally Indian footpaths].

A year later, a few of the original six roommates were moving out. One week before their leaving, Mrs. N. had to rise early to catch a train. Without an alarm clock, she asked Dick to set his for six and wake her.

Precisely at six, there was a rap at her door. Mrs. N. said thank you and instantly returned to sleep. A short time passed and there was a second rap at the door. Mrs. N. answered that she was getting up. Afterwards, she thanked Dick for waking her, twice.

He looked at her rather embarrassed for he had slept through his alarm and had not wakened Mrs. N. as agreed.

The helpful specter made sure Mrs. N. did not miss her morning train.

82 Jane Street

Jane Street is named for a Mr. Jaynes, on whose land it ran.

Shauna Lazarus provided via telephone interview this story of her former residence.

Lazarus lived at 82 Jane Street in the early 1970s, subletting an apartment from a woman who had moved in with her boyfriend.

When Lazarus would see the woman, she repeatedly asked Lazarus if she "felt safe" in the apartment.

There were frequent power outages. Lazarus' friend related that, when her boyfriend would light candles to check out the problem, he often heard noises, like tapping and rapping throughout the apartment. She would then say aloud:

"Don't want to see you. Go away."

Months later, a man was visiting Lazarus from California. He arrived at the apartment one morning at 8 A.M. and let himself in, Lazarus previously providing the keys, for she had already left for work.

When Lazarus returned home, the guest pointedly asked her:

"Why didn't you tell me you had a ghost?"

Her guest was psychic, and had seen a long-haired ghost sitting in Lazarus' rocking chair. He also picked up a feeling of harmlessness about the specter.

Alexander Hamilton, after his infamous duel with Aaron Burr, died next door in #80, which is so indicated with an historic plaque on the front of the building. Perhaps it is Hamilton who still clings to #82 as a result of his untimely death.

Chapter V

Ĕast Sĭde

Gramercy Park

Running from 14th to 23rd Streets, Park Avenue South to Third Avenue, the Gramercy Park area hosts the only private Park in the City. The gates are bolted to all but residents and their guests, the keys changed every October 1st. You not only need a key to enter the park, but a different one to leave. There are those, including locals, who take umbrage with the exclusivity of the Park.

Located in the Gramercy Park Historic District designated by the City in 1966, the Park is open to the public one afternoon a year, usually the first Saturday in May, with one exception. In 1863, troops were quartered in the park while the Draft Riots raged in the City.

The park is overseen by a handful of trustees. Children are safely locked inside the park, the sidewalk inside is cleaned daily and jogging only allowed at specific hours.

Originally swamps, what is today's Gramercy Park was purchased by Samuel Bulkley Ruggles who emptied the swamps, planned the streets and in 1831, broke up the land into 108 lots. The Park encompassed forty-two lots and homes were constructed on the final sixty-six lots. Ruggles created the Gramercy Park indenture, which originated a trust to not only govern the Park, but also the real estate surrounding it.

Gramercy Park contains the oldest existing co-operative apartment building in the City, 34 Gramercy Park East, which also featured the last hydraulic elevator, outfitted with electricity in 1994. The City's largest Victorian mansion, the National Arts Club, is located at 15 Gramercy Park South and is the City's first private club to allow women in on an equal par with men, in 1898. The 1857 Brotherhood Synagogue at Gramercy Park South was originally a Quaker meeting house.

It is at 19 Gramercy Park South that our Gramercy Park ghost story takes place.

19 Gramercy Park South
The "Evyan House"
(former Benjamin Sonnenberg mansion)

Constructed in 1845, #19 once belonged to railroad, insurance and banking baron Stuyvesant Fish. Jack Finney's time-travel novel *Time and Again* featured a fictional character, Si Morley, a twentieth century commercial artist who lived, for a time, at #19 in the nineteenth century.

But a writer would be hard-pressed to dream up Benjamin Sonnenberg, later owner of #19.

The "consummate" public relations man, according to a *New York Times Magazine* article, Benjamin Sonnenberg bought the house in 1945 and lived there until he died in 1978. Sonnenberg immigrated to the United States from Brest-Litovsk when he was nine. In 1926, he went into public relations, amassing such clients as CBS, Lever Brothers, and Federated Department stores. He carried enough weight to garner covers of *Fortune* and *Time* for his clients.

Sonnenberg thoroughly enjoyed throwing parties but not being a guest himself. A great dinner party for him might include a person of the cloth, an author, a woman of "questionable" virtue, a millionaire and a model.

In stark contrast to his glorious home, his menus were adequate, often boring. Once he held a reception for friends like Hedda Hopper and they were offered champagne and roast beef on white bread from Pepperidge Farm™, one of his clients.

The 2000 *Times* article related that later owner Richard Tyler, following a dinner party at his home, could not get to sleep. At 3 A.M., he got up and roamed through his 37-room house where:

> "[B]ehind some paneling in one of the living rooms, I found an old radio. I turned it on, but there wasn't any power. I walked away, and suddenly I heard music. Big-band music..."

Tyler checked the radio. In spite of having no apparent source of power, music was, indeed, playing.

He did not tell a soul except for his sisters, visiting from Australia, who also heard the music and remarked on it the following morning.

Tyler would like to believe that the music was a housewarming present from the ghost of Benjamin Sonnenberg.

East 26th Street
The Barker House

The Barker House, a brownstone apartment building, was erected in 1859. Its entry in *The National Directory of Haunted Places* states that its first owner, Alanda Hanna Barker, resided with her two sisters there for over fifty years.

In the 1970s, the structure was turned into a bordello and "voted one of the ten most interesting bordellos in New York," by one magazine. In 1978, the old Barker House was bought by Carole Boyd and Sandi Summer, who refurbished it for use as a town house.

Soon enough, their belongings started to move on their own. The strains of classical music were heard wafting through their house, played by spectral hands. Frequently, the heavy odor of lavender would be noted, which was not worn by either woman.

Finally, Sandi met the specter of a long blonde haired twelve-year-old girl attired in a night-gown standing in her bedroom.

The women called the American Society for Physical Research (ASPR) who looked into the paranormal happenings of the house. The result was a twenty-nine-page report stating that the Barker House was haunted, the third floor back room being the apex for the visitations.

Following the ASPR's investigation, other apparitions began materializing in the house, including a tall, thin man in 1700s garb, a man who constructs boats in the garden, a mourning woman in black, a deranged woman, and a fluffy dog.

And neighbors have beheld spectral streetwalkers trying to drum up business in front of the brownstone.

Murray Hill

Murray Hill runs from approximately Madison and Third Avenues, from 34th and 42nd Streets, and is named for Robert Murray. Murray's country home was located at today's East 37th Street and Park Avenue during the Revolutionary War.

According to an oft-told tale, following the British invasion at Kips Bay during the War, Mrs. Murray so delayed General Howe and his chief officers at tea, American troops positioned in lower Manhattan were able to flee up the West Side to Harlem Heights.

Third Avenue at 34th Street
Second building on northeast side of Third Avenue

America's Haunted Houses tells us the ghost story that took place in the early 1960s, of John Gray, successful advertising account executive, popular with co-workers and managers alike.

In the then world of Madison Avenue, white people held all the top positions in agencies. As such, Gray did not even consider disclosing that he was a very light-skinned black man "passing" as a white man.

Gray developed cancer. Due to his illness, he was not able to work in advertising. As a result, Gray took a city job with unusual hours which normally had him home in the middle of the afternoon. He passed away at thirty-three.

When his family gave him a genuine southern funeral, it became quite obvious to his friends that he was black. Gray, instead, would have chosen cremation, his ashes sprinkled over those areas of the city that he knew would not have let him live in as a black man in those days.

In 1961, Bob and Frank, also in advertising and promotion, took over Gray's former apartment three months following his death. Frank was white, Bob black.

Not long after they moved in, Frank was alone, in bed, reading a book. He distinctly heard the front door open and close followed by a man's footfalls on the uncarpeted floor.

"Who is it?" he called out.

Frank could not think of anyone who would visit his apartment in mid day.

No one answered, and the footfalls proceeded deliberately to the bedroom door. Frank heard the customary sound of the door opening and closing and the footfalls steadily marching into his room in the direction of his bed where they suddenly stopped, at 3:00, followed by absolute quiet.

Frank was frightened – he could see nothing. Soon the invisible footfalls resumed, turned and slowly walked out again, followed by the sounds of the door opening and closing once more. Frank thought it best to not tell Bob.

About six weeks later, Bob had the same encounter. Alone in bed, he heard the sound of footfalls. The door opened and closed but it did not seem to bother him.

Bob, more psychic than Frank, felt that the presence was the late John Gray visiting his old apartment. Bob stated in a hushed but distinct voice toward the invisible caller:

"May your soul rest in peace John."

Afterwards, the sound of footfalls were no more in the room. The men compared notes and realized they had identical supernatural experiences. In time, they moved out.

Three years passed. Frank was at a party in the same neighborhood when he overheard a guest talk about a friend, Vernon, who had just vacated a "haunted apartment," apparently being too scared to stay. Frank knew they were referring to his old apartment.

In 1964, when Hans Holzer investigated the haunting, the present inhabitants were a film editor and his wife. Both had experienced paranormal happenings in the apartment but decided to stay in spite of it. Holzer was accompanied by medium Ethel Johnson Meyers in an attempt to make contact with what seemed like an uneasy spirit.

As soon as Meyers went into a deep trance, she reported that a "dark complexioned" gent was gazing seriously at Frank and his old apartment roommate Bob, who had joined in the séance. In trance, Gray assumed the body of Meyers, talking in a most fervent and deep voice to his old friends.

Initially, Gray could not fathom why they were unable to see him, protesting sharply that they had not called upon him as of late. Delicately, Holzer told Gray that he had died. Gray balked at this, vehemently swearing they were all insane to even think such a thing. As in the case with many spirits, Gray did not realize he was dead.

Slowly, Gray finally acquiesced, but this did not allay his pain. He kept asking where was he to go and kept protesting that they were in his home. Eventually, all present coaxed the restless ghost to let go.

As Meyers resumed her own body, John Gray entered the next world, completely.

Yorkville

In the latter part of the 18th century, Yorkville was a little town located between New York and Harlem. Its country manors lured rich Germanic families, such as the Schermerhorns and Astors. But the largest group of Germans in the City lived on the Lower East Side, especially around Tompkins Square in "Kleindeutschland" ("little Germany").

By 1900, as scores of Eastern Europeans and Italian immigrants streamed in, downtown Germans left the Lower East Side for Yorkville. This exodus was further accelerated by the *General Slocum* tragedy of 1904.

Packed with vacationing revelers, mostly women and children from Kleindeutschland, the excursion steamer *General Slocum* caught fire and sank in the East River, taking more than a thousand women and children to their deaths. (Until the 9/11 attack, it was the single greatest loss of life in the City of New York).

Most of the surviving spouses, not taking part in the excursion due to job demands, felt they could no longer live in an area where they had lost so much. They relocated to Yorkville to be with their countrymen. In the years prior to World War II, Yorkville was a hub for both Nazi and anti-Nazi activity.

It is at 7 East 80th Street in Yorkville that filmmaker Alfred Hitchcock decided to throw a haunted house party.

7 East 80th Street

A *New York Times* of 1956 ran an article which stated that film maker Alfred Hitchcock was in the market for a genuine haunted house in which to host a party. He hired publicists Young & Rubicam to come up with a suitable haunted site.

After being turned down by the heirs of the Old Merchant's House Museum (which we will cover in the "Museums" section) who were horrified at the thought of a party at their venerable old mansion, Hitchcock settled on a "lovely old cobwebby mansion at 7 East 80th Street." The work then commenced, including setting up a coffin bar and installing spectral voices by way of a "hi-fi" located behind the drapes and oil paintings.

The following week, the *Times* reported that invitations were printed on menus done up on stationery resembling dark tombstones. The menu was headed: "Carte de Morts." Aperitifs included Morbid Morgue Mosels, Suicide Suzettes, Consomme de Cobra, and Vicious-Soisses.

The entrees featured Home-fried Homicide, Ragout of Reptile, Charcoal-broiled Same Witch-legs, Corpse Croquettes, Barbecued Banshee au gratin, Opium Omelette en Brochettes, Stuffed Stiffs with Hard Sauce, Gibbeted Giblet, Monster Thermidor, Tormented Tortillas, Ghoulish Gou-lash, and Blind Bats en casserole.

The final "nail in the coffin," so-to-speak, were the memorable desserts: Python Pudding, Morphine Meringue Glace, Fresh-cut lady Fingers (in season), and finally, liqueurs: of course, Bloody Marys, Anisette d'Arsenic, Hennessy's Heroin, Dead Grand-dad, and Formaldehyde Frappe.

There was no subsequent report as to how the guests survived the night's festivities, if, in fact, they did.

86th Street
Third floor
Front flat [apartment] on building's west side

A *New York Times* of 1936 stated:

"Banshee Turns up in 86th Street Flat."

An old empty tenement, with the exception of a janitress and "a wistful bean sighe (banshee) who walks o'night in pallid cerements," was related to the head of the Universal Council for Psychic Research, Joseph Dunninger, as a "testing ground" on the subject of hauntings.

Two weeks prior, Dunninger, in a letter to the *Times*, stated he would bet $10,000 that no one could come up with a haunted house in New York City, or within a plausible distance of the City.

To Dunninger's amazement, he received a letter from H.S. Pretty, Esq., of 1,685[sic] York Avenue, accepting the bet. Pretty stated that he had resided in a haunted house "and had close acquaintance with the bean sighe."

The house in question was an "old-style tenement" at East 86th Street, in which Pretty resided from 1924 to 1932. The address was withheld to keep the curious away.

Pretty wrote that while an occupant of a flat in the house in question, and due to many phenomenal incidents he had experienced while living there, Pretty conducted a probe, inquiring if other tenants had experienced similar incidents as to those he had encountered.

In response to Lawyer Pretty's inquiries, it was learned that the revenant [ghost] was that of an Italian women who once resided in the front flat on the building's west side, third floor.

The senior tenant, Mrs. Schreiber, resided on the top floor fourth rear, north side, when a disaster befell the Italian woman.

Schreiber related to Pretty that in 1917-1918, the Italian woman's husband shot her in a jealous rage. Schreiber's apartment was underneath the shooting flat.

Making her way downstairs after nightfall one evening, Schreiber saw the spirit of a woman floating by the entry of the building. Apparently attempting to dodge Schreiber, the ghost vanished into the wall on the north side.

Pretty went on to write that a Mrs. Moran, who also resided in the tenement, asked him one morning what he was doing at 11 P.M. the prior night. He replied that he was reading in his kitchen.

Moran said:

"And you saw and heard nothing?"

"Nothing," Pretty replied.

Moran stated:

"At that time, I saw a woman go down the hall and disappear through your kitchen door."

Odd occurrences continued to befall Pretty, especially one night in 1927.

Pretty, his son, aged seventeen, and his pal of about the same age were out for the evening and returned at 8:45. Pretty came home first, then his son, and then his pal.

Pretty unlocked the door and stepped into the kitchen. Almost in the center of dark room was the form of a woman of Pretty's own height, draped in white that hung closely to her. Pretty moved toward her, until within one foot of the phantom. Neither spoke and each was separated from the other by about two feet.

"The face of the figure was concealed by drapery, and it furnished its own light. I watched for about ten seconds and than, instantly, it was gone," Pretty related.

In retrospect, Pretty was sorry he did not try to communicate with the specter for he felt no fear. When they turned, they saw in the bedroom, heading through the floor rapidly, the phantom, which measured up to Pretty's chest.

"This my son can attest. His chum Howard...was so alarmed, he would not sleep as he did occasionally with my son in our flat."

There was much more in Pretty's letter, including the statement that the $10,000 offer for a genuine haunted house was not the prime motive for the disclosure of the ghostly stamping grounds of the "Lady in White" or vanishing specter of Yorkville.

Two days later, the *Times* reported that at midnight the night before, not only did Dunninger come to witness the "Lady in White" walk, but also fourteen police of the East 104th Street station house, who were under the mistaken impression that were hunting for "goats," along with five hundred locals who were looking for ghosts. They began collecting at ten in front of the old red-brick front building. Pretty had been there but left, unable to bear the crowds.

Dunninger entered the old building and poked around the crumbling walls and old apartment. But the Lady in White did not appear and Dunninger refused to pay up. The report did not indicate if Lawyer Pretty took Dunninger to court, for although Pretty gave the ghost story, he could not guarantee an appearance on demand for Dunninger, five hundred locals and fourteen police officers, New York's Finest.

Gracie Mansion
88th Street & East End Avenue

Gracie Mansion, the formal home of the mayor of New York City, was built in 1799, with reception and conference rooms added in 1966. Originally constructed as Scottish merchant Archibald Gracie's country home, the 16 room mansion features leaded glass, a semicircle fanlight over the main doorway, and graceful railings, characteristics of The Federal United States architecture period.

Gracie, a founder in 1801 of the *New York Post*, received in his mansion, among other notables, Louis Phillipe, later King of France; the Marquis de Lafayette; Alexander Hamilton; John Quincy Adams; and Washington Irving. Irving, in Mary Black's 1984 book, *New York City's Gracie Mansion: A History of the Mayor's House*, depicted the Gracies as "a charming warm-hearted family, and the old gentleman has the soul of a prince."

During the War of 1812, Gracie's shipping concern collapsed. Broke, Gracie sold the mansion in 1819 and the City purchased it in 1887. Gracie Mansion eventually became the home of the Museum of the City of New York from 1924-30. In 1942, Gracie Mansion was christened the mayor's residence due to the machinations of formidable then parks commissioner Robert Moses.

In 1981, Mayor Edward I. Koch created the Gracie Mansion Conservancy, which, in 1984, undertook a vast refurbishment of the venerable Mansion. The yellow wood-frame house was once again renovated in 2002, the exterior portion of the renovation running $85,000, put up anonymously, although many speculate that it was paid by Mayor Michael R. Bloomberg. Mayor Bloomberg does not reside in Gracie Mansion but in his East 79th Street town house, using Gracie Mansion for official entertaining.

The private rooms, where former Mayor Guiliani and his former wife slugged out the tattered remains of their marriage, have been opened for tours. Caroline Guiliani, the former Mayor's daughter, etched her name on a library windowpane, just as former Mayor John V. Lindsay's daughter Margie had done in 1964, and Millie, granddaughter of Noah Wheaton, the private citizen in longest residence at Gracie Mansion.

There are tales of specters in Gracie Mansion and it is no wonder. Where the Mansion is situated is somewhat secluded and gives views of the Hell Gate, a dangerous expanse of water in the East River. Hell Gate's battling tides were responsible for the wreck of scores of ships which rest on the River bottom, most notably the *Hussar*, Revolutionary frigate which was hauling a payroll of $500 million in gold and silver coins for British troops in America.

Chapter VI

Roosevelt Island

The first settlers of Roosevelt Island, a two-and-a-half mile strip of land in the East River, were thought to be the Leni Lenape Indians. In 1637, Dutch Governor Wouter van Twiller purchased the island from the Leni Lenapes. Due to the Dutch using it as a pasture for pigs, it was called Varcken (Hog) Island.

Hog Island became Blackwells Island, for the family who resided and farmed there from the late 1600s to 1828. Their reconstructed house still exists, now overshadowed by high rises. New York City purchased the island in 1829. Prisons, poorhouses, hospitals for infectious diseases, and asylums were constructed. Sadly, Blackwells Island, once home to farmland, fast disintegrated into an island of horror.

Charles Dickens visited Blackwells Island in 1842 and was horrified by the conditions he encountered. A completely opposite view was held by Clergyman J.F. Richmond in his 1869 book *New York and Its Institutions*. Richmond wrote that although the island was cut off on both sides from the rest of the world by a swift-moving current, he thought that the island's new use as a haven for the hapless and those in anguish, a site of tranquil reflection for the violent, was heaven sent.

Smallpox, once believed wiped out, was the cause of 25.4 out of each 1,000 deaths in 1850, according to the book *The Encyclopedia of New York*. In 1856, the Smallpox Hospital was erected, facing the east channel of the River. The Hospital replaced wooden shacks on the riverbanks where smallpox victims were previously quarantined.

Immigrants, wary of the City's vaccination policies (due partially to their immigrating from countries where men in uniforms usually meant trouble), were regular victims, while others carried the disease over from their homelands, resulting in the 1871 epidemic.

An 1872, *New York Times* editorial griped that patients were discharged "uncleaned," in the identical clothes in which they had arrived, spreading smallpox throughout the City. The isolation of the hospital empowered the prisoners and indigent, who acted as nurses and workers, and demanded money from the patients who had some, while ignoring those who had none.

In 1886, a new neo-Gothic hospital for quarantining smallpox victims was constructed on North Brother Island, (where the ill-fated *General Slocum*, already mentioned, steamed to her demise). The new hospital reduced the chance of spreading the contagion to Blackwell's Island population of 7,000 by the end of the century. Contractors refused to work on the southern tip of the Island, fearing contagion. The facade of old Smallpox Hospital still stands today.

By the end of the nineteenth century, the Island hosted a workhouse, poorhouse, madhouse, and a penitentiary where "Boss" Tweed did time. Another famous inmate was Typhoid Mary. The workhouse was packed and antiquated, and the prison run by the most hardened inmates who lived high on the hog, so to speak, because they were drug lords, despite their prison home.

Nellie Bly, famous newspaperwoman (for which an amusement park in Brooklyn is named for), got herself committed from Bellevue to the Lunatic Asylum to write about what she experienced. Joseph Pulitzer pulled strings and her expose came out in 1880, shocking all those who read of the horrors of the Island.

The former Blackwells Island was renamed Welfare Island in 1921. Mae West (said to haunt an apartment at 266 West End Avenue), did eight days in the penitentiary in 1927 for what was then considered risqué, a play Sex she produced and starred in.

In 1934, Commissioner of Corrections Austin H. McCormick led a raid on the infamous prison and finally wrested control from the criminals. Welfare Island, in 1935, became a haven for the old and sick, with a hospital for chronic diseases, the New York City Home for Dependents, cancer and charity hospitals.

In the late 1960s, planners for the City, loath to have so much good real estate lie dormant, began designs for redevelopment, and called it Roosevelt Island to spruce it up its image. By the 1970s, an "Instant City" was born, a planned neighborhood. Politically part of Manhattan, Roosevelt Island offered a home to 5,100 of varied economic backgrounds with 2,138 rentals, and the Roosevelt Island Tramway transported Islanders to Manhattan.

The old City Hospital, built in 1859, was the City's biggest and perhaps the United States' largest charity hospital. Following the Civil War, the Hospital treated thousands of Union soldiers, as well as the City's poor. In 1873, it cared for up to 8,000 patients yearly, with wards for the treatment of tuberculosis, syphilis, and leprosy, among other ailments. Although listed on the National Register of Historic Places, the Hospital was never granted City landmark status and was torn down in 1994.

In that same year, Composer and choreographer Meredith Monk presented American Archeology No. 1: Roosevelt Island. Performers sang and acted out the infamous history of the Island. The performance piece opened at the northern end of the Island in Lighthouse Park, where a small stone lighthouse believed to be built by an asylum inmate who feared a British invasion stands, and closed at the Island's southern end, usually not open to the public, where the spectral remains of the Smallpox Hospital offer an eerie backdrop.

In an article in the New York Times, Lynne Abraham, a spokesperson for the Roosevelt Island Operating Corporation, stated that funds collected by the Friends of the Roosevelt Island Landmark enabled the Roosevelt Island Operating Corporation to light the Manhattan side of the remains of the Smallpox Hospital at night since February 1995, giving it a spectral prominence. The entire southern end of the Island is fenced off.

The only remains of the Lunatic Asylum is the elaborate octagon tower. A New York architectural firm is intending the tower, a City and state landmark listed on the National Register of Historic Places, to be the centerpiece of new residential housing. The $100 million construction is planned to resemble the asylum as it was at the end of the nineteenth century. Finally, the site of so much suffering will be put to a better use – to house middle-income residents.

It is not surprising that with Roosevelt Island's history of suffering and madness, there are ghosts that roam the Island.

In a phone conversation with Eugenie Martin, Director of Roosevelt Island Research, who lived in one of the new buildings, Martin related that she had seen flickering forms out of her peripheral vision and felt "womped" on the shoulder in her sleep by an unseen hand. A neighbor was tapped on the shoulder and a babysitter was so scared, she performed a séance.

During the séance, the words "art is beautiful" came up, along with an image of a man "with a Lord Byron shirt," which would indicate attire from the early nineteenth century. A bearded man was "seen" chasing a woman and strangling her. Thought to be an insane artist, he tried to kill the woman when she broke off their engagement.

The specter identified himself as Carl Wentworth. Both he and his former fiancée had dark blonde hair. When he asked for wine, the woman conducting the séance demanded that he quit tapping on her shoulder. He indicated that he was placed in the Lunatic Asylum as a result of his gruesome action.

As a result of the séance, the babysitter was never troubled by him again.

Chapter VII

West Side

Soho

Soho's name is dervied from its location, "SOuth of HOuston Street." The Mercer Street area, in the mid-1800s, was filled with brothels. In the late 1960s to early 1970s, Soho was an area in which rents were inexpensive, and comprised mainly of art galleries. (My brother, artist Thomas Lanigan-Schmidt, got his start in a gallery in Soho.)

Today's Soho, like so many other formerly "funky" neighborhoods in New York City, has given way to a more expensive lifestyle, hosting boutiques over art galleries, many of which have moved into the western reaches of the Chelsea neighborhood.

Haunted Houses USA tells us that 60 Mercer Street, put up in the late 1880s, has been the site of a haunting.

60 Mercer Street
Broadway between West 8th and Canal Streets

Serving as an office building, bank, Western Union office, a series of restaurants, a retail shop and presently an art gallery, 60 Mercer Street has been visited by many psychics who report that a shining, white form is often beheld.

A calm ghost had been reported on the balcony, stairway, and in an office at the site.

There is speculation that the spirit is folksinger/songwriter Phil Ochs, who owned the Breezin' Restaurant located at the site in the 1970s. Another psychic investigator felt a presence, but maintained it predated by decades the 1976 death of Ochs.

Ochs committed suicide, when he purportedly left a note stating:

"The words wouldn't come anymore."

131 West 14th Street

131 West 14th Street. *Courtesy of Richard DeSilva, President, Desco Vacuum.*

Desco Vacuum is presently located in the storefront of 131 West 14th Street.

But in 1881, the brick, four story structure was a boarding house, with as many as thirty lodgers at a time, owned by Mrs. Mary Carr, "a widow lady."

Two scary specters busy day and night at the house were having a damaging effect on Carr's livelihood.

According to a 1881 *New York Times* article, boarders were leaving as soon as they discovered that the building was haunted, including many of Carr's best tenants. When interviewed by a *Times* reporter, she burst into tears, saying that an enemy aimed to ruin her.

The two phantoms never appeared to her. But from the time she took possession of the house, one or both specters materialized in front of the servants and scared them away. As a result, Carr was unable to hold onto a chambermaid or cook for more than a week. In some instances, the help fled the day after they were hired.

Initially, the ghosts only appeared to the servants. So Carr, grateful at least that the apparitions had not bothered her bread and butter, "kept the gloomy secret in her own bosom." Aside from the great burden of constantly having to hire new "help," no physically destructive results came from the ghostly callers.

The phantoms were said to be a man and a woman. He was tall, somewhat stooped, sporting English side whiskers, a moustache, and had extremely large black eyes, which "strike terror" to all who gazed upon him.

The woman, "a maiden lady," had a "lovely" face that was wounded by scars that showed "a life of dissipation." She was blonde, and often seen in front of the front parlor mirror. The ghosts apparently roamed freely in the apartments.

In time, the spirits apparently tired of appearing solely to the help. Wanting a change, they began to display curiosity in the boarders.

The ghostly man was seen by a "colored" waiter seated quietly at the window of the dining room in early afternoon. The waiter's hair stood on end as the specter disappeared. The female phantom did her toilette [old-fashioned word for washing up] in the parlor in the morning. Both phantoms were seldom seen together, and appeared to have no contact with each other.

Two weeks prior to the *Times* report, between midnight and 1 A.M., a gent who had been a boarder since Carr began the boarding house woke in a cold sweat. He beheld the male ghost standing by his bed, scowling down on him contemptuously with his large black eyes.

When the man tried to gain his senses, the ghost grasped his bedclothes, wrenched them from the petrified boarder, hurled him to the floor and disappeared.

The *Times* reporter noted that:

> "The gentleman is not a coward, but a visitation of this unusual character in the dead of night is not calculated to increase one's confidence in his surroundings."

In the morning, the border told Carr of his frightening meeting with the unknown. Believing it was only a nightmare, however, he paid no attention and shrugged off the incident.

But the phantom would not be ignored and returned the following two nights, until the petrified boarder quickly packed his trunk and ran fast away from the haunted house.

A week before, another man took a room. The following day, he too, grabbed his bags and left in a great rush. The male specter had paid him a call and the boarder said he did not wish "to risk a repetition of the visit."

Carr reported the hauntings to the then 29th Precinct officers who conducted a thorough search of the house. They noted that when the front door was bolted, there was no way for anyone to gain access to the house, except if theft was committed.

One night, the male ghost "played his trump card, and created such an excitement that the fact of the mystery could no longer be kept from all of the house."

The chambermaid retired at about 10 P.M. to her room on the top floor. Just before midnight, she woke to a strangely cold feeling. A fleeting light from the hall entered her room, enabling her to see large objects but nothing else.

She suddenly saw a man standing a few feet from her bed, his back toward her. The chambermaid, who had never heard about the hauntings, was terrified. "Her heart stood still," the *Times* reported. The male ghost turned and faced her. He was tall, slightly stooped, with side whiskers and a moustache, and had large black eyes. His hand was held up to his face.

The chambermaid screamed and fainted. When she came to, the phantom was still in the room, but had floated to a corner where he stood, looking at her. She again passed out and again came to. He shrank in height to half size, steadily growing smaller until he vanished.

The chambermaid jumped out of bed and ran wailing down the stairs to Carr, to whom she told her scary story. This roused the entire house, including passers-by outside, who wanted to know what the girl's screams were about, and collected about the door.

The police officer on duty was called into the house by Carr. The chambermaid sat in the basement, trembling in terror, "rocking herself to and fro." The Catholic cook sprinkled holy water on the floor and all the furniture in the house to protect against evil spirits. Guided by Carr, the police searched the house from top to the basement but discovered nothing out of the ordinary. Officer Clinge took over for Officer Chapman who also inspected the house.

They concluded that no one could have entered through the door without breaking into the house and there was no sign of forced entry.

"Spaniard" Mr. Piette, who roomed at the house, related his meeting with the ghost to Officer Clinge.

One night while in his room reading, he heard footfalls climbing the stairs. He looked up and standing at his side was a tall man dressed in a black coat and light pantaloons, sporting side whiskers and a moustache, with large black eyes. The form disappeared but Piette thought he heard it running upstairs.

After a séance was held to make contact with the ghosts, the boarders lived in total fear. Officer Chapman induced Harry Paine, formerly an advertising agent of Haverly's Fourteenth Street Theatre, to stay in the house and be on the lookout for the phantoms that Wednesday night.

Armed with a loaded whip stock [gun], "intended to test the corporeal nature of the male ghost" should he show himself, Paine came to the house and began his vigil with Carr and some of the servants.

At about 2 A.M. with no ghost appearing, Paine thought it time to get some sleep to be alert for an encounter with the specter, should it "suit his convenience to appear." Paine laid down in one of the bedrooms with his clothes on, and clenching his trusty "whip stock," dozed off into a light sleep.

Suddenly, he felt two large hands seize his ankles. With one mighty yank, he was thrown to the floor. Paine tried to fire his whip lock but was not quick enough, for as he lifted his arm to shoot, he saw what appeared to be a solid shade move through the open doorway and disappear. Paine sped into the hall and explored it, but could not discover a trace of his eerie visitor.

Aside from seeing the specters, strange noises and lamentations were heard in the house by servants and others. Often, it sounded as though a heavy body fell against a door, followed by horrible moans, which caused the scared servant girls to shake in fright.

Carr heard the strange rustling of clothes and felt unexplained currents of cold air. Once, when heading upstairs, she felt an icy hand upon her face.

Years prior to these events, another family resided in the house. One of the daughters was a young lady of twenty-four, very pretty, but being slowly ravaged by alcoholism. She was engaged to a merchant who sailed for Europe, and sadly, as was too often the case in those times, drowned during the voyage.

Afterwards, she increasingly drank more, finally dying of the effects of the drink. The young lady had a brother who committed suicide by poisoning.

Officer Clinge, who knew the young man and woman well by sight, stated that the depiction of the male phantom was that of the young suicide, and that the female ghost resembled the appearance of the unfortunate young woman.

Did the brother and sister haunt the house where their last melancholy days were spent?

There was a follow-up story in the *Times* to "The Fourteenth-Street Ghosts."

Captain Williams, upon close scrutiny, found that since approximately 1869, the house had a strange fame. It was the habit of help in nearby houses to inquire of the servants at the "ghost house" if, upon the moving in of new boarders, they had yet seen the ghosts.

At that time, the Brown family were boarders. Mrs. Brown was a spiritualist and she and her husband and their four children resided in the house for about a year.

A man, not a boarder or having any other business with Landlady Carr, was described as resembling the male specter seen in the building on different times by people "whose nerves [we]re steady." Once, a police officer followed a man with side whiskers into the house. The officer questioned a servant as to the man's business but she had no idea what the officer was referring to. Again the house was searched, but no man was found.

Many of the boarders who quickly left were not thought superstitious. One was a well-educated, "...trusted employee of Macy's." After he left, he swore the house was haunted, and nothing could induce him to ever return.

Carr utilized many "strong-minded persons" to maintain a look-out for the male phantom, and if caught, "he will not be treated very gently."

The 29th Precinct was quite busy investigating hauntings in that year, for the *New York Times* related the story of "Officer Quinns's Specter."

32 West 31st Street

One morning at daybreak, Officer Quinn observed that the basement door of 32 West 31st Street was ajar. He came in, lit the arc [gaslight] in the hallway and headed to the basement's main room. He found a woman seated at a table. Thinking she was help in the building and had left the door open by mistake, Quinn said:

"Do you know that your door is wide open?"

The woman said nothing, gathered up her skirts and walked to the door of a small pantry into which she entered. But when the officer opened the door, she was not there.

He ventured into the hall to a small room where he found a "negro girl." He asked her who the woman was.

The girl cried out:

"What! Have you seen her too?"

She reported seeing the eerie woman several times and that, as a result, had difficulty sleeping.

Captain Williams later maintained that he is not responsible for the ghosts in his precinct. They must have set up housekeeping prior to his assignment at the 29th. As for Officer Quinn, the Captain affirmed that he was "a clear-headed officer, not a drinker, and his tale of the ghost of the pantry can be completely counted on."

19 West 68th Street
Second Floor
(James Dean House)

19 West 68th Street. *Courtesy of Carmen Bonilla, Property Manager, Company Secretary, Fine Times, Inc.*

The ghost of actor James Dean calls on the second floor of his former rooming house, according to a *New York Daily News* article.

Dean kept an apartment at 19 West 68th Street in the early 1950s, even after moving to Hollywood. It was the closest thing he had to a home.

In the 1970s, massage therapist Russell Aaronson, who lived in Dean's old apartment, would often find strangers at his door, inquiring if they could see Dean's old apartment. They came to somehow connect with the ghost of young Dean. Memorandums from "Deaners" are left on the vestibule walls in French, Japanese, Italian, and German.

When Paul Alexander, author of the Dean biography, *Boulevard of Broken Dreams*, visited Dean's old "haunt," he noted that he could feel Dean's presence.

471 Central Park West
at 107th Street, top floor apartment,
northwest corner

Hanz Holzer's *Ghost Hunter* provides us with "The Central Park West Ghost."

In the 1930s, this area was (and still is) a prime residential neighborhood. As such, when Mrs. M. Daly Hopkins and her husband needed a new apartment, they headed over to Central Park West.

When the Hopkins were looking around at apartments in the area, they luckily came upon a man putting up an "Apartment for Rent" sign. He was the superintendent of the building and they took the apartment on the spot.

It was a huge eight room apartment, which suited the Hopkins fine. They needed a lot of room for themselves, their young son, and his nurse. In November, they moved in.

Nothing uncommon occurred initially, save the times Mrs. Hopkins heard her housekeeper cry out, like someone – or something – had startled her.

According to Mrs. Hopkins' 1954 *Fate* magazine story entitled, "Ten Years with a Ghost," the housekeeper said to Mrs. Hopkins that she frequently sensed someone standing behind her but when she would turn around, no one was there.

For two years, the housekeeper suffered the "unseen visitor." Finally, she could take it no more and quit, stating:

"Somebody keeps turning my doorknob...you have a ghost here."

After Annie left, Josephine, a "colored woman," was employed as live-in help. She too kept crying out in fright, the same as Annie had done.

Finally Josephine said to Mrs. Hopkins:

"This apartment is haunted."

Mrs. Hopkins had to then acknowledge that there was an "unseen guest" at the apartment. But, being a practical woman with a huge apartment in the City of New York, Hopkins said they would simply have to live with the unseen visitor.

Josephine thought they were dealing with a female ghost. So, for the next seven and a half years, she oftentimes spoke aloud to the phantom, calling her "Miss Flossie" and appealing to the unsettled specter to let her know what was distressing her.

Ultimately, Josephine told Mrs. Hopkins that she discovered why "Miss Flossie" still walked in the mortal realm, unable to move on.

Miss Flossie had killed herself.

Josephine never saw the ghost, for it always disappeared in an instant faster than she could turn to take a good look.

Interestingly, for some reason, children often can see ghosts while adults cannot. And this was the case with the Hopkins' small son, when he was four.

He was sleeping for some time that night when Mrs. Hopkins heard him cry out. Because her son's "Nanna" was out for the night, Mrs. Hopkins dashed to his room. He told her a, "lady visitor waked me up when she kissed me." The only others in the apartment at that time were the Hopkins. Their son related that the "lady visitor" looked like a doll, the kind young girls played with.

Mrs. Hopkins calmed her boy. After he returned to sleep, Hopkins informed her husband of the haunting.

It took many years before "Miss Flossie" paid another visit.

One evening, her son in boarding school and her husband out of town on business, Mrs. Hopkins was alone in the apartment. After retiring for the night, Hopkins woke to someone calling her name:

"Mrs. Hop-kins! Mrs. Hop-kins!"

It sounded important. Immediately, she heard another noise coming from above. Footsteps on the roof – a burglar! Hopkins attempted to phone the superintendent but the line was severed. She fast locked herself into the bedroom.

The next day, the superintendent told Hopkins that the top floor apartments in two other buildings on the block had been robbed that night. But curiously, her apartment was not. While the superintendent could not figure out why the Hopkins' apartment had been spared, Mrs. Hopkins knew that "Miss Flossie" had a spectral hand in it.

One night, when the Hopkins came home from the theatre, they discovered a tiny kitten mewing on their front doorstep. Mrs. Hopkins took the kitten in, thinking it was another tenant's cat, but when no one came forward to claim it, the Hopkins called the kitten their own.

But the kitten acted bizarrely from the moment she entered the apartment. Flying through the eight rooms with her fur bushed out like a Halloween cat, she appeared petrified of something.

A week later, Mrs. Hopkins was alone, reading in the evening. The kitten was curled up, motor on, snoozing happily nearby.

Suddenly, the kitten rose, staring at the doorway leading into the hall. Her eyes followed as if someone entered the room, glided by Hopkins, and eventually stood right behind her.

The cat was paralyzed with fear. Hopkins reassuringly told her not be fearful of "Miss Flossie" and the kitten finally calmed down and returned to sleep. But Hopkins felt a curious chill.

When her husband returned, Mrs. Hopkins insisted they move, their unseen guest proving too much for her. Two weeks later, they moved into another apartment.

One evening at dinner, Mr. Hopkins said he had discovered additional information in regard to their former apartment from one of the long-standing tenants with whom he had recently met up with.

At the time they took the apartment, the superintendent informed them that the prior tenants had vacated "ten minutes before." What he failed to tell them was that the Hopkins had moved in ten minutes after the funeral of the prior tenant.

The wife of the prior tenant had committed suicide in the living room.

Mrs. Hopkins decided it was time to pay a call on Mrs. Foran, who lived in their old building just below where their former apartment was.

Hopkins inquired of Foran as to the type of woman the suicide had been.

Foran related that she was part of a unmarried couple that resided elsewhere before their marriage. After they wed, the couple moved to the apartment the Hopkins would later live in, and then vacate, out of fear.

Still depressed in spite of getting married, the woman, living there three years, thought the other tenants were talking about her and about their living together, considered amoral in those days. Foran said that "Miss Flossie" did not belong there, for she sported bleached hair, something else considered amoral in those days.

In July, 1960, Hans Holzer thought it was time to call on "Miss Flossie."

Holzer sent the Hernandez family, who were then living in the haunted apartment, a letter stating that he would be visiting them in three days and would they kindly allow him into their apartment, having the consent of the landlord to see them and their apartment. (To gain entry, Holzer had written that "a famous literary figure" had once lived there).

Mr. Hernandez, his wife, and child, greeted Holzer, medium Mrs. Meyers, and Mr. Lawrence, a newspaper writer, to act as witnesses. Hernandez guided them through the big apartment to the living room, the room Holzer wanted to focus his visit on.

The Hernandez family reported never seeing or hearing anything out of the ordinary. No "phantasm" had visited them. But they granted permission to Holzer and his associates to garner any feelings they could.

Meyers picked up the image of a gaunt older woman with gray hair, long nose, wide eyes, and bushy eyebrows. There was also a black cat and a heavy-set man with a mustache and "a booming voice" who recited lines and wore a cutaway coat that featured a stand-up collar with wings. Meyers picked up the impression of a wedding band and that somebody there lived with the departed for quite some time and acted as if they were still alive.

"...[I]f I go out, he is not going to come back again...I...see him coming out of the carriage..." Meyers, in a trance, related one of the spirits saying.

She began breathing quickly, a look of terror upon her face. Meyers picked up the letters "M.B." or "B.M." and that an unseen person walked around outside and wished to enter by the window. Meyers also "saw" a black-clothed body in a casket in that room but few flowers, the name on the casket's silver plaque reading "Steves" or "Stevenson," and that the police had business there.

Holzer inquired of Meyers if she sensed any uneasy spirits still in the apartment. She responded that the agitation was fading, due to the fact that a religious person once resided there.

According to the information Hopkins had related in the 1954 Fate article, Holzer theorized that the young son, and the depiction of the "older woman," is the Hopkins son and Mrs. Hopkins, respectively. The kitten was the black cat and Meyers' impression of the wedding band summoned the time when the couple had been living together for years prior to marriage.

The funeral after "Miss Flossie's" suicide was accurate. "M" is Mrs. Hopkins' initial, and "M.B." may have been "M. D." which is M. Daly, Hopkins maiden name. "Someone walking on the outside" recalled the robbery of the other buildings. Police and the coffin added up to when there is a suicide.

Not long after the séance, Mrs. Hopkins passed away. Holzer wondered if Mrs. Hopkins and "Miss Flossie" might then finally get to know each other and Hopkins could then personally thank "Miss Flossie" for giving her warning of the impending burglary.

Chapter VIII

Times Square and Broadway

Times Square

Times Square.

When Times Square was Longacre Square, horse exchanges, carriage factories, stables, and blacksmiths' businesses were the principal enterprises of the area. At the turn of the century, advertising gent O.J. Guide is thought to have originated the name, "The Great White Way," when he saw the future profitability of electrically-lit billboards. Only when the IRT subway reached Times Square in 1904, that Times Square as we know it today really started taking off.

On 42nd Street's north side is the triangle made by the intersection of Seventh Avenue and Broadway. Enveloped around One Times Square, three stories up, is the Motogram, a moving sign 360 feet long, sporting letters five feet tall. The Motogram's 14,800 light bulbs notifies those passing by from the streets of newsworthy happenings.

Replaced by a colorful, electrically-lit billboard on the building's north end, One Times Square is perhaps most well known at New Year's Eve. Times Square is clogged with revelers who flock to watch as the great illuminated apple drops from the top of Times Square to signal in the new year.

The Times Square/Broadway theatre district has seen many changes over the years. From horse stables to electrically lit advertisements, to theatres which evolved into vaudeville houses, burlesque houses, movie houses, and XXX theatres.

The XXX theatres are mostly gone, replaced by an extravaganza of neon that, at night, looks like the wild lights of a giant pinball machine. And while it is safer now to walk down 42nd Street, the area has become a sanitized version of what it once was. Although more attractive to a degree, Times Square has lost much of its originality.

It is in Times Square that Oswald Reinsen had an odd encounter with two Royal Air Force officers during World War II, according to *The National Directory of Haunted Places*.

Reinsen came to New York on business matters frequently. Because he graduated from Harvard University, when in the City, he took a room and his meals at the Harvard Club.

One night, Reinsen was crossing 45th Street near Times Square. He waited for the light to change before crossing the street en route to the Harvard Club, where he was dining alone.

He noticed two uniformed men also waiting at the light whose uniforms were those of Britain's Royal Air Force.

While it was not out-of-the ordinary to see RAF men in New York then, these gents seemed to be lost. They looked around, as tourists do, but repeatedly checked their watches against the large flashing sign on the *New York Times* building.

One officer turned to Reinsen and inquired if they were in Times Square. Reinsen told them indeed they were. They appeared to be heading in the same direction as Reinsen so he made a few cordial remarks and soon enough they were gabbing away.

The RAF men had never been to New York and had many questions. They thought the City electrifying and "alive," following the gloomy constraints the war had forced upon England. Reinsen noted that at every block, one of the RAF men glanced at his watch. He assumed they had an appointment, but upon questioning them, they said they had no plans that evening.

Reinsen asked if they would like to be his guests for dinner at his club. The RAF men were elated at the offer, but only after one peeked at his watch and gave the go-ahead to the other.

Reinsen took the men to the Harvard Club. After they finished dining, the RAF expressed their thanks for a superb meal, noting that they had not eaten that finely since before the war.

The three spoke of the war, but the RAF men appeared loath to talk of their own experiences. And they continued checking their watches.

Reinsen, exasperated, inquired again if they did in fact have an appointment – anything to stop that infernal peeking at their watches. Again, the RAF men told Reinsen they had no other plans.

Their discussion resumed. They spoke of the contrasts between England and America, and also their common interests, and projected what they thought the world would be like following the war. Reinsen, enjoying their stirring talk, almost forgot about the men's practice of checking their watches so frequently.

Five minutes to midnight, both men took one final glance at their watches and got up from their seats. They thanked Reinsen for an enjoyable and unforeseen night, adding that it might be the most unusual evening they ever had.

Baffled, Reinsen stated he did not comprehend what the man was driving at.

One of the RAF men explained that, only twenty-four hours ago, he and the other RAF man were flying a mission over Berlin and were shot down and killed.

They excused themselves and once again thanked Reinsen for his hospitality, strolled to the dining room door and disappeared through it.

And Reinsen never saw them again.

Broadway

The city's theatre locale grew around Times Square in the first thirty years of the twentieth century, moving uptown from the Herald Square area. Oscar Hammerstein, whose resume included being an opera promoter, composer, maker of cigars, and plasterer, was the pioneer of the theatre district, pushing it north of 42nd Street from Herald Square. Hammerstein is often credited with being "the man who created Times Square."

42nd Street's first theatre, the *Republic*, was built in 1900 by Hammerstein. Certainly a visionary but not a man of business, Hammerstein was soon in financial straits and leased the *Republic*, with the exception of roof rights, to David Belasco, who quickly and quite modestly renamed the theatre after himself.

Later named the *Victory Theatre*, it eventually became a XXX-rated porn movie theatre. But, like many other venerable New York institutions, the *Victory* was once again reborn, this time as the *New Victory Theatre*, dedicated to productions for children. (If you look closely enough, you will find the "B's" in its decor – "B" as in Belasco, a testament to David Belasco's outsized ego.)

The theatre world, as evidenced by the long tradition of wishing an actor to "break a leg" rather than good luck, is a rather superstitious place. Frank Rich, described as "the Butcher of Broadway" for his often acerbic pen while drama critic for the *New York Times* from 1980-1993, wrote in his autobiography, *Ghost Light*:

> "Sneaking into a lonely, darkened Broadway theatre, he saw the crew strike the set, leaving behind a naked light bulb on a tall pole – a "ghost light," meant to ward off spirits."

Our first haunted theatre is the *Belasco*. It is of no great surprise that David Belasco, larger than life, would want to be even larger – in death.

The Belasco Theatre
111 44th Street

Belasco Theatre.
Courtesy of The Shubert Organization, Peter Entin, VP-Theatre Operations.

"Notes on Madame Butterfly," from the Metropolitan Opera's *Stagebill* fills in the details of David Belasco's life.

Belasco, a Portuguese Jew, was born in San Francisco to a showman and his wife. As a child, he ran away to join the circus and eventually ended up on Broadway.

Partially due to his circus training, Belasco originated the visionary sequence of lighting and "scrim" later called "montage," as well as his use of the elevator stage, far ahead of its time. Many of the rich images and fantasies on Broadway stages today are due to David Belasco's ingenious imagination.

Always a showman, always his own publicity department, playwright/director Belasco presented *Madame Butterfly* in 1900 London. He related that when the great Giacomo Puccini beheld the show, he went backstage and implored Belasco for the rights.

"I agreed at once...it is not possible to discuss business arrangements with an impulsive Italian who had tears in his eyes and both arms around your neck," Belasco stated.

The book, *Supernatural on Stage: Ghosts of the Theatre*, related that Belasco, often called "the Bishop of Broadway" or "The Wizard," kept apartments on the theatre's top floor, reached by a private elevator, where he invited "special" female visitors. The elevator, no longer usable, once lifted guests, the majority of them women, to the private apartments and Belasco's "casting couch."

There were tales of wild parties, peepholes into the women's dressing rooms, and other ribald shenanigans at the *Belasco* when David manned the helm.

Belasco, one of the most eccentric personalities in the history of New York theatre, customarily wore a monk's robe with a cowl covering his almost bald head and decorated his office like a monastery although he adorned it with erotic chachkas (bric-a-brac).

Ghostly occurrences include hearing the whirring of the no-longer used elevator's cables, in addition to footfalls in the apartment, late at night, when no one is about. In 1992, at 4 P.M., a custodian heard the elevator chains leading to Belasco's old apartment clattering. The custodian's dog grew extremely anxious, as if he saw a ghost.

Stagehands working on the 1995 production of *Hamlet*, starring Ralph Fiennes, related to a stage doorman they heard "strange sounds." Other crew members wondered if there were interlopers in the house, for draperies moved on their own. Actors rehearsing their scenes have seen the spirit of David Belasco sitting in his box seat, frowning if he did not like their performances.

Customarily, when the last theatre-goer has left and the lights dimmed, the stage curtain stays down. Not at the *Belasco*. Witnesses say it goes up halfway, stops and once again lowers, as if Belasco himself is "taking his own special bow."

When there are rehearsals or performances at the *Belasco*, actors and theatre-goers alike report that they sometimes see the ghost of David Belasco lurk in the cathedral-like study – "his spirit which, in the dead of night, sends a phantom elevator on its vertical journey – to the horror of those working late," and others who hear a hazy voice hum, croon, and wail.

One person who worked at the *Belasco* swore he knows of at least one employee, actor, or theatre-goer who has described beholding the specter of David Belasco – twice. The employee related that those who have witnessed the ghost of Belasco refer to him as "the monk" due to the fact he always dressed like one. One witness reported seeing a ghostly being with white, tousled hair.

Another witness described a spectral encounter at the stage door in the alley of the Theatre.

Between the window and the door, an apparition was looking around. The witness was peering through the gate out onto 44th Street, and invited it to come in.

The ghost looked at him and vanished.

Tina Skinner related this story in a fax to me about Steve Altman, electrician in the Schubert Theater chain, which includes the *Belasco*.

In 1982, Altman stated that a phantom once stood behind him at the *Belasco*. In fact, he encountered two different manifestations while working there, one benevolent, the other not.

It was 11 A.M. and Altman was working on the stage. He turned and saw "her" glide across the back of the mezzanine. "She" was attired in a blue evening gown and walked by quickly and "business-like" to the far side without looking around.

"She seemed completely neutral. You didn't even exist for her," Altman said. "She had dark hair and very white skin, but not ghostly pale."

When Altman witnessed a second act of the specter's mezzanine-crossing performance, he decided it was time to look into the matter. He discovered that the woman in the blue evening gown had perished in an elevator mishap en route to Belasco's secret apartment to get a job.

The apartment, Altman reported, was where you never saw anything, but always sensed a male presence. Someone or something was watching you. The impression — an uneasy feeling — was greatest by an old mirror that hung in the apartment. As a result, he did not like venturing into the old apartment alone.

"He seemed to be watching you. It was uncomfortable," Altman related.

He stated that a doorman once was speaking to someone who suddenly vanished.

It has been thought that the colorful David Belasco still frequents the secret apartment where he gave personal auditions for hopeful actresses and welcomed his many female friends. Belasco, 5' 2", was a world-class womanizer.

David Belasco died in New York in May, 1931, but apparently has never left his beloved *Belasco* theatre.

And he probably never will.

New Amsterdam Theatre
214 West 42nd Street
Between 7th & 8th Avenues

In its heyday in the mid-1920s, the ten-story *New Amsterdam Theatre*, the only 42nd Street theatre with landmark status, attracted the swells of the City. The Theatre's Art Nouveau design was embellished with an orange interior of marble, mahogany, and classical friezes. Plasterwork displayed themes of Shakespeare and Wagner, and shows featuring Fred Astaire, Fanny Brice, and Eddie Cantor were commonplace, according to a *Time* magazine and *New York Daily News* articles.

Owner Florez Ziegfeld's Midnight Frolic revues supper club, believed to be one of the most wondrous clubs of its time, was performed in the Aerial Gardens, a roof garden featuring an enclosed space, glass balconies, rainbow lighting, and a movable stage.

Built in 1903, the Theatre opened with A *Midsummer Night's Dream*, light years away from *Blood Beach*, one of the last movies shown before the theatre closed in 1983 for twelve years, as reported in a *New York Times* article. The Ziegfeld Follies played from 1913 to 1927, burlesque in the 1930s, and, in 1937, movies arrived at the *New Amsterdam*.

In 1995, Walt Disney & Company took over the old *New Amsterdam* as part of the 42nd St. Redevelopment Project. Their aim was to keep the Theatre's original Art Nouveau style as much as possible, in spite of the fact that rubbish was as deep as snowdrifts and white mushrooms thrived under the platform near the stage.

From the flashy hues and flower etchings in the wooden balustrades, to the men's loge lounge murals portraying New York's history, the restoration team had their hands full. But the rewards were always finding the delightful remains of the Theatre, such as a light fixture in the shape of a woman's head, and light sockets emanating like tendrils of hair.

Today, *The Lion King* is running in the refurbished *New Amsterdam*. But before the *New Amsterdam* was brought back to life, workers who took part in the restoration had many uncanny experiences in the *New Amsterdam*.

According to *The National Directory of Haunted Places*, many have described seeing a young woman, sobbing, wearing a white dress trimmed in silver. It was the spectral Olive Thomas, a star of the Ziegfeld Follies, the centerpiece of the Theatre. After a run with the Follies and fleetingly being one of Flo Ziegfeld's mistresses, Thomas went west and became a silent film star.

Thomas wed Mary Pickford's brother, Jack, thus insuring her prominence in the world of silent films. But in 1920, she collapsed on a Paris hotel room floor, the result of a poisoning. The specific facts of her death were never revealed and Olive Thomas was interred in a white dress trimmed in silver.

When her specter was sighted, Thomas appeared to be attired in one of Flo Ziegfeld's *Follies*'s costumes, holding a blue glass in her hand. Was it the glass that held the poison that took Thomas' life? There were also rumors that she had died of syphilis in the 1920s. The ghost, sporting a sash with the name "Olive" on it, looked perplexed as she strolled around the-then gutted theatre.

The Palace Theatre
1564 Broadway at 47th Street

The *Palace Theatre* was built in 1913. In its heyday, the *Palace* was considered the height of vaudeville. Anytime you "played the Palace," you had hit the big time.

Supernatural on Stage relates that in 1990, the *Palace Theatre*, a Walt Disney & Company theatre currently running Elton John and Time Rice's *Aida*, was both refurbished and absorbed by the forty-three-story Embassy Suite Times Square Hotel.

But prior to the Disney takeover, a tightrope walker's specter was observed swinging on the dress-circle rim. Louis Borsalino, one of the "Four Casting Pearls" act, fell and died while balancing on the tightrope in the 1950s.

Borsalino's screams and a man dropping to his death have been related by those peeking through the *Palace*'s curtain peep-holes.[74-90]

Chapter IX

Off Broadway, Off-Off Broadway, etc.

The Joseph Papp Public Theatre
(formerly the Public Theatre)
425 Lafayette Street

Joseph Papp Theatre. *Courtesy of Carol Fineman, General Press Representative.*

The renowned Joseph Papp (born Yosl Papirofsky of Williamsburg, Brooklyn) began the New York Shakespeare Festival in the 1970s at the now Joseph Papp Public Theatre, after acquiring the Old Astor Library from the Hebrew Immigrant Aid Society in 1965.

A *New York Times* article stated that a developer was ready to tear down the old Astor Library when the newly created Landmarks Preservation Commission came up at bat for its first major success. Arrangements were made for Papp's *New York Shakespeare Festival* to purchase the structure for $560,000 for use as indoor theatres, in addition to his existing success with outdoor presentations of Shakespeare in Central Park.

The *Public* launched such ground breaking musicals as *Hair* and *A Chorus Line*. After Papp died in 1991, the Public Theatre was named in his honor.

First constructed to house books, the construction of the immense, elaborate structure that would become the Astor Library began in the mid-1800s after real estate giant John Jacob Astor saw the need for a library in the expanding city. Astor bestowed the project $400,000 and the facility opened as the non-circulating, Astor Free Library in 1854.

The Astor Free Library actually thwarted the needs of the working class and poor in their use of the library. Library hours were only when most people were at work. In many cases, certain users were actually dissuaded from using the "free" library by making them feel like "interloper[s] and intruder[s]," according to an article in the *New York Daily Tribune*.

During the first years of the Astor Library, a learned ghost story came from its not-really-opened-to-the-public stacks, as related in *The Diary of George Templeton Strong*.

Famous lawyer, originator of the Union League Club, and trustee of Columbia University, George Templeton Strong kept an articulate, haughty and often racist journal that gave specific insights into more than four decades of nineteenth century New York City, albeit from a upper-class point of view.

Attorney Strong's diary hazarded into the spectral realm twice. It is with his second story that took place in the Astor Library that he wrote about in 1859 we will deal with now.

Astor librarian Joseph Green Cogswell met the ghost of the late Austin L. Sands, lawyer, insurance man and merchant.

The night was clammy and the wind cutting, as New York City winters often are. "Old Sands' spook" was seen strolling through the Astor Library. It relaxed in the corners, yawned and futilely searched for something that would catch his eye by the cover.

"It walks the Astor alcoves, having naught else to go. It is staring at shelf 30B, blasé and tired and blue," Strong related.

On three different nights, Cogswell saw the ghost of Sands and tried to address it:

"Mr. Sands...you have no business here tonight.....You never came in while living, and you shan't come now you're dead."

The specter looked at the doctor sharply. Cogswell, annoyed by the fact this literary ghost had interrupted his sleep, looked straight back at the phantom. Sands' specter grew flustered. Unable to come back with a snappy retort, Sands' phantom silently vanished.

Strong's postscript to that journal entry gives every indication that Librarian Cogswell did, indeed, meet up with the specter of Sands. Strong wrote:

"That's the true narrative of the apparition of Austin L. Sands, Esq., deceased, to Cogswell at the Astor Library on three separate occasions, as detailed by him to Mr. Burns and Hoppin...at D.B. Fearing's dinner table."

On one of the three appearances, ghost Sands responded to Cogswell's questioning as to why it was making its appearance known. It simply said:

"For variety."

Does the ghost of Mr. Sands still roam about the old Astor Library, now the Joseph Papp Public Theatre?

Jean Cocteau Repertory Theatre at the Bouwerie Lane Theater
330 Bowery at Bond Street

Jean Cocteau Repertory Theatre at the Bouwerie Lane Theater is located in the NoHo Historic District, as defined by a New York Times article, as Bond Street from Lafayette Street to the Bowery, featuring everything from 1830 row houses, 1890s lofts, modern storefronts and vacant lots.

In the 1830s-1840s, this area was synonymous with fashion, but the invasion of business along Broadway put an end to its social prestige. Its grand homes evolved into boarding houses and offices.

The 1870 census revealed that the block included an actress, a minstrel, and a reporter. Less than one hundred years later, tenants at #26 had to hide their mattresses in the morning because it was illegal to live there. But new legislation in the 1970s protected residential loft tenants.

Jean Cocteau Repertory Theatre at the Bouwerie Lane Theater was originally built in 1874 as the Bond Street Savings Bank. Converted to a theatre in 1963, the theatre seats were purchased for $1.00 apiece from a movie theatre being torn down. The box office window, as well as the chandelier, are holdovers from the bank.

A deceased member's presence of the Jean Cocteau Repertory Theatre at the Bouwerie Lane Theater is said to be felt by the present members, according to an usher.

A letter to me from Quiche Lloyd-Kemble, Executive Director of the American Renaissance Theatre, gave details on the Provincetown Playhouse, Duplex, Thimble, African Grove, and the old Union Square Theatres from their Dramatic Art's 1994 Haunted and Historic Walking Tour:

Provincetown Playhouse
133 MacDougal Street
South of the intersection of Washington Square South

In 1915, a circle of hopeful actors and writers created a Cape Cod summer theatre. The next year, Eugene O'Neill met up with the young thespians, toting along plays that filled a suitcase. One such play, Bound East for Cardiff, garnered enough acclaim that they opened a New York season in 1916 utilizing the parlor floor of 139 MacDougal.

In 1917, they refurbished a four-story, pre-Victorian structure that was once a storehouse, stable and bottling works at #133 into a theatre seating 182 people. Among the plays first shown there included *The Emperor Jones*, which launched Paul Robeson's career and *The Hairy Ape*, both by O'Neill. The theatre was also home to Gertrude Stein and Edna St. Vincent Millay. Bette Davis appeared there early in her career.

Still a working theatre, long-time staffers swear it is haunted. They have noted odd sounds and a cold, opaque form that passes them on the steps.

Thimble Theatre
10 Fifth Avenue basement

The Thimble Theatre was located in the basement of the 1845 brownstone that still stands at 10 Fifth Avenue. Home to the ghost of the theatre's founder, Guido Bruno, a Greenwich Village eccentric usually identified by his flashy, ill-fitting plaid suits. Bruno is recognized as the originator of performance art and his theatre presented the U.S. debut of Strinberg's *Miss Julie*.

After Bruno's death, an occupant of the former theatre (which is now a basement apartment) recounted peculiar happenings, such as music playing from no visible source and objects sailing across the room.

The Union Square Theatre
100 East 17th Street

Union Square Theatre. *Courtesy of Margaret Cotter.*

Union Square was originally called Union Place in 1811. During the late nineteenth century, 14th Street was the midway point for Ladies' Mile, a walkway of swanky shops that extended from Broadway and 8th to 23rd Street. By the turn of the century, businesses and art galleries traveled uptown to Madison Square.

In the years prior to World War I, Union Square evolved into a forum for anarchists, socialists, 'Wobblies,' and Communists, where they took to soapboxes to espouse their political leanings. Ten years later, these large assemblies oftentimes grew into clashes with the authorities.

The most well-known confrontation was a Depression-era workers protest of 35,000 that led to public outcry after police attacked one hundred of the protestors. Union Square was thereafter the soul of militant political movements in the City.

Once the center of the City's first theatre districts, the old Union Square Theatre (not to be confused with the present theatre of the same name) stood at 14th Street between Fourth Avenue and Broadway. That has its own ghost story and is covered in the "Ghosts without a Home" chapter.

The present Union Square Theatre, according to a *New York Times* article, was reportedly haunted by a phantom that lived in a crawl space and had eyes like a cat that glowed in the dark. Windows and a chandelier once started making a racket on their own, and did not quit until the maintenance man demanded that whoever – or whatever – knock it off so he could get some sleep.

And the sounds stopped.

Cherry Lane Theatre
38 Commerce Street

A converted barn and former brewery (or malt house), the Cherry Lane Theatre was founded in 1924 as an experimental theatre by a group including Edna St. Vincent Millay.

The Cherry Lane Theatre is haunted by numerous ghosts, according to *Supernatural on Stage*. One phantom is said to materialize in white at the top step of the lobby staircase. Another thespian haunt stays close to the dressing room hallway.

It is theorized that the specter may be either Aaron Burr or Thomas Paine, publisher of *Crisis*, a Revolutionary War publication on the side of the colonists, for both lived in the area. One local believes it is the ghost of Washington Irving, who grew up on William Street but resided briefly on Commerce Street near the location of the present Cherry Lane Theatre.

Cherry Lane Theatre. *Courtesy of Elliot Fox, General Manager.*

Chapter X

Clinton Court and its Environs

Hell's Kitchen
30th to 57th Streets west of Ninth Avenue

Blue Guide New York tells us that "Hell's Kitchen" was once a ghetto. Its dwellings contained many of the City's most notorious tenements (a word derived from unrelated tenants living under one roof). The name "Hell's Kitchen" is thought to have originated when two of New York's Finest were observing a neighborhood brawl on a typically sultry, New York City summer evening.

One remarked to the other that the neighborhood was "hot as hell." The other officer responded that hell was cool, that this was "Hell's Kitchen."

Territorial gangs victimized the railroad grounds of the Hudson River (later the New York Central Railroad) down Eleventh Avenue. They so terrified the area that police from the area's 20th Precinct would only go out in details greater than three to handle problems that arose from the gangs' terrors.

The gangs had such names as "the Hudson Dusters," "Gophers," "Gorillas," and "Battle Row Annie Ladies' Social and Athletic Club." These and other gangs gave Hell's Kitchen its disreputable fame as one of the most threatening neighborhoods in America.

Following 1910, the New York Central Railroad enlisted a group of thugs who crippled the gangs by use of brute force and arrest. The neighborhood enjoyed a brief respite from the violence, which recommenced full-throttle with the coming of Prohibition in the 1920s, whose sway is still carried on today with the "Westies," well known for their gangster behavior.

Hell's Kitchen (called "Clinton" by newer residents) is now a stabilized neighborhood, where residents coexist with the many restaurants of "Restaurant's Row" that cater to a predominately theatre-going crowd.

We begin our Hell's Kitchen ghosts at what was once known as the "Havoc House."

428 West 44th Street
and 9th Avenue
(The Havoc House)

Actress June Havoc lived in the basement apartment of this townhouse from 1962 to 1969. She heard unusual sounds coming from the back of the apartment, such as rapping and poundings in the kitchen, like someone was searching the cupboard for food. As such, residents nicknamed the ghost "Hungry Lucy."

Havoc, sister of Gypsy Rose Lee, heard pounding noises from under the floor but plumbers said the pipes were in perfect working order, and carpenters said there was nothing wrong with the wooden floor. Tenants in the upstairs and downstairs apartments heard nothing.

June Havoc called in Hans Holzer, who wrote about the experience in a *New York Daily News* article. Holzer arranged, with renowned English medium Sybil Leek, to have a séance in the apartment.

Leek sat in a chair adjacent to where the sounds were emanating from and went into a trance.

"Hungry," Leek mumbled faintly..."I want some food, some food," she cried.

"Who are you?" Holzer asked.

"Lucy Ryan."

"What year is this?"

"1792."

A Morse code of sorts began to be tapped out on the table:

"L-e-a-v-e."

Leek also communicated with the ghost of a soldier, Alfred, who was under Colonel Napier in 1792. Napier was commander of a garrison posted in the area when it was part of former British Governor George Clinton's estate, only two blocks north of Havoc's house.

Lucy Ryan had apparently gotten involved with a soldier during the Revolutionary War. They made plans to run away, but the War came. The soldier was commanded to battle and hid Lucy in an underground hideaway, where she swore to wait for him. But he was killed in action.

Lucy, forever faithful, and with no way of knowing what befell her young man, starved to death in her hideaway. Ryan explained, through Leek, that the steady pounding was her sole way to get attention to her great hunger.

Leek told Lucy that her beau had passed on and that it was time to join him, that she would never again have to pound for food.

420-422 1/2 West 46th Street (Clinton Court)
Between Ninth and 10th Avenues

422 1/2 West 46th Street (Clinton Court – outside gate). *Courtesy of Clinton Court.*

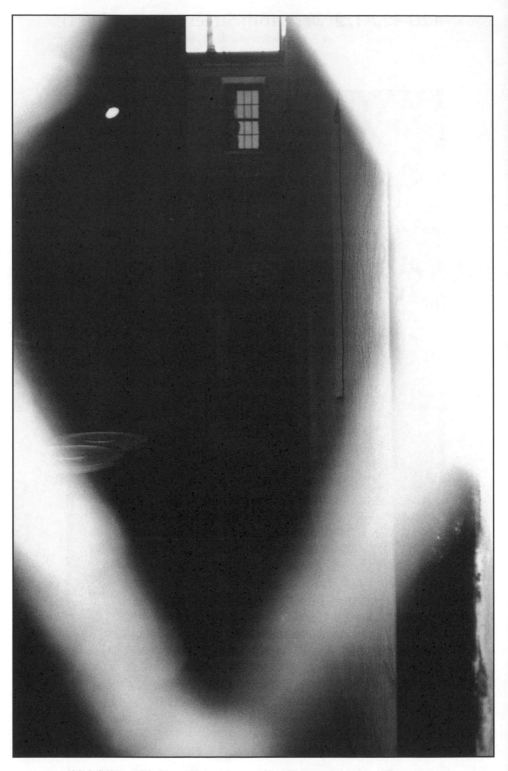

422 1/2 West 46th Street (Clinton Court – through gate). *Courtesy of Clinton Court.*

The Clinton Court area was once an old potter's field and is haunted by many specters.

Clinton Court, a split-tiered carriage house of former Governor George Clinton, is hidden in back of the main house on 46th Street.

Hans Holzer thinks that 422 1/2 West 46th Street is presumably "the most haunted house in New York," according to a *New York Daily News* article.

In the early eighteenth century, a sailor was hung after being convicted of mutiny by the British on board a New York-bound vessel. His body was interred in a potter's field near present-day 46th Street and Tenth Avenue in an anonymous grave.

Afterwards, odd occurrences befell those who passed the old graveyard.

The sailor was seen rising from his grave and terrifying passers-by. He was called "The Old Moor" and for years, the tale of the Old Moor's specter scared the willies out of anyone in the vicinity.

The Old Moor was the first reported spirit to materialize in the area of Clinton Court. In the 1820s, Old Moor's ghostly visit so horrified a coachman's wife that she accidentally tumbled down a winding stairway. She died from her injuries, and soon become one more specter haunting the courtyard.

The Old Moor also terrified one of Governor Clinton's children. For many years, the family's grandchildren made believe they were ghosts as a game until a phantom appeared to them one night. In her rush to escape the apparition, one grandchild fell from the stairs and died of her injuries. In more recent times, the spirits of the child and a colonial officer named Walker have been observed in the courtyard.

In addition, the ghosts of a wailing woman, an elderly gent named Joe, and a young girl bearing a single red rose, have also been seen in Clinton Court.

Tom Winberry and his wife, Pam Beckerman-Winberry, resided on the ground floor of the carriage house. In 1983, when they first moved in, Tom saw a "hooded, shadowy figure, female in sense," that traipsed through the hallways and floated over his bed one night.

It was about 2 A.M. Winberry saw the form of a woman in a hooded cloak with cowl waft by the opened door and head in the direction of the bathroom. The form stood, head bowed, in the archway for a moment. Winberry, not afraid, stood still, watching in awe.

One time, Winberry was sitting with a friend in his house and they saw what appeared to be blue-green lights dripping from the ceiling in his living room. Television lighting director Winberry could not figure out a basis for the odd green light. Holzer observed that dripping blue-green lights often signify the presence of "new, confused ghosts, trying to orient themselves to their new dimension."

Pam stated that she had also noticed curious occurrences in the house. One time, Tom was asleep and she was standing by the refrigerator. Pam jumped. She saw something in the hallway.

Finally, they summoned Hans Holzer to investigate.

Denis Hamill, author of this *Daily News* article, tape recorded Winberry as he told of the hooded ghosts. A new tape in his recorder suddenly jammed and the writer had to fast replace the tape. Holzer stated that specters enjoy sabotaging cameras, televisions and tape recorders (and, also, from my own experience, computers when I am writing of things ghostly).

> "...[T]he figure approached me," says Winberry. "It stood next to the bed. I put out my hand to touch and it went into her. The part that went into her essence was in shadow and the rest of my arm was in light. Then she moved over the bed, hovering for a full two minutes...pop, she was gone..."

Holzer stated that Winberry met the Coachman's Wife, an active ghost.

Trent Gough, a theatrical director who resided at the carriage house for seven years prior to the Winberrys, remembered one night when he heard, "the voice of a small child playing with one of my girlfriend's dogs in the kitchen."

When he entered the room, the sound ceased. The dog looked at Gough as though he had invaded a private moment, which apparently he had.

A small courtyard and stables are visible through an iron gate of the cooperative apartments at 420 West 46th Street. The charming structure at 422 1/2 West 46th Street is the former carriage house. The winding stairway to the second floor still exists.

343 West 47th Street

Rob Warren, who lived at 343 West 47th, related to me in 1995 of strange happenings in the basement of his building during the first three months of his living there.

Whenever he did his laundry, any time, day or night, he would spot a "dark-jacketed figure with light gray hair who walked from right to left in a stooped fashion." Warren had no idea who the figure was but believed it to be an apparition.

Chapter XI

The Dakota and Central Park

The Dakota
Corner of 72nd Street and Central Park West

In the late 1800s, apartments were just beginning to gain approval with the wealthy of New York City. When Singer Sewing Machine heir Edward S. Clark contracted for construction of the Dakota in 1882, his selection for the site was bold – uptown, encircled by shanties and empty land, so far north and west that naysayers deemed it "Clark's Folly," one commenting that the structure "might as well be in the Dakota Territory."

The Singer Sewing Machine heir appreciated that view so much he advised the architect to decorate the building with ears of corn, arrowheads, and a bas relief Indian's head above the main entrance.

From its inception, the Dakota has been a lavish ten-story building, its sections originally fitted with sculpted mantles of marble, paneling of oak and mahogany, marble floors, and solid brass hardware.

The eighth and ninth floors, considered unsuitable for tenants in days prior to elevators, held the servants' rooms. The basement was home to the boilers and generators that illuminated the Dakota, for the Edison Company lines stretched only as far as Spruce Street at that time. Once completed, the Dakota was said to be architecturally one of the City's finest apartment buildings and socially unrivaled West Side address.

Rex Reed, Robert Flack, Lauren Bacall, Yoko Ono, Connie Chung, and Maury Povich have all called the Dakota home, among other notables.

New York City Ghost Stories has an entry on the Dakota.

Edward S. Clark is one of the many ghosts of the Dakota. He appears to be unable to give up overseeing work in the building, for his specter has been seen shaking his toupee fiercely at workmen in the basement of the building. Clark is described as a man sporting wire-rimmed glasses and a closely-clipped beard.

Another basement inhabitant for years was actor Boris Karloff. Every year, Karloff tried to enjoy Halloween, but due to his *Frankenstein* fame, when he hung a bag of candy outside his door for the children of the building, it went untouched.

Contrary to popular thought, The Dakota is where Roman Polanski filmed only exterior shots from *Rosemary's Baby*, in spite of the fact the castle-like structure long had a reputation for being a haunted building.

In 1965, workers refurbishing apartment 77 met the specter of a ten year old boy walking in a hallway between two bedrooms. His arrival is always preceded by a "strange outdoorsy, fresh-yet-musty odor." He has been seen often by numerous witnesses.

Ghosts of former occupants include Rudolf Nureyev, who defected from Russia in 1961 and Leonard Bernstein, buried in Green-Wood Cemetery in Brooklyn. Other ghosts yet to be identified are a crying woman, an elderly gent, and a young girl holding a single red rose.

When John Lennon and Yoko Ono bought into the famous building in Robert Ryan's old apartment on the seventh floor, some of the more traditional residents were put off. Soon, in spite of John's sporadic shenanigans, the couple's sometimes curious clothes, and the never-ending attempts of fans to invade the well-guarded gate of the Dakota, they proved to be rather unexceptional neighbors.

Immediately after settling in, John and Yoko hired a psychic to "read" their apartment. The medium was said to have communicated with the ghost of Ryan's former wife, who died in the apartment.

Lennon was killed by a deranged gunman in the 72nd Street entrance doorway on December 8, 1980. A New York Daily News article mentioned that, earlier in the day, fellow Dakota resident Lauren Bacall had alerted security that there was something amiss about waiting autograph seeker Mark Chapman, who would later that night take John Lennon's life. Lennon's spirit materialized at the foot of the bed of many leading psychics and parapsychologists in the weeks after he died.

Accounts of Lennon's manifestations by disc jockeys and other people in the music business frequently take place on the anniversary of his death. Psychics maintain that Lennon epitomizes an enormous supply of positive energy in the beyond.

In addition, a lamenting specter refuses to leave the Dakota. Over the years, many workers and inhabitants have described noticing a spectral girl in a nineteenth century yellow silk dress bouncing a red ball. She keeps repeating, tearfully:

"Today's my birthday."

And with that, wearing a sheepish grin and uttering a soft cry, she vanishes.

It has been said that she is a harbinger of death and was spotted the night John Lennon was murdered.

During a séance with Lennon, he corroborated that the Dakota was haunted. In that conversation with Lennon's specter, he stated that his supernatural body does "visit" his old apartment. Lennon's spirit has been spotted crossing from the 72nd Street entrance of the Dakota, across Central Park West to the "Imagine" mosaic at Strawberry Fields, a memorial to him.

Strawberry Fields.

Central Park

In 1844, poet William Cullen Bryant and other notables started to call for a public park, noting that business was eating up much of Manhattan, and the population what was left of it.

The Board of Park Commissioners, created in 1857, announced a design contest, and Frederick Law Olmstead and Calvent Vaux's plans won out. The Irish and black squatters who long called that area home were removed forcibly, along with their pigs and goats, from what would become Central Park.

In spite of the fact the Park was designed as a respite for city dwellers, the overseers of Central Park, much like those of the Astor Library, initially created so many onerous rules to thwart the needs of the working class that it was obvious it was really meant for the City's elite. Over the years, many have tried to tamper with the initial designs of the park, including Robert Moses, but today, it is indeed, a Park for all the people.

It is in Central Park that the ghostly Van der Voort sisters still do their figure-eights on the frozen lake, according to *Ghosts in American Houses*.

Rosetta and Janet Van der Voort owned a brownstone mansion in the 1800s. Inseparable, in the winter they loved doing figure-eights on the Central Park ice skating pond. They grew old together, living alone in their massive house. Never bothering with anyone but each other, they had no friends or close relatives and passed away within months of each other in 1880.

But they could never leave behind the ice skating they so cherished in life.

Rosetta and Janet's specters were first sighted ice skating during World War I. They were dressed in large bustles, quite the thing — when they died. One sported a red dress, the other purple. The ghostly ice skaters have been seen on several occasions, endlessly doing their figure-eights, even unto death.

Chapter XII

Aaron Burr and Family

Aaron Burr is a most interesting figure in American history. And apparently, given the number of hauntings he perpetrates, Burr seems quite reluctant to leave New York City. Maybe it is because he was so busy in life. A brilliant lawyer with the nasty habit of attempting armed insurrection against the United States government, he shot Alexander Hamilton dead in a fair duel in 1804.

Burr was never tried for Hamilton's death but instead for treason, for which he was surprisingly acquitted. In his 70s, Burr remarried but died the same day Eliza Jumel, his wife (the ghost of the Morris-Jumel Mansion in Washington Heights), divorced him on grounds of adultery.

The Battery

Battery Park.

New York City Ghost Stories states that, for over two hundred years, the ghost of Aaron Burr has been sighted keeping a sad, spectral vigil at the water's edge of the Battery, watching seaward for his daughter, Theodosia, who died in a shipwreck en route to visiting Burr when he was imprisoned for treason.

But Burr and Theodosia finally did have their long-awaited reunion, but only after death, as attested to by the following story.

One If By Land, Two If By Sea Restaurant

17 Barrow Street
Between 7th Avenue & West 4th Street

One if By Land Rest. *Courtesy of Rosanne Manetta, General Manager.*

Barrow Street was first called Reason Street in honor of political writer Thomas Paine, whose *Age of Reason* was published in the 1790s. When people took to calling it "Raisin Street," Trinity Church took umbrage and had enough political clout to have the street renamed in honor of artist Thomas Barrow, nineteenth century water colorist who sole celebrity was based on a painting he made of Trinity Church in 1807, widely issued as a print at that time.

One If By Land Restaurant is one of the most romantic and beautiful restaurants I have ever visited, especially during the winter holiday season. The first time I walked into Burr's former carriage house, my eyes were drawn immediately to the back right of the balcony room, where the ghosts of Burr, and his daughter Theodosia, are often seen by the windows. He is said to yank chairs out from guests and snatch items from tables, according to Lance, a former waiter.

Once, my husband and a friend, both attorneys, were having dinner at One If By Land. There were discussing the merits of scaffold cases in personal injury law. Later that week, our electrician fell from a scaffold and sustained injuries. Though not serious, he was able, through our friend, a plaintiff's lawyer, to be awarded enough of a settlement to relocate his family to Puerto Rico where he and his wife were born.

We all wondered if Burr, astonishingly never disbarred for any of his wrong doings and practicing law in the City of New York until well into his seventies, had a hand in that scaffold case.

129 Spring Street

Spring Street was named for a spring tapped by Aaron Burr's Manhattan Water Company. Seemingly set up as a late eighteenth century utility, the Water Company, in typical Burr fashion, curiously evolved into a bank instead.

The then area roughly abutting modern SoHo was known as "Lispenard Swamp" or "Lispenard Meadows." Named after property owner Leonard Lispenard, it was a region of small farms, rolling hills, creeks, and wetlands. The site carried fresh water, "the Fresh Water of Collect Pond," already mentioned, from the new wells to the City.

Many thought that "the Collect" was bottomless, that fantastic monsters lurked in its murky depths, ready to grab the unwary bather. This was a tale that was backed up by the many deaths in the waters of the Collect.

The Collect, a fresh-water source for the City of New York, had become polluted. By 1810, the Pond was drained, filled in and vanished. New sources of water were needed in a City where epidemics from the result of drinking dirty water abounded.

Forever-enterprising Burr rushed to the aid of the City's thirsty denizens. On December 22, 1799, he formed the Manhattan Water Company (sometimes known as the Manhattan Company). The plan was to use steam engines to draw water through wooden pipes, (samples of which are now housed at the New-York Historical Society), to a reservoir on Chambers Street.

But sly Burr had something else in mind.

Within the Water Company charter was an easily-missed clause that provided investors the authorization to start a bank. While the Manhattan Water Company did lay many miles of wooden pipe to carry water, its primary purpose was banking, finally evolving into the Chase Manhattan Bank.

It is in Soho where the ghost of Elma Sands still roams.

On January 2, 1800, Juliana (or Gulielma) Elmore Sands was found floating in a well at the corner of Broadway and Spring Street, without her shoes, hat and shawl. The police had been conducting an investigation for the missing Sands since after Christmas.

They interrogated her beau, Levi Weeks, who swore that he had not been with Miss Sands that night. But others had witnessed Weeks taking Elma Sands away on his sleigh that winter night.

A *New York Daily News* provides more details for what later was known as the "Manhattan Well Mystery."

Sands had lived with her sister at the Greenwich Street Quaker-run boarding house of her cousins, their children and boarders, which included Weeks. Many lodgers believed that Weeks and Sands were lovers, for he was often seen attired only in a nightshirt as he quietly made his way to Sands' bedroom for brazen nightly visits.

Sands, (until young Weeks pressed his affections), was thought virtuous, while Weeks was viewed as an unprincipled beau. Matrimony was believed pending and Sands assumed that she would a Christmas bride, that she and Weeks would be wed on December 22, 1799.

As Christmas 1799 neared, Sands happily told her sister and cousin that she was leaving at 8 P.M. December 22nd – to wed Levi Weeks. Weeks later stated that he and Sands had argued outside the house, and that, as a result, he went off alone and spent the evening with his brother Ezra.

Levi Weeks' neighbor maintained she heard a sleigh leave the house just prior to 8 P.M. Others stated they saw a sleigh with two men and a woman, perhaps the Weeks brothers and Sands.

Later, two different witnesses heard a woman call out for help from the location of Lispenard's meadow well.

The second witness saw from a window a male skulking by the well. Others swore they were almost run over on Broadway (then called "the Broadway") by a sleigh with no bells that speeded by with a horse at full gallop coming from the direction of the well. The sleigh looked like the one owned by Ezra Weeks.

At 10 P.M., Levi returned home. He inquired of Sands' cousin if she was asleep and learned that she had yet to come back.

The following morning, Sands' sister, Hope, challenged Weeks as to where Elma was. Weeks said he knew nothing of Elma's whereabouts. When pressed about his intentions toward Elma, he swore he had no intention of marrying her.

Boot prints and sleigh tracks were found in the snow by the well and its wooden cover was not righted. Regardless of this evidence and the cries heard the previous night, no one investigated the well, even after boys playing around it on Christmas Eve discovered a muff floating in the water.

On December 28th, Levi requested that Hope Sands sign a letter verifying that his association with Elma was not of a serious (i.e. matrimonial) nature. Sands would subsequently state that the gist of the document was that Weeks paid no more interest in Elma than any other females in the boarding house, and that there was nothing between them that would result in marriage.

Hope responded by not signing off on the document.

The following day, Elma's cousin Elias used grappling hooks to drag the Hudson River near the docks west of Lispenard's farm in the hope, or fear, of finding Elma's body.

On January 2, 1800, he inspected the well using hooked poles. He discovered the body of Elma Sands in icy water, a swelling at the crown of her head. A coroner's inquest ruled the death a "willful homicide."

On January 2, Weeks was formally charged with the murder of Sands.

Levi implored his well-connected brother, Ezra, to provide him with the best lawyers. Ezra, a builder hired by Alexander Hamilton to create a country mansion in Harlem, coaxed Hamilton, Aaron Burr, and others to defend Levi Weeks, they were essentially the nineteenth century counterpart of a "dream team," to present Levi's case.

The trial commenced on March 31st. In three lengthy days, the jury heard seventy-five witnesses, one who stated that he saw a man who resembled Weeks dipping a pole in the well a week prior to the slaying to check its depth.

Prosecutor Cadwallader Colden told the jurors that Elma Sands was a "woman of virtue" until she took up with the likes of Levi Weeks. And that Weeks, pretending to have honorable intentions toward Sands, came to fetch her on the pretense of marriage, but instead brought her to the well where he murdered her.

Aaron Burr and Alexander Hamilton then took up the defense. They slandered Elma as immoral and suicidal, stating that she most likely threw herself down the well in repentance over her wicked life.

In *Burr, A Novel*, there is a fictional conversation between Washington Irving and the book's narrator about the Manhattan Well Mystery.

In the book, Irving remarked that by the time Burr gave his summation:

"...[T]he jury and the judge...no doubt the devil himself — were convinced that Elma Sands was a woman of no virtue while Levi Weeks was a young Galahad..."

Burr and Hamilton slammed the reliability and memories of the witnesses, by illustrating that, with their "common" backgrounds, they could not be counted on to recall what really happened.

And Judge John Lansing, if not in the pockets of Burr and Hamilton, certainly had much to learn about fair jurisprudence. He disallowed statements that Sands anticipated wedding Weeks. Judge Lansing also seemed to have not been up on the proper methods of charging a jury.

He stated to the "gentlemen of the jury" that Sands most likely drowned, that young Weeks did not possess a killer's nature, and that the testimony given did not sustain a guilty decision in the case.

At that time, trials continued without a break until their completion. As a result, the jury who, at one juncture during the testimony implored the judge for a sleep break, was exhausted by the end of the proceedings.

Not wanting to rock the mighty judicial boat in front of them and also suffering from sheer exhaustion, the jury came back with a "not guilty" verdict in five minutes.

New Yorkers were enraged. The victim's cousin, Catherine, was so angered upon hearing the jury's findings, she put a curse on the defense lawyers and the judge. She pointed at Alexander Hamilton and cried:

"If thee dies a natural death...there is no justice in heaven."

Levi Weeks, knowing it was in his best interests to leave town, fast, promptly resettled in Natchez, Mississippi. Judge Lansing disappeared in 1829, never to be seen again. Hamilton perished in the duel with co-counsel Burr. Burr, after the duel, was arrested for treason in an attempt to create a new country in the western United States. When President Jefferson pardoned him, Burr traveled to Europe where he aimed to procure an army to invade Florida.

And Elma Sands? Her ghost returned, as a *New York Times* article related, revisiting the area and fervently indicating to all where she was killed around Christmas, 1799. The specter of the slain woman has been seen coming from nearby Burr's Manhattan Well.

Many, many years later a restaurant, The Manhattan Bistro, sprung up on the spot of the former well. Elma Sands' body was found where the present basement of the building is under an alleyway beside a loft building on Greene Street north of Spring Street.

And that brings us to the haunting of The Manhattan Bistro.

The Manhattan Bistro
129 Spring Street

Manhattan Bistro (exterior). *Courtesy of Michael Meyer-Wakneen, Manager.*

Michael Meyer-Wakneen, Manager, in front of Manhattan Well (basement of Manhattan Bistro). *Courtesy of Michael Meyer-Wakneen, Manager.*

The Manhattan Bistro has been at the same site since 1954, quite an accomplishment in the fast-changing world of New York City restaurants. When I visited the Bistro, old liquor and wine bottles were featured on a shelf above the bar, having been excavated from where the Manhattan Well sits.

Both Marie DaGrossa, owner, and Michael Meyer-Wakneen, manager, were kind enough to allow me to photograph the old Manhattan Well, which is quite impressive and is situated in their basement. But Meyer-Wakneen noted that, at the time of its construction, it was really on street level.

Meyer-Wakneen stated that:

"Once a paranormal investigator wanted to take a look at the old Manhattan Well. But when I tried to open the door that leads to the basement and the well, it would not open. It only did after the investigator left."

Owner DaGrossa often hears banging when no one is about, while working at her desk, situated right next to the well. The area is used as both office space and an ideal setting to cool their wine.

The spirit of Sands has been seen many times in the area of the old Manhattan Well. A man was shocked one night by the ghost of what he characterized as a young woman with long hair and a dress dirtied by moss and wet weeds. Elma has been heard crying for help, according to a *New York Daily News* article.

Another sighting was by a sanitation worker who saw the misty form of a woman in the alley in back of 129 Spring Street. In 1974, a local stated that a gray-haired ghost attired in mossy garments rose from his waterbed. About this same time, a woman residing at #122, across from the Manhattan Bistro, peered out her window one early December morning and beheld a woeful, floating entity.

[Was the murder of Elma Sands the genesis for Theodore Dreiser's *An American Tragedy*? In Dreiser's novel, a young woman having an affair with her upper class employer, who promised matrimony after getting her pregnant, was drowned by him to cover up their affair and so preserve his social standing.]

In any event, justice often prevails. Soon after the "Manhattan Murder Mystery," Washington Irving concluded in *Burr, A Novel*:

"...[Burr] lives on...under the dread mark of Cain...,"

Burr's cherished daughter, Theodosia, named for Burr's wife, was lost at sea in 1812 while sailing to meet him on his return to New York, as mentioned in the "Battery" piece. Theodosia's specter has been seen walking the Cape Hatteras, North Carolina beaches.

She left Georgetown for New York aboard *The Patriot*. The vessel presumably strayed off course and was lost. Some have speculated that it vanished into the Bermuda Triangle, for no remains of the ship were ever found. Many think her confused ghost came to Cape Hatteras to wait for another ship to take her home to her father.

Perhaps Elma Sands finally has attained complete justice.

Chapter XIII

Churches

St. Mark's In-The-Bowery
131 East 10th Street at 2nd Avenue

St. Mark's in the Bowery. Courtesy of the Rev. Julio O. Torres, Priest-in-Charge.

Erected in 1799, St. Mark's In-The-Bowery (from the Dutch "bouwerie" or farm) is New York City's second oldest church, after St. Paul's Chapel. A National Historic Landmark, St. Mark's first catered to a wealthy, traditional congregation. An Episcopal church since its inception, St. Mark's is also thought to be the location of New York's first governor, Peter Stuyvesant's, private chapel.

New York City Folklore fills in more details on Governor Peter Stuyvesant.

The final and most colorful Dutch governor of New York City, Peter Stuyvesant is interred in St. Mark's. He passed away in 1672 on the farm where the church now stands. Stuyvesant lived an almost hermit-like existence after the English defeat of New York. His remains were laid in a crypt in the chapel he had constructed in 1660, which has been re-fashioned into St. Mark's in-the-Bowery.

The graveyard of the church, often locked, was the site of a macabre kidnapping in 1878. Department store millionaire A.T. Stewart was dug up and hauled away, a $20,000 ransom demanded for his safe return. His remains were finally retrieved — two years later. Other dearly departed interred in the graveyard include Commodore Matthew Perry, Daniel Tompkins, and members of the Fish, Schermerhorn, Stuyvesant, and Livingston families, all old New York names. A plaque on the church commemorates writer W.W. Auden.

The old church bell tolled the passing of President John F. Kennedy, Robert F. Kennedy and Rev. Martin Luther King. Since King's murder, it has pealed for the end of the Vietnam War.

From virtually the moment Stuyvesant died in 1672 at eighty, household help and workers described seeing the ghost of Peter Stuyvesant "hobbling" about his old farm. Stuyvesant had a wooden peg-leg and walked with a cane and was often referred to as "Peg-leg Peter" or "Old Silver Nails."

Any meddling with the graves of St. Mark's, even the laying of a street nearby, has caused peculiar and often terrifying happenings. Rappings, as if by Stuyvesant's famous wooden leg, are heard emanating from the bowels of his crypt.

In 1774, his old estate burned down. In the middle of the night, a spectral shape was seen hobbling about the wreckage. Was it the irate ghost of Stuyvesant surveying the destruction?

Again in the early nineteenth century, when houses were constructed and roads cut around the graveyard, odd and scary occurrences took place, including spectral moaning and tapping. In the 1960s, a church sexton came to the chapel late one night only to run away in panic. Stuyvesant had proceeded toward him.

When a sacrilegious commissioner ordered the cutting of Second Avenue through the graveyard in the 1930s, the church bell started to madly toll at midnight. The sexton and others, woken by the wild tolling, rushed to the church, which they found well bolted. As they searched for who was tolling the bell, the ringing stopped.

In the midst of the Civil War, a sexton "was chased from the church by the repetitive clunk of Peter's peg-leg," his "shrieks" so shrill that nearby occupants were roused from their beds.

They congregated at the church and the sexton related what happened to him. At that instance, the bells of St. Mark's started to ring and the people, along with the sexton, were well aware that not a soul should be in the church at that time.

After the pealing stopped, the bell rope was inspected and found to be torn in half. Located high above their heads, it was not possible for any living soul to reach it. A length of bell-tower rope was located the next morning by the busy church sexton, atop Peg-leg Peter's grave.

"Old Silver Nails" let construction workers know not to encroach on his former property during the Second Avenue building project when it grew too close to the St. Mark's graveyard.

The pealing of the church bell was heard once again.

Many thought that Peter's soul may finally have found peace in the early 1950s. His last direct descendant was placed in the Stuyvesant vault at St. Mark's and it was sealed.

But prior to Christmas, 1995, an unidentified woman who never heard of the ghostly stories was strolling across the front of the church. She:

> "...[H]eard what sounded like a soft shuffle and then a distinct thump...It was...echoey...like something out of an old pirate movie-some pirate shuffling along with a wooden leg!..."

When the woman learned that Peter Stuyvesant was entombed there and that he sported a wooden leg, she "was a little spooked."

Another time, the woman was nearing the church when she heard the thumping again "as if it was coming from the churchyard." She headed to where she thought the sound was coming from. Out of the corner her eye, she thought she saw the ghost of Governor Peter Stuyvesant, walking at a fairly brisk rate.

The woman further noted that if anyone wanted to perhaps encounter "Silver Nails" themselves, they might want to pay a visit to the churchyard on Christmas Eve (a magical time for many), when, she heard, Peg-leg Peter would be sure to check out his old environs.

But old "Silver Nails" does not have a monopoly on the haunting of St. Mark's.

In 1943, a former rector noted that each time he was on the pulpit, there was always one parishioner who came alone, and sat in the same pew.

When he inquired of the man why he had a special fondness for that seat, the man said it was the ideal seat for viewing the specter of a woman who always materialized in the midst of every service in the center aisle of the nave and quickly vanished when services were completed. She has also been spotted in the church balcony and tower.

Another female specter stands by the rear entrance, and a spectral shape had also been seen in the balcony next to the organ.

Many psychics have corroborated that there is tangible energy of the specter and the investigator stated that he had recorded the energy on photographic film shot in the old, haunted church.

A member of the Arts Project, a current series of dance, poetry, and theatrical training and shows at the "cathedral of the East Village" said she also heard the tales.

> "I have...talked to two people who say they've sensed the energy here. One said she detected a very sad spirit, while the... gentleman said he felt the presence of a very content ghost."

The Bowery was originally the road to Stuyvesant's farm, and it is thought that "the stubborn Dutchman" would not relinquish what he felt was his land without a fight. After he died, the ghost of Peter Stuyvesant had been seen strolling about his former home. Today, those who reside in the area, tourists, and the homeless describe meeting his phantom ambling down the sidewalks.

Interestingly, the same church that served the needs of New York's conservative affluent, St. Mark's In-The-Bowery is now the site for artistic performances that have included, among others, Isodora Duncan's dances, and a Robert Frost poetry reading.

Poets & Writers Magazine had an article about The Poetry Project at St. Mark's.

Started in 1966, The Poetry Project features public literary events and is a resource for writers. It is the site of the only joint reading by Robert Lowell and Allen Ginsberg and had been used for historic memorials to such writers as Frank O'Hara and Ted Berrigan. William Carlos Williams read his poems in the church's main sanctuary, as did parishioner and poet W.H. Auden.

Other writers and performers have included William Burroughs, Sam Shephard (who produced his first plays there), Alice Walker, Amiri Baraka, Virgil Thompson, Adrienne Rich, Yoko Ono, and Patti Smith. Every year, the Poetry Project has a New Year's marathon poetry reading that begins on New Year's Eve, runs throughout the night and well into the next day.

As long as St. Mark's in the Bowery is active, you can be sure to see the ghost of Peter Stuyvesant, most often strolling down Stuyvesant Avenue toward Cooper Square, his peg-leg keeping an unsteady gait.

Peter Stuyvesant bust (St. Mark's in the Bowery). *Courtesy of the Rev. Julio O. Torres, Priest-in-Charge.*

The Church of the Ascension
12 West 11th Street

Built in 1840, The Church of the Ascension is thought to be a wonderful example of "brownstone Gothic revival" architecture.

The church was the site for an atypical (at that time) wedding two years later when President John Tyler ("Tippecanoe and Tyler too") wed Julia Gardiner, thirty-five years his junior. The bride, whose family still owns Gardiner's Island at the edge of Long Island Sound, was thought to be Long Island's most beautiful woman.

According to *Sidewalks of New York* walking tour, when workmen were renovating the church a few years ago, the massive mural by John La Farge that hangs above the alter almost fell, injuring them. They had the distinct impression that someone did not want them to disturb the original placements within the church, some designed by Stanford White.

St. Luke-in-the-Fields
487 Hudson Street

St. Luke-in-the-Fields. *Courtesy of Paul Kline, Dir. Finance & Operations.*

"...He sprang to his sleigh, to his team gave a whistle,
And away they all flew like the down of a thistle..."
Excerpt from "The Night Before Christmas"
by Clement C. Moore (or was it?)

Erected in 1822, St. Luke-in-the-Fields is the City's third oldest church. And it is a very charming church, evoking what the area must have looked like in the early nineteenth century.

When I took pictures of St. Luke-in-the-Fields, I ventured upstairs, and marveled at the bell rope that simply hung through a hole in the ceiling, leading to the cupola. Not long after, a custodian rang the bell to call the faithful to services. When I asked the strapping man if it was hard to pull the bell, he replied that yes, indeed it was.

For many years, St. Luke-in-the-Fields was the recipient of Leake's Dole, a weekly present of bread to indigent parishioners who came to the ten o'clock Saturday service. Granted by a gift in the Will of John Leake who died in 1792, Leake bequeathed that one thousand pounds "put out at interest to be laid out in the annual income in sixpenny wheaten loaves of bread are distributed...to such poor as shall appear most deserving."

St. Luke-in-the-Fields' parish house is the home of the ghost of Clement C. Moore, states *New York City Ghost Stories*.

Moore, St. Luke's first pastor, assisted in drawing up the plans for the first building which was destroyed in a fire. Moore was also bequeathed all of what is now Chelsea from 24th Street to 19th Street, and Eighth Avenue to the Hudson River.

But he is said to be most famous for writing the timeless "A Visit from St. Nicholas," thought to be an 1822 Christmas present for his daughter. But a *Los Angeles Times* piece stated otherwise.

English Professor Don Foster of Vassar College (New York), who wrote *Author Unknown: On the Trail of Anonymous*, (which unmasked the "Anonymous" of *Primary Colors* to be Joe Klein), wrote that a Major Henry Livingston, Jr., an obscure bon vivant and Revolutionary War veteran, actually wrote "The Night Before Christmas."

Maybe that is why the spirit of Clement C. Moore has not been able to leave the parish house of St. Luke-in-the-Fields. He has been found out, and it only took less than two hundred years, thanks to Prof. Foster of Vassar College.

Chapter XIV

Hotels and Apartment Buildings

Hotel Thirty Thirty
(formerly the Martha Washington Hotel)
30 East 30th Street

The story of the ghost of the Hotel 3030 occurred when it was the Martha Washington Hotel, a women's residence. A 12th floor room is said to be haunted by the obstinate phantom of an elderly woman who once resided there. Subsequent occupants related they could hear the ghost turning news pages late at night.

The book *Haunted America* elaborates further.

Eileen Courtis, a Londoner, came to New York at thirty-four, and thought she might find a peaceful hotel and a job. She found an office position and the Martha Washington Hotel where she rented a room on the 12th floor.

Instantly, upon crossing the threshold, she was sickened by an offensive smell emanating from the room. She thought at first to demand another room, but did not feel like making a stir and kept the room. She thought she would stay for only a few days but after six months she was still there and not yet unpacked.

All her life, Eileen had many occurrences of ESP. Her initial feeling of her room was that someone had passed away in it.

One night, she was awakened "by what sounded like... someone...sitting in the chair at the foot of her bed reading a newspaper." Immediately, she flipped on the light. No one was there. So, she went back to sleep.

At once, the sound resumed, along with that of someone walking across the floor, starting from the chair and heading toward the door. When Eileen switched on all the lights, the sound ceased. Worn out, she nodded off again.

The following morning, she examined the room meticulously. Maybe it was mice. The odd smell was still there and she asked management to fumigate the room. All the manager did was give her a droll grin and no one ever fumigated the room. The rustling sound kept up, night after night. Eileen slept with the lights on for the next three weeks.

Her ESP conveyed to her that the presence was a iron-willed, spiteful old woman who took umbrage with others living in what she still viewed as "her" room. Eileen thought it time to fight her and stay. The same pattern continued, the rustling of pages and the walking, and every morning Eileen woke, completely fatigued, from all the action of the night. Her co-workers wondered why she looked so worn out but Eileen needed that room and was determined to fight for it.

One night, she lay in bed, knowing something would once again happen. Instantly, two bony but powerful arms reached over her head, clutching a large pillow to smother her. Eileen fought back, with all her might, to push the pillow from her face.

Eileen was resolute about staying in her room. Maybe she was being as stubborn as her tormentor.

One evening, she came home from the office and felt a quick pain in her back, as if being stabbed. In the night, she woke feeling completely crippled, unable to move her arms, legs or head. Eventually, after a seemingly never-ending moment, she grabbed the telephone and called for a doctor but none came. She called a friend who hurried over, to discover Eileen in a state of shock.

During the following days, she had a complete examination by the company doctor, which included X-rays. She was fine. Her vigor had finally returned and she thought it time to throw in the towel.

She rested in Florida and ultimately returned to New York and the Martha Washington Hotel. She no longer wanted the room that caused her so much grief on the 12th floor and resided in another room with no problems for more than a year.

One day, a neighbor who remembered Eileen from her days on the 12th floor ran into her in the lobby and pressed for a visit. Eileen, who kept her own company, finally, reluctantly agreed.

They spoke of many things when the neighbor suddenly mentioned that Eileen had rented, "that haunted room across the hall."

Eileen had never mentioned to anyone what she had gone through and was therefore baffled by what this woman said. The neighbor acknowledged that she had meant to caution Eileen while she was living in that room, but could never gather up sufficient courage to do so.

Eileen demanded that the woman tell her what ailed her former room.

"The woman who had the room...before you...was found dead in the chair...the woman who had it before her was also found dead, in the bathtub."

Eileen gasped and left quickly. She then knew that the pillow threat was not a delusion and that she was lucky to be alive.

The Empire State Building
33rd and 34th Streets at 350 Fifth Avenue

The land marked Empire State Building is once again New York's tallest skyscraper, due to the attack on the World Trade Center.

Demolition for the building of The Empire State Building began just two months shy of the 1929 stock market crash. The Empire State Building cost just under $41 million to construct due to the harsh economic times in which it was built and was put up in record time.

The great 1933 movie *King Kong* (one of my favorites), thought to be an extraordinary example of composite motion picture photography, used the Empire State Building for its climax, the legendary Kong battling army planes, to his death.

That same year, Irma Eberhardt jumped from the top of the Empire State Building and achieved the sad distinction of being its first suicide.

On July 28, 1945, after weaving its way among the towers of midtown Manhattan in a fog, an Army B-52 smashed into the 79th floor, killing fourteen. Two British parachutists, in 1986, jumped from the 86th floor and perched safely near Fifth Avenue and 31st Street, no doubt into the arms of New York's Finest. The Empire State Building's staircases yearly are transformed into a race as climbers vie in the Empire State Run-up, the winners making times for the eighty-six flights in eleven-and-a-half minutes.

A New York Daily News article relates that the Empire State Building has a ghost.

A young woman in 1940s attire rambles through the halls, forever expecting the young man who swore he would meet her at the top of the building during V-J Day.

57 West 57th Street
(Medical Arts Building)

A malicious specter in the penthouse apartment of 57 West 57th has been attributed with causing inhabitants to lose their minds.

The heavy feeling that is associated with this haunting is linked to socialite Edna Champion and her French lover, Charles Brazelle. They resided in the building and had a concealed passageway joining their apartments.

Their hostile rows apparently resulted in their deaths for both died from injuries at each other's hands.

The book I Believe in Ghosts fills is more details.

Edna Crawford Champion (of Champion spark plug name) inherited $12 million dollars from her husband, who died from, presumably, a heart attack after a fierce beating by Brazelle in Paris' Hotel Crillon bar in 1927.

Edna yearned to buy the penthouse apartment of 57 West 57th Street for her lover Brazelle. Brazelle in turn yearned for not only the penthouse but also Edna Champion's millions. When Champion attempted to purchase the penthouse, her offer was rejected. Edna, not to be deterred, instead bought the entire building, paying $1,300,000 in cash.

Edna, described as a "luscious blonde beauty," had come to New York for just such a catch as Albert Champion. But she did not cotton to the idea of simply being Champion's mistress – she wanted to be his wife. As such, Champion gave his then-wife $1 million to get lost so he and Edna could get married.

Champion, like many other older husbands of young brides, was ridiculously possessive of Edna. He gave her clothes, furs and jewelry but did not give Edna her own bank account, or even large amounts of cash, evidently afraid she might become too independent of him.

Traveling to Paris on business, Champion made plans for Edna to follow him at a later date. Once in Paris, through a friend of Champion, Edna met Charles Brazelle, charming, handsome and much younger than Edna. Brazelle was a "fortune-hunter with a way with women," and Edna, never one to turn down the attentions of an attractive younger man, was an easy mark for Brazelle.

It was not long before Champion found out what Edna was up to when he was at business meetings. Even though Champion threatened to cut Edna off financially, even refusing to give her everyday spending money, she willfully continued to meet with Brazelle on the sly.

One night, while Edna and Brazelle were having a romantic moment at the Crillon Bar, Champion found them together. A tumultuous commotion ensued and Brazelle hit Champion, who wobbled away. A few hours later, he was found dead in his hotel room. Brazelle's story to the Paris authorities was that Champion "had a weak heart."

Following a cursory inquiry, no doubt accelerated by the greasing of well-placed palms, the authorities abandoned the case. Champion's death was said to be from natural causes.

In spite of Edna instantly being fabulously wealthy, wedding bells with Brazelle were not on the horizon yet, for he was already married. Edna would have to settle with being Brazelle's lover, for the time.

Back in New York, Edna and Brazelle were soon enough having a grand time wasting Champion's money. One of Brazelle's fancies was to reside in a what was then considered a "newfangled apartment with a penthouse." As such, Edna, wishing desperately to please Brazelle, bought the building at 57 West 57th Street.

Stained glass windows were installed, in addition to imported marble mantels and rare tapestries from Europe. For the playroom, Edna directed that a forty foot mural be painted, featuring a scene from a Venetian carnival, the main figures being Brazelle and Edna, naked, save for a mask, a domino, and a pair of high-heeled shoes.

A secret stairway was constructed to couple Brazelle's apartments on the lower floor with Edna rooms above. *I Believe in Ghosts* relates that:

> "[I]nside, fountains bubbled under artificial moonlight; monkeys and peacocks in gaudy colors scampered over gold and silver walls."

In the top floor penthouse, a unique room was erected to house a superb carved bed, over which floated a pure gold cloth canopy. Those religious vestments, pilfered from a Russian church, were worth $30,000.

For many years, Brazelle held Edna practically captive in the apartment, enlisting spying French servants to note her every move.

Their love nest took five years to decorate. It was not even finished when Edna was on her death bed, a pathetic casualty of drugs, alcohol and a blow caused by a telephone hurled at her by Brazelle in one of their many plastered fights.

Following the telephone melee, Edna's irate family was finally able to contact Edna and throw Brazelle out. Bodyguards were hired to prevent Brazelle from seeing Edna but he still attempted to get to her several times, secreting himself for days in the doctor's offices situated in the building, for which he had duplicate keys.

Brazelle tried one final time to see Edna the night she died.

Blocked by her bodyguards, terribly beaten and tossed from her bedroom window to the terrace below, Brazelle died soon after, and his body lay unclaimed in the morgue for ten days until an estranged brother claimed the remains of Brazelle.

Brazelle was said to have directed his business affairs quite efficiently. He collected rents from the hospital building and established a brokerage office on the second floor but neither Brazelle's banker or broker could explain the great quantities of money that he possessed and quickly threw away.

It was thought that Brazelle had squirreled away the bulk of the loot in the apartment behind the myriad secret partitions that filled the walls, or upstairs, in the engine room on the roof where, for some unexplained reason, he spent much of his time.

Following Edna's passing, her relatives undertook "treasure hunts" to find the missing loot, but with no luck. Brazelle took his monetary secrets to his tomb.

Following their deaths, the penthouse and everything in it remained vacant for some time. Carleton Alsop, at that time a sound recording company executive, wished to purchase the penthouse. Alsop, without any prior knowledge of its macabre atmosphere, thought the penthouse the right setting for an "urban honeymoon" with his bride, a former Princess and rich American widow of a Russian nobleman and relative of Mrs. John D. Rockefeller, Jr.

What attracted them most of all was the terrace that would be a good dog run for Alsop's four Great Danes.

Alas, the Alsops' bliss was fleeting. Arguments, irrational and brutal, were common in circumstances which, Alsop would later report, were not part of the customary challenges of newlyweds. Any of their parties involving liquor, (which was usually all of them), often had rather unforeseen and devastating outcomes.

Soon the ambience began to change Mrs. Alsop so curiously that her husband grew concerned. She would sit for hours before a mirror, regretting that she would shortly lose her youth and loveliness. In spite of being from a wealthy family and soon to come into her own fortune, she would brood about money, demanding everything be done on the cheap, and insisted taking her breakfast in the butler's pantry rather than in the fancy breakfast room.

She would have notes delivered to her husband mid-day that sadly stated that she could not be alone, while the house was swarming with servants. Mrs. Alsop was once discovered roaming on the 15th floor in an almost frantic state. Alsop soon learned that Mrs. Champion, oddly, had acted in the same manner.

A psychiatrist was summoned. On his counsel, they thought it wise to make certain alterations in their way of living.

They relocated to the top two floors, leased the lower floor and shut the secret stairways that Brazelle had utilized. They also tore out the fanciful decorations of the Russian boudoir and converted it into a stylish new bedroom. But to their dismay, all the paint and renovations could not alter the sour environment.

But it was the actions of the four Great Danes that was the most difficult to explain.

At night, they were placed in the penthouse bedroom. When the newlyweds often awoke to their whimpering, the Alsops assumed the dogs simply missed them. But when they put the lights on, the Great Danes would be "...standing four abreast, with taut muscles and hackles on end, gazing through the bedroom's glass doors – at nothing."

Two of the Danes appeared to be completely losing their minds. They were brought back to the kennels, leaving one adult and puppy. The puppy often hid under the bed and refused to venture out.

The Great Danes and the Alsops heard sounds like the agitated click of high-heel shoes on the floor under them, and the din of odd, incomprehensible fights that wafted up the stairs.

Before the year was out, Alsop's wife left, swearing she would never come back to their penthouse. Alsop continued to live there, along with the housekeeper who had been in the employ of the Champions, and attended to the Champion's dog, an elderly chow that would not move for hours in the center of a room, whining sadly for no apparent cause.

After Mrs. Alsop left, Alsop thought he might lift his spirits with friends and nights of drinking. At one such party, a guest went to the upstairs bathroom. When he rejoined the party, he was ashen and trembling, unable to say what happened to him. Another time, a woman guest swore that someone – or something – had trailed after her down the stairs.

Great Danes are said to be one of the most congenial, as well as fearless, of dogs. But these poor dogs cowered before their master when Alsop, either alone or with friends, tried to get to the bottom of the odd footfalls on the floor below. Nothing could induce the Great Danes to venture downstairs.

When Alsop would go to that floor, whether by himself or accompanied, the noises stopped, only to restart instantly on the floor he had just left.

As a result, Alsop finally had to be hospitalized – at the hospital under the haunted penthouse. When he had convalesced enough, he thought it best to sublet the quarters, in spite of great financial loss, and look for a more serene environment in which to live.

Many years later, author Danton Walker, author of I Believe in Ghosts, visited the apartment with Alsop, who was gratified to learn that the feelings within his old home had altered immensely for the better. Perhaps the negative vibes of Champion/Brazelle were finally put to rest.

And in a storeroom was the forty foot mural of a Venetian carnival in which Brazelle and Edna modeled as the dominant figures, Edna naked but for her mask, domino, and high-heeled shoes.

The Osborne Apartments
West 57th Street between Seventh Avenue and Broadway

The book, Gotham, tells us that by the mid-1970s, the New York City Buildings Department accepted "French Flat" as a formal listing. Like "apartment house," "French Flat" suggested a grander and higher-choice structure than "tenement." To further emphasize their class rank, the new buildings boasted names with "attitude," such as the Osborne, perhaps named for the piano manufacturer.

An article in the New York Daily News tells us more about the Osborne.

One of the City's first high-end apartment buildings (or French Flats), the Osborne was constructed in 1885 by, and was also home to Stanford White. The Osborne had that unique old world grandeur that lured the artistic and wealthy.

The Osborne also has quite a macabre history. Movie star Gig Young shot and killed his wife Kim Schmidt before using the gun on himself. And because it was the interiors of the Osborne, and not the Dakota where "Rosemary's Baby" was shot, it seems only appropriate that the Osborne would have its share of ghosts.

Doorman Constans Matsoukas had an encounter with the supernatural at the Osborne.

In 1973, he was asleep in the basement and woke at 2:30 to what sounded like a door opening. Matsoukas opened his eyes and saw what he thought was a man and demanded to know whom he was and what his business was.

But the form simply smiled and did not reply. Matsoukas knew something was amiss, got up, and the form vanished.

When Matsoukas recounted what the form looked like, a woman who had resided in the Osborne for many years stated that it fit the description of a man who was discovered dead in his apartment on the ninth floor.

Matsoukas related that often, when he was in the lobby, he had a feeling of someone watching him. The other doormen and porters felt it as well, so he assumed the phantom was still there. A night doorman stated that he sometimes responded to an elevator call late at night, only to discover no one there when the elevator reached the floor, always the ninth.

One of the Osborne's most acclaimed residents, Maestro Samuel Margolis, a voice teacher whose students have included Robert Merrill, Jose Ferrer, and Gertrude Lawrence, was frequently visited by apparitions. The phantom seemed to cling to three of Maestro Margolis' eight gigantic, high-ceilinged rooms, packed with costly antiques and memorabilia of the maestro's profession.

A voice student and member of the household, Tom Bertram, often beheld phantoms in the apartment. One time, he awoke to see a man with a pleasing face and short hair approaching him. During another visitation, a hand took hold of Bertram's ankle and shook him heartily. Bertram was convinced it was the work of the phantom.

Bertram had a canvas suitcase in his room. One night, it was abruptly thrown down the stairs. He ultimately vacated that room, so ill at ease from its unseen visitors, stating that he would never sleep there again.

Margolies questioned whether there were ghosts in his apartment, but could not account for how, one night, all the living room pictures fell off their nails and smashed simultaneously to the floor.

Hotel Des Artistes
1 West 67th Street

Hotel Des Artistes. *Courtesy of Gerard Picasso, Managing Agent.*

Built in 1917, the 1920 census revealed that fourteen artists, musicians, or writers, eleven actors or movie executives, twenty-two stockbrokers, engineers, and other businesspeople resided at the Hotel Des Artistes. The most recurrent job listed, household staff servants, totaled twenty-six, according to a *New York Times* article.

LeRoy Neiman, Richard Thomas, Joel Gray, Noel Coward, Zasu Pitts, Edna Ferber, Isadora Duncan, Norman Rockwell, and former mayor John V. Lindsay have all called the Hotel Des Artists home.

Directors Alan Crosland, of Al Jolson's 1927 "The Jazz Singer," and George Fitzmaurice who directed Great Garbo in the 1931 "Mata Hari" were also occupants. In 1925, Fitzmaurice surmised that, because movies were then being shown on Paris-to-London planes, they would soon be available on the New York City subway system.

The ten-floor, $1.2 million structure was the largest studio building in the world, with a swimming pool, squash court, sun parlor, ballroom, and restaurants. The gothic style façade is often thought to be the cornerstone building on a block of artists' studios.

The New York Daily News has an article about "The Mad Spirit of Des Artistes."

Author Margaret Widdemer purchased her apartment from a Mrs. F. Widdemer, whose friends and cleaning woman all had weird experiences in her apartment, ranging from sounds from no discernible source, the slamming of doors, and abrupt feelings of horror and terror.

Hans Holzer was summoned and came one night with his tape recorder and a few friends with supernatural abilities, including designer and actor Barrie Gaunt.

As Gaunt strolled about the apartment, he grew agitated and bewildered.

"Someone came up these stairs, stopped about here and turned around – hate in the eyes. It's a woman," he indicated.

His left hand felt strangely stiff and he had a feeling that someone was murdered there, zeroing in on the staircase where it curved. He picked up a tormented wailing, and in the room just above, utter chaos. He stated that there was:

"A very beautiful woman, also a man, and I feel there's been a death here, a death by violence. The woman is fighting for her life, but not physically. Rather, she his fighting for her sanity. The person who is dead in this apartment is the man."

In the following days, Widdemer spoke to many of the other occupants and learned that the F. family's daughter was a tall, beautiful, blue-eyed blonde. When she was roughly seventeen, she went insane, and grew so wild she had to be placed in a mental hospital.

There was a history of mental illness on both sides of the family. The girl's loathing was aimed at, for reasons not understood, her mother. As such, the mother was not able to visit her daughter in the asylum, so violent was the unfortunate girl's reaction to her. The girl passed away in the asylum.

Was it her father trying to control his wild daughter that Gaunt picked up on the stairs? Or the specter of the pathetic girl still trying to hold onto her old home, fighting the awful power of untreated mental illness that would tear her away forever?

The Hotel Des Artists is also ghosted by a specter who enjoys touching people. The extroverted apparition has been seen by several occupants and some wonder if it the ghost of silent film star Rudolph Valentino.

Valentino died in 1926. His funeral drew throngs of frenzied fans, some of whom even threw themselves out of windows, so despondent over his death. Valentino's specter is said to float by, as indicated by a bluish color in a hallway mirror and trail of "exotic cologne."

The Ansonia
2109 Broadway between 73rd and 74th Streets

Built in 1904, The Ansonia was an apartment hotel that offered restaurants and a complete domestic staff. Once the New York City home of Caruso, Toscanini, Ziegfeld, and Stravinsky, among others, the Ansonia to this day still attracts an artsy crowd. Developer William Earl Dodge Stokes penned ducks, chickens and a pet bear on the roof. On a much, much lesser level, Plato's Retreat, one of the swinging clubs of the 1970s, was housed there, until it was swept away, a casualty of AIDS.

The 1992 psychological thriller, "Single White Female," was filmed at the Ansonia. An article in the *New York Daily News* stated that it is home to many clairvoyants and spiritualists. The Ansonia also hosted a phantom family of Russian royalty, and a child's ghost attired in old-fashioned clothes.

Chapter XV

Museums

Old Merchant's House Museum
29 East Fourth Street

Old Merchant's House Museum. *Courtesy of Margaret Gardiner, Exec. Dir.*

Listed in the National Register of Historic Places, the Old Merchant's House Museum is a three story brick townhouse built in 1832. A beautiful and uncommon "survivor" from when the Bond Street area was the City's most desired address (as attested in the Bouwerie Lane Theatre entry), the old Merchant's House Museum was originally constructed by a hat dealer (who used to put scripture quotes in the hats), trying his hand at real estate.

New York City Ghost Stories tells us the House was bought in 1835 for $18,000 by Seabury Tredwell, a merchant on the way up. Seabury and his wife Eliza had children, three of whom married.

Mary, the dreamer, often doodled men in top hats in her tablets, which are still in the possession of the Museum. The three remaining daughters were Phoebe, Sarah, and Gertrude. Called Gitty when young, Gertrude was the last child, born in 1840. There were also two boys, who managed to do not much of anything, surprising considering how status meant everything to their father.

The Tredwell family filled their home with fine fashionable furniture, some late Federal, American Empire and a few Victorian pieces, which are still there today. The townhouse was kept in the family until the last immediate Tredwell – Gertrude – passed away there in 1933.

Luckily for the City of New York, Gertrude, like her father, was frugal, evidently never tossing anything out. At the end of her life, Gertrude lived in respectable impoverishment which would have limited her from altering the house profoundly.

The Old Merchant's House Museum is a splendid museum, not well known to many New Yorkers or tourists, but well worth the trip. Their newsletter tells us that it is the lone family home of the City of New York maintained unimpaired from the nineteenth century and, surprisingly, Greenwich Village's sole historic house museum. The landmarked Museum has been open to the public since 1936.

Because the Museum is available for private parties, corporate events, still photography and film shoots, Jackie Plant, a food editor, utilized the space for a food photo shoot in 1994.

It was a ten hour shoot for a Thanksgiving meal layout, and Jackie was cooking in the somewhat workable kitchen. The dining room was made festive by her staff who showed great respect for the surroundings and were in awe of all the original items of the mansion.

Jackie plugged in a hand mixer and the fuse blew. Not so unusual in an old house, but in an old house completely rewired, it was not common to repeatedly have fuses blow.

Food Editor Plant felt a presence in the old Tredwell kitchen.

When she and her Senior Editor were joking, they sensed that an unseen third person did not like the way they had cooked the potatoes for the shoot.

Plant told me that:

"When I stood by the black horsehair couch in the hallway on the first floor, I felt the skin on the back of my neck rise up, as though something was letting me know I was not allowed to sit on the couch."

Lights frequently blew out, and there were ongoing problems with the cameras for the shoot, necessitating the use of batteries.

Plant, who grew up surrounded by antiques, admired the Tredwells' taste in furnishings and bric-a-brac. When she ventured upstairs to look around, Plant reported:

"I picked up the presence of a family – a stern father who had a ram-rod straight back and frolicking children."

In spite of Plant's feeling that Seabury had stern ways, she did not sense that the children feared him.

The Old Merchant's House Museum is quite savvy about its ghosts. While some haunted New York sites are not so forthcoming with information as to their unseen guests, the Old Merchant's House Museum hosted a talk on April 25, 2001 entitled, "Is the Merchant's House Museum Haunted?" The talk was presented at the Museum by Carlos S. Alvarado, PH D., Chairman of Domestic and International Programs of the Parapsychology Foundation.

It was only their second talk that garnered a standing room audience (including me), the other talk on "Edith Wharton at the Merchant's House."

Dr. Alvarado spoke of staff members relating such incidents as the piano in the Museum playing itself, misplaced objects that reappeared, and the odor of fresh flowers being detected when none are present. The sounds of giggling girls and a ghostly woman singing have been heard. In April 2000, the dining room door slowly opened by itself. Alvarado reported this is referred to as "slow scale phenomena."

In November, 2000, staff member Joseph Esposito was working alone late in the office. He went to the supply closet for a folder and was paralyzed by the sound of two or three children running on the stairs, lasting four to five seconds. (In the midst of my 2002 phone interview with Esposito, he reported that their photocopy machine inexplicably turned itself on). In December of the same year, a staff member at the base of the staircase thought someone was coming down the stairs. She moved to allow the person to pass, but no one was there. (Interestingly, Phoebe Tredwell's passing is the only known tragic death to have occurred in the Old Merchant's House. She fell down a flight of stairs and broke her neck).

Equipment failure often takes place, primarily with phones and staple machines, "seen with enough frequency, it puzzles you," Alvarado reported.

Alvarado remarked:

Old Merchant's House Museum (plaque).
Courtesy of Margaret Gardiner, Exec. Dir.

"I believe enough is happening in this house to warrant a scientific investigation."

Joie Anderson, through the Jr. League Committee, stated:

"Once or twice, I was aware of a presence feeling happy that I was working there."

Some say Gertrude Tredwell's ghost has never quit the Old Merchant's House. Alvarado noted that given Gertrude's ninety-three years in the Old Merchant's House, going about her daily routines day in and year out, she imparted a magnetic energy onto her every day objects of the house and she is there still, in the only home she ever knew.

The National Directory of Haunted Places reports that Seabury Tredwell wanted a proper home befitting his growing financial status in the city. He was an old-fashioned man, as attested to by the front parlor portrait of him. The portrait was made from a photograph following his death, his hair in a queue, more in the style of the 1700s than the 1800s.

In accordance with Seabury's old-fashioned ways, he presented to Gertrude a few prudently evaluated men, young as well as old, in the desire that she might possibly select one. She reasoned that there had to be a man she could choose – and love – whom Seabury would also welcome, and that she would wait for him.

In spring, she took a walk in their garden [where high tea is now offered every Mother's Day]. Gertrude was noticed by a young man walking past the Tredwell house. They introduced themselves, something unheard of in those times of strict adherence to Victorian etiquette.

Gertrude was elated and persuaded the young man named "Lo" to gain admission into her house. Seabury welcomed Gertrude's young man, a poor medical student.

Gertrude beseeched her father that her "Lo" would make a very good doctor one day. But Seabury's retort was to ask what Lo was going to live on until then? His money?

Tredwell assumed, and maybe not without cause, that everyone in New York City knew his daughters were heiresses who would have substantial dowries. This concept was so firmly entrenched in Seabury's mind that he distrusted every young man (not previously sanctioned by Tredwell) who came a' calling as being a gold digger. Lo was, he maintained, not after Gertrude's love but only her money.

Gertrude had an inescapable allure and confidence. Small, blue-eyed, and dark haired, Gertrude resembled Great Britain's Princess Margaret when she was in her late twenties.

Tredwell steadfastly balked at welcoming the young medical student as a potential mate for his Gertrude. In addition to his low financial holdings, he was Catholic. Tredwell did not cotton to supporting wedlock out of the family faith. Even if Louis suggested conversion to Gertrude's faith, it was unlikely Seabury would ever change his mind.

Despite Gertrude's love for this young man, and in firm observance of Victorian mores, Seabury told Gertrude that she could no longer see the man she loved. Seabury, plagued with the suffering and pains of encroaching age, begged her not to let him down in his twilight years. All he wished was that she choose someone who could take care of her in the style to which she was accustomed, and that Louis could not give her that.

Regardless of her heart, Gertrude eventually gave in to her father and sent the young man packing, giving up her life for her father, never again receiving a gentleman caller.

Seabury Tredwell died in 1865. The two remaining sisters, Gertrude and Phoebe, carried on living in the house. Gertrude ran the house and the sisters only ventured outside at night, when they absolutely had to purchase food.

The windows were kept shuttered. Even minuscule bits of light were hidden with felt or other cloth to prevent light and cold from penetrating their inner sanctum. As Gertrude and Phoebe severed themselves completely from the outside world, myths abounded about them and their lives.

After Phoebe died, Gertrude was then alone in "her father's house." At age ninety-three, she died. The two servants who discovered her dead in her bed soon departed, abandoning Seabury Tredwell's once-fine house to new owners, or just plain neglect.

The sisters clung to the past, for there was neither electricity nor telephone in the house and the original furniture and all fine works of art were still there. The sole heat emanated from fireplaces, of which the house has many. The garden, at that time, was long gone. Only the house was still there, between a garage and ordinary modern building.

The Tredwell house was in dire need of renovation. Gertrude had willed the house to her niece, Lilly Nichols. But, as she was getting on in years and it was only a matter of time until she too would die, a relative, George Chapman, made arrangements that the title be transferred to him, with an eye to the future.

The Tredwell mansion had the makings of an ideal museum, for it was one of the few houses in the United States that offered all contents— from furniture to personal items and clothes – still untouched just as it was when the Tredwells resided there in the nineteenth century. Eventually, the old Seabury Tredwell mansion evolved into the Old Merchant's House Museum.

When the first custodian came to reside in the house, it was found that thieves had stolen a pair of Sheffield candelabra, a first edition of Charlotte Bronte, and the Tredwell family *Bible*. But the rest of the house was in good order, in spite of the fact that much cosmetic work had to take place right away.

One of the women helping in this was alone in the house one afternoon. She had been hauling some of Miss Gertrude's clothing downstairs in order for it to be appropriately exhibited in a special glass case.

She took a breather from her work, gazed up and saw a woman on the stairs eyeing her intently.

The woman resembled Princess Margaret of England. But she noted the odd, old-fashioned garments the woman wore and knew immediately she was part of a bygone time. The stiff-fitting bodice had a row of small buttons and the long, straight skirt fell to the floor. As she gaped in shock, wondering who this strange person was, the woman on the stairs disappeared.

This happened many times to the volunteer, invariably when she was the only one there. She started to doubt her senses, until another volunteer, a writer who had wandered past the stair-case on her way to the library to do some research, had a similar experience.

There was an inescapable uneasiness throughout the house at nightfall, but the sounds did not actually scare the volunteers. There was much to do to ready the house for its transformation as a museum, admission fifty cents.

The volunteer attempted to create order out of the great amount of personal effects, such as dresses, gowns, shoes, and hats. The Tredwells left all their worldly possessions intact, as though they thought they would return to their corporal bodies one day and pick up where their lives had left off.

Writer Mrs. R. knew how significant it was to keep the house just exactly the same for future research of that era. She began by an taking inventory of Gertrude's wardrobe. As she examined the immense wardrobe one piece at a time, she had the strange sensation of being watched.

At that time, the house was threatened by burglary and vandalism, but what the writer feared was being followed by an unseen force on her trips from the third floor to the basement and back again for more clothes. Often a cold sensation grazed her as she walked through the halls, but she thought that was caused by the dank atmosphere in the old house.

One day when she walked into the front bedroom – Gertrude's old bedroom – from the hall bedroom, she had the feeling of another being close by. Something was sweeping by to reach the other door that opened into the front bedroom before the writer did.

When this took place another time, Mrs. R. started wondering if the tales about the house being haunted had some truth to them. Absolutely, there was something there, along with the sound of another whisking past her.

Finally, something happened that convinced her she was never quite alone in the house.

One morning many months after first coming to the house, she walked into the kitchen toting items to be displayed along the wall opposite the fireplace. Out of the corner of her eye, she saw what appeared to be the form of a tiny, graceful woman in front of a huge fireplace.

While Mrs. R. saw the brown taffeta gown the apparition was wearing, she could not make out her features, for her head was turned away, but she did see the cascading brown hair. Everything was muted and somewhat hazy but with substance. The ghost's hands, exceedingly beautiful and well defined against her dark gown, held a cup and saucer.

Mrs. R. was petrified, fearful to turn her head and gaze at the phantom. Abruptly, the ghost turned around and swiftly left the room and went into the hall. The writer was in a cold sweat, her hands trembling so much she had to put down the items she was carrying.

Gertrude Tredwell was still in the house, and appeared the way she was happiest, in the days of seeing her young man before her father forbid her to do so.

When Mrs. R. realized who the phantom was, she was no longer afraid. It was Gertrude's home, where she had relinquished her love to appease her father.

Soon thereafter, Mrs. R. was alone, arranging flowers for the front parlor table. The door was open to the hallway. Mrs. R. was so busy with her work she did not notice she was no longer alone.

She heard an odd noise and glanced up from the table. It was the swish-swish of a taffeta gown rushing by quickly. The writer followed the sound and beheld a woman ascending the stairs. It was the identical tiny form she had first seen at the fireplace, wearing the same taffeta gown. The figure rounded the stairs and vanished from sight, leaving the sound of the gown lingering for but a moment, and then all was still.

Mrs. R. did not feel any terror, only a cordial affection between her and the phantom. As it was all in a day's work, she carried on with her flower arranging.

At that time, the Old Merchant's House Museum's curator was experienced antiquarian Janet Hutchinson, who divided up the appointments with her friend Emeline Paige, Editor of the *Villages*, a local paper, and Mrs. Hutchinson's son, Jefferson. Emeline often felt uncomfortable in the back bedroom.

Another who picked up the heavy feeling of the Museum was novelist Elizabeth Byrd and her friend Mrs. B. who paid a call on the house one night in 1964. As Byrd stood in what was Gertrude's bedroom, she saw that the bedspread was indented – as though someone had just gotten up from it. As she gaped in wonder at the bed, she smelled an odd scent. Those with her noted the scent also, but it faded away before they could find the source.

Mrs. R., the force behind the Historical Landmarks Society, is quite sure Gertrude no longer has to oversee restoration of her home now that everything is in its proper place.

The Old Merchant's House is now a private museum, no longer threatened by the ever-changing landscape of the City. An old tunnel was walled up to keep rats out but still remains.

Apparently Gertrude Tredwell and her siblings have never completely quit "their father's house," but perhaps they have all finally found lasting peace within its gracious walls.

Murray Hill Morgan Library
29 East 36th Street, between Madison and Park Avenues

The Morgan Library. *Courtesy of Marilyn Palmeri, Mgr., Photography and Rights.*

The Morgan Library was built in 1906 by McKim, Mead & White. Instead of using mortar, marble blocks were joined, much like the wonders of ancient Greece and Rome. Expenses were not spared. The marble lionesses protecting the front entrance were made by Edward Clark Potter, who later situated a more well-known pair, Patience and Fortitude, to guard the front entrance of the New York Public Library.

Set up as a museum in 1924, the Morgan Library includes an invaluable assortment of Middle Ages' manuscripts and the Renaissance, artists' drawings prior to 1800, a Gutenberg Bible permanently on display, and the "Christmas Carol" manuscript by Charles Dickens that is exhibited only during the holiday season. The Library is a testimonial to the supreme ability of Morgan to use his robber-baron wealth to his advantage.

The Morgan, not a circulating library, is one of those little-known museums of the City of New York. In the East Room, the ceiling is inlaid with the signs of the Zodiac, somewhat rivaling, but on a much smaller scale, the constellation ceiling of Grand Central Station. Morgan's study, a Renaissance-style private library, is exactly as it appeared when Morgan was alive.

The book, *Morgan Library Ghost Stories* relates that, in 1987, Supervisor of the Reading Room, Inge Dupont suggested a ghost story writing competition, one stipulation being that the tale involved the Morgan Library. In fall of that year, Charles E. Pierce, Jr., recently appointed Director of the Library, and James H. Heineman, member of the Board of Trustees, evaluated the tales to choose for a public reading which took place in December of that year.

One story by Richard Priest was entitled "Non Furtrum Facies," the story of William Bucher and a book he coveted.

The Morgan Library has four copies of the *Horae* by Aldus, dating back to the sixteenth century. William Bucher, however, had none, which he felt unjust. So he planned to pilfer one of the Morgan's copies, rationalizing that the Library still would have three others. What would be the harm?

He thought out the theft with much diligence. Bucher determined that the book was tiny enough to slide right into the side pocket of his jacket. Also, because he frequented the Morgan, they would not search him when leaving the reading room. It was so simple. All he had to do was use a substitute for the book he was lifting. Bucher made an imitation of the book, and he was so pleased with the results, he thought anyone would be hard pressed to discover the forgery.

Bucher came to the reading room at opening time, knowing full well he would most likely be the sole reader and also that only one staff member would most likely be working. He had filed the call slip the prior day, and so the book he wanted was retrieved quickly.

After the librarian turned, Bucher had the original book in his right hand while he dove the other hand into the left pocket of his jacket to take out the bogus book. Instantly, an excruciating pain blasted through his right arm, causing temporary paralysis. His cry caused the librarian to turn and look at him and Bucher knew then that his carefully laid out plans would not work.

On his way out, Bucher thought it best to put aside his illegal thoughts. As he started to descend the short flight of steps to the sidewalk, he was passed by a lady ascending the steps. Turning, she gazed right at him. Her lips did not move and Bucher heard no sound, but he somehow knew she said:

"It was indeed a prudent decision, Mr. Bucher."

She looked familiar but from where? He had seen her face – recently – in a painting? A photograph? Then he remembered.

She was Miss Greene, the first director of the Morgan Library.

The only problem was that she had been dead those twenty years.

Bucher turned to the door and asked the guard about the lady was who had just left the library.

The guard, startled, said:

"Mr. Bucher, no one had gone through this door since you did."

The Frick Collection
One East 70th Street

Henry Clay Frick, Pennsylvania Dutch trailblazer in the business of coke and steel, began amassing his art collection that would later evolve into the Frick Collection around 1895. Later, he bought the Flemish, Dutch, Italian, and Spanish paintings that currently adorn the collection. In 1905, Frick thought it unwise to go ahead with plans for a new house and gallery in Pittsburgh, fearing that pollution from his steel mills would be hazardous to his art.

The Frick Collection is housed in a mansion fashioned in an eighteenth century motif and it situated at the location of the former Lenox Library. Following Frick's death in 1919, both the house and art were bequeathed in trust for the creation of a public gallery. In 1935, the house, expanded and refurbished, was opened to the public.

The Library features, among other art works, one of Gilbert Stuart's paintings of George Washington. And it is in the area of the Library that the hauntings of the Frick have been noted.

An employee stated that anytime staffmembers attempt to use the library elevator, it inexplicably stops at floor 2, whether the button for that floor is pushed or not.

The second floor was where "Miss Frick," (as she is always referred to) daughter of Henry Clay Frick, kept her bedroom, along with those of her father and mother's. (Interestingly, as opposed to the fashion of the upper crust in those days, wherein husband and wife's bedrooms had connecting doors, Henry Clay's bedroom connected only with Miss Frick's.)

Miss Frick never married and only lived in the Frick mansion all her days.

Perhaps it is Miss Frick who always brings employees back to her quarters, forever reminding them she is ever diligent in watching them go about their tasks.

Metropolitan Museum of Art
82nd Street and Fifth Avenue

Our final museum entry is the Metropolitan Museum of Art.

Founded in 1870 by a group of civic leaders, art collectors, and philanthropists, the Metropolitan Museum is the largest art museum in the western hemisphere, with 3.3 million objects.

An article in the *New York Daily News* relates that there is a streaker phantom who sprints nude across a basement storage room.

Morris-Jumel Mansion
Roger Morris Park
65 Jumel Terrace at 160th Street

An historic site bought and preserved by the City of New York in 1903, the Morris-Jumel Mansion is one of the City's few intact pre-Revolutionary structures. Erected in 1765 and remodeled in 1810, the Morris-Jumel Mansion was originally the summer home of Lt. Col. Roger Morris and his wife Mary Philipse, rumored to have been involved with George Washington prior to her marriage. At the advent of the Revolution, the Morrises went back to England, along with numerous other rich loyalists.

George Washington turned the house into his headquarters between September 14 and October 18, 1776 during his fruitless defense of the City. The mansion slowly disintegrated, being made into a tavern until Stephen Jumel, rich French wine merchant and his wife Eliza (originally Betsy Brown) purchased and refurbished it in 1810.

Mme. Jumel was known for her haughty ways, shocking love affairs, and endless social climbing. Originally Jumel's mistress, she lead him to the altar by faking a fatal illness, according to a New York Times article, that also noted she had been a Rhode Island prostitute.

Upon Jumel's death in 1832, she became one of the wealthiest women in America. Roughly a year after Stephen died, seventy-seven-year old Aaron Burr married the fifty-eight-year old Eliza, evidently for her riches.

Their union was tempestuous. They finally separated after one year, after Eliza accused Burr of adultery, whereupon she was granted a fast divorce. Burr passed away on that same day of a broken heart, at the loss of Mme. Jumel and her wealth.

Jumel, in spite of her great wealth, was shunned by the New York City elite for her past indiscretions. Alone in her impressive mansion, she eventually lost her mind and died in 1865 at age ninety-three.

The wraith of a hateful elderly woman is often seen in the Morris-Jumel Mansion. Some speculate it is Eliza Jumel, who many whispered murdered her aging husband, Stephen, in order to wed Aaron Burr.

There have been numerous sightings of Eliza, her mentally unbalanced specter marching about her former home through the years, as well as reports of both Eliza and Stephen's specters rambling through their Mansion. Eliza's apparition has been sighted at the third floor windows yelling at playing children on the street below.

A book, The Jumel Mansion, was published in a limited edition (800 printed, 750 sold) in 1916. The author, William Henry Shelton, recounted several of the odd happenings of the Mansion in 1832 and 1833.

The earliest record of spectral occurrences in the Mansion was in a description by a Mme. Nitschke, governess of Matilde Pery, the child of one of Eliza's nieces who lived in the Mansion in 1868.

Not long after her employ, she was moved to the Lafayette Room to be closer to Pery, who was in total fear of Madame Jumel's specter, which she believed responsible for a dreadful tapping every night between midnight and 1 A.M.

Pery would run to Nitschke's room at night in great agitation to flee the phantom. Nitschke asked Pery if she was not concerned about leaving her daughter under the circumstances, but Pery maintained Matilde slept well and never heard it.

One night, Pery raced into Nitschke's bedroom howling. That alarmed Mr. Pery, who rushed in to learn what was going on. Nitschke stated that he had always been apprehensive in that particular bedroom, maintaining that the phantom of Madame Jumel, attired in a white dress, had appeared at the side of his bed.

Abruptly, there were loud raps similar to a mallet pounding from below the floor, under Mr. Pery's chair, from which he jumped quickly out of.

Nitschke asked the spirit if it wanted prayers said for it.

They heard three knocks. The taps that responded to yes and no appeared to be coming from the walls, from one side of the room, then the other.

"The manifestations...began with heavy raps on the floor...and they were followed by a clatter of what sounded like a skeleton hand drumming on the panes of the east front window.

"...[T]his same drumming...seemed to come from the room where Matilde slept, but the clatter seemed to be on some object of tin instead of on glass."

Nitschke peered into the room. The rapping continued on the tin slop-pail and then stopped completely. Matilde never awoke and Mrs. Pery admired Nitschke's courage in venturing into that ghostly room.

According to Hans Holzer's *Great American Ghost Stories*, the most well known "sighting" of Eliza's phantom took place in January, 1964.

Over a dozen students from nearby P.S. 164 came to the Mansion grounds prior to 11 A.M., looking forward to their field trip to the local historic site. But the Mansion was not yet open. And so, the boisterous kids ran and frolicked, shouted and hollered on the grounds, as kids do.

As a few ran by the two-story columns in front of the Mansion, a gray-haired woman wearing a long dress materialized on the balcony and yelled at them:

"Shut Up!"

Four girls looked up as the strange woman eyed them sharply, took a step back and went into the house.

The building curator finally came. As the students lined up, she informed them that the custodian would be along shortly to unlock the Mansion. The four girls who were told to shut up inquired why the woman who hollered at them could not open up the Mansion for their tour. The curator was confused, for there should be no one in the Mansion at that time. The custodian came, unlocked the Mansion, and the students went on their tour. Along the way, they saw an old portrait in one of the rooms. One of the girls who had been yelled at by the woman on the balcony shouted out:

"That's her! That's the lady who yelled at us!"

It was a portrait of Eliza Jumel.

Retired and present guards and volunteers, in addition to visitors with no prior information of any sightings at the Mansion, have felt many spirits.

Two other phantoms spotted on the third floor are of a servant girl who jumped to her death from the balcony, and an unidentified ghost, perhaps a soldier or maybe even Aaron Burr. In 1993, the specter of a Revolutionary War soldier was seen two different times on the top floor by schoolteachers ushering their classes on tours through the building. But the most ever-present spirit is that of Eliza Jumel.

Jumel has been reached in séance, and many times she has let mediums know she felt rage and torment and did not want them pestering her anymore. As she harangued, the spirit spoke of Napoleon and also her high-flown illusions. At one reading, Jumel demanded that a questioner leave or she would summon the authorities. She maintained she was the "wife of the Vice-President of the United States of America," which Burr had been.

Many times, spirits are held captive in a supernatural time-warp until they repent for a grave action on their part. One particular occasion in Jumel's life might explain her inability to move onto the spirit world.

There have always been doubts over the precise nature of Mr. Jumel's death. It was said that the coroner's report indicated that he sustained a mortal injury when he accidentally fell onto a pitchfork. That might have taken place, but what comes into suspicion is what Mme. Jumel's motives were for reportedly prematurely ripping her husband's bandages from his injuries, which resulted in his bleeding to death.

And then there were the whispers that Eliza was having an affair with Burr at the time of the "accident" and that Burr was part of scheme to get rid of Stephen Jumel.

In the Mansion, five months following the students' encounter with the ghost of Eliza Jumel, a séance held by Hans Holzer and medium Ethel Johnson Myers yielded the quite frank soul of Stephen Jumel.

Jumel swore that yes, his wife did away with him. In addition, the spirit of Stephen Jumel maintained that he was buried alive in the cemetery of the Old St. Patrick's Cathedral on Mott Street at the behest of his wife and with the participation of a doctor.

Stephen Jumel's spirit is thought to finally be at rest. But it remains to be seen whether the ghost of Eliza Jumel will ever give up her former home at the Morris-Jumel Mansion.

Chapter XVI

Concert Halls

Radio City Music Hall
Avenue of the Americas at 50th Street

Samuel Lionel (Roxy) Rothafel began his career playing movies in a bar back room and grew to be a show business titan, presenting radio programs and stage productions and overseeing many New York City theatres, including the sumptuous *Roxy*.

Due to his innate sense of knowing what his audience demanded, Rothafel was granted almost free artistic license by the RKO Corporation, subsidiary of RCA, who made him Director of the Music Hall, built in 1932. He not only had input into the plans for the construction of the Music Hall, he also was instrumental in originating its procedures.

Rothafel so disliked the three nudes sculptures that graced the Hall, (odd considering his ribald reputation,) that he demanded they be removed. And they were, only to be returned to their original locations at the insistence of art connoisseurs.

The auditorium of the Music Hall seats 6,200 people, and the egg-shaped ceiling is what Roxy insisted upon to provide acoustic excellence. And it is beautiful, from the auditorium to the lobby to the restrooms.

The classic, art deco layout of Radio City is uncommon. It is said that Rothafel toured Europe for inspiration from their opera houses and music halls but came up empty. On his return voyage to New York City, he was sitting in a deck chair, watching the setting sun over the great expanse of ocean. That wondrous vision was what he carried back to Radio City Music Hall.

Supernatural on Stage tells us that Roxy Rothafel had his preferred seat for Music Hall shows, aisle D, front row center, third mezzanine. Informed tour guides often let visitors know of the ghostly Roxy's sporadic visits to the Music Hall. Sporting top hat and tails, Rothafel would amble down the steps, but disappears before taking his customary seat.

Carnegie Hall
154 West 57th Street at 7th Avenue

Carnegie Hall. *Courtesy of Rachel Alexander, Senior Director.*

Built in 1891, the original auditorium of Carnegie Hall seated 2,760 and had renowned acoustics, enthralling audiences and performers alike, beginning with Tchaikovsky, who was a guest conductor opening week. Carnegie Hall was originally constructed as an Oratorio Society by Andrew Carnegie, then president. Carnegie, a frugal man who viewed money as the never-ending bottom line, did not make money on the Hall.

Almost threatened by the wrecker's ball in the early 1960s, a panel of preservationists, led by violinist Isaac Stern, rescued Carnegie Hall.

Carnegie Hall, restored in 1986, not only offers classes but also studio housing for such past illustrious denizens as Walter Damrosch, Carnegie Hall backer; Isadora Duncan; Evangeline Adams, astrologer; Fanny Hurst, author; Martha Graham, dancer; Andre Kostelanetz and Leonard Bernstein; musician Gerry Mulligan, and actor Marlon Brando.

Stagebill describes Johnny Mathis as "the world's greatest living romantic singer," (and whom Glenn and I have seen almost a dozen times). While rehearsing for an October concert in 1993, Mathis spotted the ghost of Carnegie Hall. When he mentioned this on "Good Morning America," a television talk show, the hosts abruptly changed the subject.

Chapter XVII

Restaurants and Bars

Many of New York City's restaurants had former lives as private dwellings or carriage houses. The dead only know that they cling to what was once their home, not aware of the fact that they might be scaring someone out of enjoying their dinner or drink, or perhaps, adding to it.

Bridge Cafe
279 Water Street

Bridge Cafe. *Courtesy of Adam Weprin, Proprieter.*

The landmark Bridge Cafe is the oldest wood-frame commercial structure in Manhattan, dating back to 1794.

Under the same roof since 1826 and thought to be the oldest continuous saloon in New York City, the present Bridge Cafe, in past lives, had featured infamous taverns, dance halls, a shanghai bar (where too much liquor would result in your being "shanghaied" – conked over the head to wake up aboard a ship out to sea, wherein you were pressed into service) and was said to be the home of a popular brothel in the mid-1800s.

A census of 1856 listed that, included among other occupants of 279 Water Street, were six prostitutes, of no great surprise considering the location's close proximity to the waterfront.

Since 1979, it has been the home of the Bridge Cafe, formerly McCormack's.

Owner Adam Weprin, in a telephone conversation, related several ghost stories for the Bridge Cafe.

A neighbor who lived across the street and often ate at the restaurant told Weprin that he often saw a face in the window at closing time when no one was left in the Cafe.

Roughly ten years ago, a previous manager left his keys in the office door, and ran downstairs to get coffee. When he returned, he found the keys bent and laying on the floor. He was the only living soul there at the time.

Adam recounted that over seven years ago, he and a friend were having beers at about 11:30 P.M. There was no one else in the Cafe, the gates were locked but the alarm system not yet turned on. Suddenly, they heard footsteps coming from the upstairs storage room. Adam said:

"Let's get the hell out of here."

His friend told Weprin that every time he visits the restaurant, he gets chills.

John Hesse, Executive Chef, had to fix a refrigerator in the Cafe. The son of an electrician, he was very comfortable working with electricity. Hesse went up to the storage room, removed an old chair and took it downstairs. Hesse returned to his electrical repairs and got a shock from what should have been a dead line. He wondered if his removing the chair had something to do with it. The next morning, at closing, he said aloud:

"This chair is staying here. Leave me alone."

After the attack on the World Trade Center, Lower Manhattan was all but shut down, including the Bridge Cafe, for eleven days. One day, Adam and one of the many rescue workers, came to the Cafe to collect any food that was still usable for relief workers. They took a break from their work, and had a glass of wine. Both Weprin and the rescue worker heard those same heavy footsteps from above, walking in the same direction as the last time, east toward the river. She said:

"I thought we were alone."

And they ran out.

Fraunces Tavern
54 Pearl Street at Broad Street

Fraunces Tavern. *Courtesy of Jennifer Eaton.*

Fraunces Tavern, New York City's oldest historic landmark (a designation which preserves the facade from unnecessary alterations), is a rebuilt mansion erected in 1719 for Stephen (or Etiene) DeLancey. A 1781 advertisement boasts that the mansion featured, among other selling points, a spring of exceptionally pure water.

The DeLanceys, one of New York City's richest and most powerful first families, stayed steadfast to the King of England during the Revolution and, as a result, endured the seizing of their holdings.

Prior to the War, the house was a warehouse and then a tavern owned by West Indian Samuel (Black Sam) Fraunces, an eminent patriot and restaurateur, perhaps of French background, who acquired the De Lancey house and opened it in 1762 as the "Queen's Head" Tavern.

Fraunces was a celebrated cook, principally for his desserts, which might have swayed George Washington in his choice of the Fraunces Tavern as the site for his farewell speech in 1783 to his officers at the end of the Revolutionary War when he momentarily retired to private life.

Fraunces' expertise later won him chief steward to Washington during most of his presidency. In 1785, Fraunces leased the structure to the Department of Foreign Affairs, the Treasury and the War Department for office space. In the nineteenth century, the building decayed, as did much of the area, until its acquisition in 1904 by the Sons of the Revolution of the State of New York who reconstructed it to its current state.

Fraunces Tavern is located in one of the few complete blocks of eighteenth and nineteenth century structures to have survived the ensuing downtown construction expansions.

The restaurant is located on the first floor and the two floors above are the Fraunces Tavern Museum.

Zagat's Survey of New York 1997, in its listing for Fraunces Tavern, writes that the specter of George Washington has never left this historical site where he said farewell to his officers.

The Ear Inn
326 Spring Street

The Ear Inn. *Courtesy of Martin Sheridan, Owner.*

Built in 1817, the land marked Federal style James Brown House is named for a former slave turned tobacconist, also a soldier in the Continental Army, reputed to have been an aide to George Washington and to be the black man portrayed by Emanuel Leutze in the painting, "Washington Crossing the Delaware."

Present owner and licensed merchant marine captain Richard Mayman, when he bought the building in 1979, blacked out part of the first letter in the generic neon "BAR" sign to rename it the "EAR." The Ear has offered music and poetry, including performances by Laurie Anderson and Allen Ginsberg.

When Mayman excavated the sandy basement (the Ear is located where the city's shoreline once was), he discovered clay pipes, a revolver, and Thomas Cloke liquor jugs imprinted with "326 Spring Street." Cloke owned the building from 1900 to the 1920s.

In the planning stages is the construction of a twenty-six story residential tower next door to the Ear. A *New York Times* article related that in a deal that encompasses moving air rights to the new tower, the contractor will fortify the Ear's soft foundation and disintegrating support beams. Also, the Inn would acquire space in the new tower for a bigger kitchen and restroom.

Would "Mickey the Sailor" like the changes coming to the Ear Inn?

"Mickey the Sailor" is a ghostly seaman from colonial times who was beached on Manhattan and is reputed to pinch women's behinds. Women who have lived in the apartments above the bar say his ghost has even crawled into bed with them.

Ye Waverly Inn
16 Bank Street at Waverly Place

"Inn's Ghost Liked Smoke, but Fire?" is the title of a *New York Times* article about the Ye Waverly Inn.

It was a fast image of a top hat and waistcoat in a mirror in 1997 that caused Maria Ennes, once general manager of Ye Waverly Inn, to finally believe in the supernatural. She "had always felt a presence at the inn, but actually seeing an image of him" was enough for her.

The restaurant reopened on February 1st of that year after a fire right before Christmas. Ennes stated that the phantom seen by customers, employees and former owners is devilish but not frightening. Stories of his mischief have been heard for decades.

Erected in 1844, 16 Bank Street was first a tavern and a bordello. Later it was turned into a carriage house for the rich and in 1920, a tea house frequented by Robert Frost and Edna St. Vincent Millay. Over time, scores have related seeing an apparition of a man sporting nineteenth century clothes.

Before Hannah Drory purchased the inn in 1993, a waitress told her it was haunted. Some of the regulars even kid about the ghost, and, when something goes wrong, Mrs. Drory would say:

"It's always easy to blame it on the ghost."

But Fire Marshall Frank Licausi stated that inquiries have come up empty for "an obvious cause" to the fire.

The blaze evidently began in a section that had no electrical outlets or incendiary substances. Licausi maintained that there is invariably a "scientific" reason for a fire, that there are those more difficult to get to the bottom than others. He swore:

"Ghosts don't start fires, we don't think."

Drory related that following the fire, she immediately thought of the phantom of the Inn. Room 16, the Inn's smoking room, was entirely unharmed.

"Room 16 is where there have been sightings as well as mischievous occurrences...It's where the ghost likes to be."

In the past, a "presence" was felt among the tables in Room 16, drifting by customers, the hair on the back of their necks standing on end as a result. Andirons and fireplace tools have moved in and out of the fireplace and sometimes, when the staff has attempted to put out the fire at closing, it has re-lighted itself. Lights go on and off by an unseen hand, and the computer keys indicating meat loaf and southern fried chicken have switched, causing much confusion, especially on busy nights. The sound of doors opening and closing and of something weighty being hauled up the back stairs are often heard.

Retired legal secretary Marilyn Dempsey was a frequent customer for over forty-five years. She maintained that the Inn's cozy feel had not changed much since she first began coming on payday in the 1950s. But over time, Dempsey noted odd sounds or a door opening and closing for no apparent reason. One happening in particular struck Miss Dempsey.

One evening, as she drank a glass of white wine while waiting for her chicken pot pie, a waitress attempted, but was unable to, light the fireplace. As she went to get a new book of matches, a blazing fire abruptly came to life. At the same moment the fire was lit, Dempsey picked up an extraordinary "presence in the room."

Ennes stated that she was rather shaken up by their unseen visitor initially. "But I'm now so comfortable with it...it might as well be another customer."

Chef Patrick Haynes noted that in the fire of 1997, the only room not affected was what they now call the Edgar Allen Poe room, which, appropriately enough, features the bar after its most recent renovation.

Chef Haynes has seen two ghosts at Ye Waverly Inn.

"One is a young lady, in her early twenties," the strapping Haynes told me. "She seems contented and wears late nineteenth century clothes. The other is a man in his forties, who often puts out candles when there is no source of a draft. And then the candles relight."

White Horse Tavern
567 Hudson Street
Between West 11th & Bleecker Streets

White Horse Tavern. *Courtesy of Jim Munson.*

The poet Dylan Thomas, a regular of the 1880 land marked White Horse Tavern, died at home after a drinking a dozen whiskeys at the White Horse Tavern in 1953. His last words were recorded as "Seventeen whiskies. A record, I think."

His spirit is said to rotate his favorite corner table, as Thomas liked to do when he was alive, as stated in a New York Times article. One report described a shadowy figure sporting a velvet cloak.

Chumley's
86 Bedford Street
Between Bleecker Street & 7th Avenue South

Lew Chumley bought what is today Chumley's in 1926. He changed the building's front so that it looked like a garage, but in actuality was a speakeasy that lured Village names like Edna St. Vincent Millay, John Dos Passos, and Theodore Dreiser. Presently, it is a restaurant behind a facade. To mark its notoriety during prohibition, it was named "Chumley's," and to this day still does not have its name displayed outside the door.

Chumley's is part of the haunted *Sidewalk's of New York* walking tour. Lee Chumley's ghost, or his widow's, have often been spotted in the old speakeasy, insuring that all is running smoothly as it should be at the former speakeasy.

Chapter XVIII

The Bronx

The only borough of New York City attached to the mainland of North America, the Bronx was originally called "Keskeskecj" by the Indians. The Bronx was bought by the Dutch West India Company in 1639. Two years later, Dane Jonas Bronck became the first white settler of the region when he bought five hundred acres between the Harlem River and the Aquahung, the Indian name for what later became known as Bronk's River, for which the Bronx is named.

Spuyten Duyvil

Spuyten Duyvil.

Physically part of the Bronx, politically part of Manhattan, Spuyten Duyvil, a narrow inlet (originally called a creek) between the two boroughs, is where the Harlem and Hudson Rivers meet, and is now the Harlem River Ship Canal.

Henry Hudson voyaged past the "creek" in 1609. Years prior to the first bridge being erected over Spuyten Duyvil in 1673, Spuyten Duyvil was bestowed its curious name. "In spite of the devil" was thought to be a very loose translation of a Dutch expression, "Spuyten Duyvil" or "in spuyt den duyvil." Others maintain, "spit on the devil" was where it derived from.

In 1693, Westchester blue bloods, the Philipses, finagled the franchise for the first toll bridge in America over Spuyten Duyvil Creek. Farmers had to fork over tolls from six to fifteen pounds sterling yearly to transport their produce to City markets. Feeling this sheer extortion, in 1758, angry citizens built a competing Free Bridge (also known as Dyckman's Bridge or Palmer's Bridge) at 225th Street and Broadway.

The farmers rejoiced when the American government seized the Philipse lands following the Revolution and made the bridge free, which remained until 1911.

Since the early beginnings of Spuyten Duyvil, youthful daredevils have dove off the steep rocks rising from the swirling waters of Spuyten Duyvil. Columbia University sculling crews train and race there. Years ago, there was a tragic drowning accident of members of the sculling crew.

Blue Guide New York tells us that Washington Irving's *Knickerbocker's History of New York* relates that in those murky, fast moving waters, Anthony Van Corlaer ("Anthony the Trumpeter") drowned in what was then an unnamed creek of whirling tides.

Van Corlaer always bragged to anyone who would listen that he could easily swim through those treacherous tides.

As such, Van Corlaer was dispatched by Gov. Peter Stuyvesant in the eighteenth century to warn settlers along the river banks of what he thought was an impending invasion by a British fleet. With a trumpet in one hand (and a jug of whiskey in the other, some thought), Van Corlaer jumped into the confluence of tides after fortifying himself with a few swigs from his jug. He swore he would cross the dangerous waters in spite of the powerful currents while shouting in Dutch:

"En spuyt den Duyvil!"

But the wild currents had their way with Anthony the Trumpeter. He drowned. The Dutch were soon defeated by the British.

According to *New York City Ghost Stories*, Van Corlaer's phantom still frequents the river and its creek banks, and is sometimes sighted on Inwood Hill. Boaters who cruise about that tip of Manhattan on the Hudson River or Spuyten Duyvil can sometimes hear a muffled trumpet forever blowing, forever warning those who no longer reside along the river and creek banks, of the impending British invasion.

FORDHAM - Loew's Paradise Theatre

Grand Concourse and 187th Street

Loew's Paradise Theatre.

The full name of the Grand Concourse is The Grand Boulevard and Concourse, laid out in 1892 by Louis Risse. Risse deemed the "Concourse" the "Speedway Concourse," and furnished separate lanes for carriages, cyclists and pedestrians who traveled on the Concourse en route to Van Cortlandt Park.

With the advent of mass transit, grand apartment buildings, some with great Art Deco facades, were built along the Grand Concourse. In the late 1920s and 1930s, the "Concourse" was the Bronx' preferred housing boulevard, "the Park Avenue of the Bronx," as some refereed to it. It seems only fitting that on such a splendid boulevard, the Loew's Paradise should be located.

Opened in 1929, the exterior land marked Loew's Paradise Theatre was designed by John Eberson in Italian Baroque style. One of the most extravagant attractions in the Bronx, this 4,000 seat movie palace was replete with carving, statuary, and paintings. The ceiling hosted twinkling stars and clouds traveling over a dark blue surface.

The book, *The Beautiful Bronx* gives us more information about the Loew's Paradise. Called the "Showplace of the Bronx," Loew's Paradise was packed every time it showed its first-run-in-the Bronx feature films. But the delight came not only from the films, but the ambience itself, which conveyed patrons "into a dreamland baroque palace."

Toward the end of Paddy Chayefsky's teleplay *Marty*, he and his friends are trying to figure out what to do with yet another Saturday night. Among other suggestions, they wonder if they should go to the Loew's Paradise. Marty, meanwhile, realizes that the "girl" he met at a local dance is who he wants to be with, and not his loser friends.

[My husband, Glenn Forman, grew up in the Bronx. He said to see a movie at the Loew's (pronounced by New Yorkers as "Lo-eez") Paradise was a great experience, for it was not just a movie theatre, but a palace, its ceilings sparkling with "lots of little constellations" to add to your movie viewing enjoyment.]

The Loew's Paradise is presently closed for renovations. The neighborhood surrounding the theatre is optimistic that, one day, it just might be restored to its former luster.

(I had never been to the Fordham section of the Bronx. When I rode a bus up the Grand Concourse, I could still make out the once splendor of the neighborhood, now a struggling working poor community. And what a pleasure it was to finally see the Loew's Paradise, although a little worse for wear, slowly, surely, coming back to life.)

On a *New York One* television broadcast about the old Loew's Paradise, security guards reported ghostly activities in the "Showplace of the Bronx." Security guard Fred Martinez told me about two night guards.

"They were both Mexican and really needed their jobs," Martinez affirmingly shook his head. "But they both refused to work after they kept hearing voices in the old theatre and seeing doors close and open by themselves."

And Mr. Martinez himself feels "something" while taking care of the old Loew's Paradise.

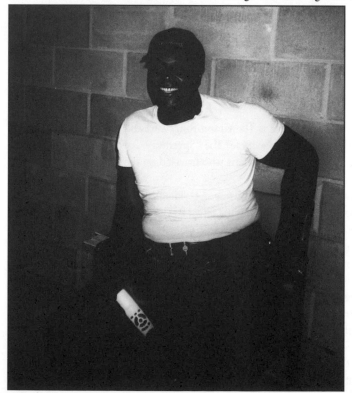

Security Guard Fred Martinez, Loew's Paradise Theatre. *Courtesy of Fred Martinez.*

Poe Cottage
Poe Park
Grand Concourse and East Kingsbridge Road

New York City Ghost Stories tells us that Edgar Allen Poe resided at the above address from 1846 to 1849, his last home, the only house left from the old village of Fordham. It was thought he wrote "Annabel Lee" and "The Bells" there for his young wife, Virginia, whom he wed when she was thirteen and they moved there hoping the "country air" would prove beneficial to Virginia, who was slowing succumbing to the ravages of tuberculosis.

They rented the small frame house from John Valentine for $100 a year. Although famous ("The Raven" had been published the previous year), it brought no relief from the poverty or misery that plagued them always.

Poe's mother-in-law, Mrs. Maria Clemm, peddled his unwanted manuscripts, and at times scoured the fields for edible herbs to feed the three of them. Although some help came through the route of public subscription, Virginia died in 1847 at the age of twenty-six and Poe, later, in a Baltimore hospital.

The Shakespeare Society saved the cottage from destruction in the 1890s, and moved the cottage from its original location on the other side of Kingsbridge Road. The City of New York acquired the house in 1912. There are four Poe museums in the United States.

The Poe mementos in the cottage are the bed in which Virginia Poe died, a locket, a wall mirror, a Bible, and a spoon. Administered by the Bronx County Historical Society, an audio-visual show details Poe's life in Fordham. The rooms are preserved-as is and some say his psychic energy is felt throughout the Poe House.

Fordham University
East of Webster Avenue between
East Fordham Road and Southern Boulevard

The Right Reverend John Hughes, subsequently New York City's first Roman Catholic archbishop, established Fordham University in 1841. John McCloskey, the United States' first cardinal, directed Fordham in its first years. Fordham, in 1846 evolved into the Jesuit university it is at present.

The Website, "Shadowlands Haunted Places Index – New York," reports that in Hughes Hall, students have noted bolted doors suddenly opening on their own accord, and a ghostly young boy who materializes in rooms late at night.

Van Cortlandt House
Van Cortlandt Park
Near the entrance of the Park at Broadway and 246th Street

Van Cortlandt House. *Courtesy of Dr. Laura Correa.*

The land comprising Van Cortlandt Park was originally a popular hunting ground for the Mohican Indians. There is also a slave burial ground in the Park. An historical society battled erection of tennis courts in the Park, stating that the courts would sit on top of those burial grounds. It is interesting to note that a Negro burial ground also once existed in the Park, next to the old Berrian-Bashford burying ground.

The Dutch West India Co., in 1646, gave Adriaen Van der Donck, the first attorney in the colony, a great mass of land which encompassed today's Park site. Following his passing, part of the land was granted to his daughter Eva and her husband, Jacobus Van Cortlandt.

Oloff Stevenson Van Cortlandt, the first American Van Cortlandt, collected one of the four largest fortunes in the colony by the time he died in 1684. Fredereck Van Cortlandt, who constructed the mansion, was Oloff's grandson.

Above the house's windows are hideous sculpted faces, exceptional for colonial architecture but more common in Holland. Visitors can view an eighteenth century kitchen, a dining room where George Washington ate, and bedrooms, most notably one where Washington slept during the Revolution.

An article in the *Kingston (New York) Daily Freeman* tells us the story of a Washington, D.C. girl who visited the Van Cortlandt mansion before its days as a public site.

She was given a bedroom with all the comforts of the mansion, while her mother paid a call on relatives. The mansion was full, for several friends and family members had come to visit. Many had been invited to stay the night.

The girl looked forward to her short visit with her aunt and uncle in the large manor house and was shown to the small room, then used as a children's playroom. It was separate from the main part of the house and one of the few vacant rooms remaining that busy night.

Before going to sleep, the girl was told that the room would be quite dark once the shutters were closed. As such, when it was time to rise in the morning, a man would rap on the door. Using candlelight, the young girl decided to read until sleepy, which did not take long. She snuffed out the candle and went quickly to sleep.

She woke to the sound of someone approaching her room from a nearby summer parlor. It was a fast, delicate step heading toward her room in a purposeful manner. Her door, closed but not locked, was opened abruptly and "someone" came in.

The night visitor stood in the doorway and the girl sat up in her bed. She saw what appeared to be a tiny woman wearing a brown skirt, a darker brown cape, and a cap, keys rattling by her side. The tiny woman had a look of sharp resolve.

The girl was lying close to one edge of the bed. The peculiar woman with the keys glided over to that side with fast, vigorous steps and tugged on her bedding. The article related that:

"[T]he figure had vanished...there came to [the girl] a strange sinking sensation of horror and terror...almost unbearable."

The girl lay shaking in her room until dawn, "[c]rouching down in the bed, she pulled her clothes up over her and lay there trembling until morning." Soon, a maid quickly opened the door of the girl's room. What she found was the young girl, clearly agitated. The maid ushered the girl to her aunt's room where she told her aunt and a cousin of her strange visitor. The girl knew that while she could recall what her visitor wore, she could not remember anything of her face. Within a moment of the ghost disappearing, there was the sound a train whistle in the distance. Her cousin responded:

"The train. Yes, that goes by at two o'clock in the morning – the very time!"

The cousin said it was the same time of sightings by others, of this very same woman in the cap. Prior to the girl's frightening visitation, another guest had related that she had the same experience. A young man heard footfalls, watched as the door slowly opened, and felt something rush by him. Although he saw nothing, he refused to ever go near that room again.

Was the playroom haunted? Before the girl went back to Washington, a friend of the family with psychic abilities visited. She was told of the young girl's ghostly visitor and said she would try to summon any spirits she could, and perhaps identify the ghost.

The aunt, the two cousins, and the psychic collected for a séance in the haunted playroom. At 11 P.M., after the remainder of the family had gone to sleep, curious events started to take place.

In the séance, the ghost was identified as a prior member of the housekeeping staff who had died with a very guilty conscience. The spectral maid said her spirit was being held prisoner in the house in retribution for her theft of a hammered silver pie dish, part of a silver set that had been in the family since they came over from Holland.

The acknowledgment of remorse finally freed the phantom maid from this earthly plane. But there are those who say the old Van Cortlandt Mansion will always be haunted by the apparition of the penitent maid.

Another Van Cortlandt Park ghost story involves Chief Nimham. Close to Indian Bridge, across Tibbett's Brook in southern Yonkers, Chief Nimham was killed and buried with his men in a field in the area. The field, at the northeastern corner of Van Cortlandt Park, is to this day haunted by Nimham's ghost, whose spectral war cries are sometimes heard in the night from the area, according to *Ghosts of the Catskills and Beyond*.

The Van Cortlandt Manor House has, along with the guilty maid, reportedly seven ghosts. Three originated in Revolutionary times when the British took over the Manor. During the occupation, a "delirious Hessian soldier" was said to have been tied to a bed. Although he was bound for his own safety, the German-speaking soldier of fortune had not way of understanding why he was tethered, and so repeatedly returned after death to what he thought to be "his final torture."

Specter Hannah hid her silverware when the British came but was not able to find it at War's end. Hannah searched until the end of her life for her silverware and apparently still continues to do so, even after death. Sounding somewhat akin to what the young girl experienced, this "hand-wringing wraith" is seen throughout the Manor.

A final Revolutionary phantom is "a Redcoat who tampers with a large wooden linen press in the upstairs hall." He may be the most unusual. The linen press was placed in the Manor after War's end, and only after its arrival is when the "phantom Redcoat" showed up. The press is now located in the family bedroom.

The other three spirits are more recent and are all women. No one knows the identity of two, "a graceful ghost whose long gown brushed the legs of guests ascending the staircase, and a laughing girl who reportedly arrives by horse-drawn carriage and gaily runs up the front steps."

The third is thought to be Anne Stevenson Van Cortlandt, one of the last family members to live in the Manor. In the 1940s, "the order-giving elderly lady, a workman heard but did not see" is perhaps vexed that the Manor was sold to "outsiders." She is thought to be Anne Stevenson Van Cortlandt.

(When I visited the Van Cortlandt House for the first time, I was quite impressed with how beautiful the site is and how well its grounds are kept. Dr. Laura Correa, who works at the Van Cortlandt House, related that she had "heard footsteps in the House, like heavy boot steps, around 10 P.M." Correa also told of a house painter who saw faces in the back windows of the House.)

Linen press, Van Cortlandt House . *Courtesy of Dr. Laura Correa.*

Chapter XIX

"Only the Dead Know Brooklyn"

From Death to Morning
-Thomas Wolfe

I have lived in Brooklyn for over thirty years, first in Kensington, then Flatbush, Cobble Hill, and now in Park Slope. The brownstone and limestone buildings of this area lend themselves to spooky stories, especially at Halloween, when Prospect Park hosts a haunted Halloween Walk, where "cadavers" pop out of coffins lent by a local funeral home, the Headless Horseman traverses the Nethermead, and ghostly music echoes up and down the hills of the Park.

In the seventeenth century, the Dutch initially colonized Brooklyn, purchasing land from the Canarsie Indians. Dutch ways, agricultural and traditional, carried on in Brooklyn even after the Revolutionary War, although many New Yorkers of British stock were lured to the waterfront. In 1898, Brooklyn voted, just barely, to join Greater New York.

The late nineteenth and early twentieth centuries were a boom time for Brooklyn, its cultural organizations, and predominate businesses like oil and sugar refining, and brewing and distilling gave employment for its large population.

By 1930, half of Brooklyn's adults were born outside the United States, most settling in ethic areas such as Bushwick, Brownsville, Bensonhurst, and Greenpoint. With economic ups and downs, Brooklyn has endured, aided by cultural organizations, families, individuals, business, and public associations.

Brooklyn Heights

Brooklyn Heights is not only New York's first suburb but also its first designated Historic District (which spares the facades of its structures from random alterations). "The Heights" came into its own after 1814 with the advent of Robert Fulton's steam ferry's scheduled crossings to New York.

The Plymouth Church of the Pilgrims
Orange between Henry and Hicks Streets

The Plymouth Church of the Pilgrims. *Courtesy of Lois Rosebrooks, Council Secretary, The Plymouth Church of the Pilgrims.*

The Rev. Henry Ward Beecher, famous pastor of Plymouth Church for forty years between 1847-1887, was well known for his fiery sermons against slavery and war, and for temperance and morality. At the zenith of his fame, "Beecher boats" transported scores of New Yorkers across the river to witness his sermons. Forever theatrical, fervently abolitionist, Beecher once featured a slave girl at his church being sold for the greatest price offered by a congregant in order to drive home the evils of slavery.

Incited by Beecher's impersonation of a slave auctioneer, his congregants bought her freedom. According to a letter from Lois Rosebrooks, Church Council Secretary, Beecher held these auctions in the early 1850s, the last known auction just prior to the Civil War. His sister, Harriet Beecher Stowe, authored the famous anti-slavery novel, *Uncle Tom's Cabin*. Beecher numbered among his friends Sojourner Truth.

The Park Slope Paper has an article that stated that the Plymouth Church of the Pilgrims was known as the "Grand Central Depot" of the Underground Railroad. Under Beecher, the congregation hid and helped runaway slaves after the pre-Civil War settlement that led to more stringent implementation of the Fugitive Slave Act.

The Underground Railroad has never been officially recognized but Senator Carol Mosely-Braun of Illinois has introduced a bill to fix that oversight. The legislation would allow the National Park Service to "link and publicize a network of thirty-eight Underground Railroad sites, including Plymouth Church of the Pilgrims of Brooklyn Heights."

Brooklyn was pro-slavery, noted Frank Decker, member of the congregation and amateur historian of the church. The *Brooklyn Daily Eagle*, helmed by Walt Whitman, was an anti-slavery publication until changing political winds brought about a new editorial view. Whitman was fired and the *Eagle* became aggressively anti-Underground Railroad. The Railroad was not only illegal, but many thought of it as immoral.

New York City's business interests in particular were often sympathetic to the south because it benefited from their exports such as cotton. Due to the necessary secret nature of the Railroad, (penalties for being discovered working for the Railroad included threats of imprisonment or worse,) personal depictions are not available.

Statue of Henry Ward Beecher. *Courtesy of Lois Rosebrooks, Council Secretary, The Plymouth Church of the Pilgrims.*

"It's a grand analogy for a railroad system," said Decker. "There were tracks, conductors, and passengers. Harriet Tubman was a conductor...a house in Brooklyn Heights was a station."

There is no way to know how many fugitive slaves escaped through the Church's intervention, or the number of Brooklyn stations arranged through the church.

Tales that have been passed down are by way of a congregation member who hid runaway slaves in a concealed closet beneath the stairs of his Brooklyn Heights home until it was safe for them to continue with their journey.

"There...was a tunnel that connected the church to other places," said Decker. "Recently, when somebody was digging up Hicks Street, they found a sizeable tunnel east-west that went under 75 Hicks Street....cut off by the basement of the house there."

The property at 75 Hicks adjoins Plymouth Church. One Brooklynite noted in 1873:

75 Hicks Street. *Courtesy of Lois Rosebrooks, Council Secretary, The Plymouth Church of the Pilgrims.*

"[Plymouth Church]'s congregation were nearly all large stockholders in the [Underground Railroad] lines."

Decker went on to say that Beecher was picketed due to his anti-slavery ideas. People marched up and down Orange Street in the 1850s with placards stating:

"Get that man out!"

The Mosely-Braun bill would link the rather spread-out locations of the Underground Railroad in a scheme denoted by a red emblem or sign. There were definitely other stations in Brooklyn, reported John Manbeck, former Brooklyn Borough Historian and a professor at Kinsborough Community College.

Plymouth Church was "a dispersing area," said Rev. Sharon Blackburn, former church minister, where runaway slaves were dispatched to sympathetic homes and other churches on the Railroad.

For all of Beecher's merits, he was accused, late in his career, of having relations with his closest friend's wife. A spectacular trial for adultery resulted, of which he was found not guilty, despite overwhelming evidence to the contrary, momentarily blemishing his career.

An article in the New York Times relates that The Rev. Henry Ward Beecher is said to haunt a house in Brooklyn Heights that pre-dates the Civil War. 75 Hicks Street was built in 1913. Is it possible that, because Beecher made his home throughout the Heights and 75 Hicks Street adjoins Plymouth Church, that the previous structure at that site has to do with Rev. Beecher?

Perhaps the Rev. Henry Ward Beecher's ghost still laments his indiscretions with a female parishioner while he was fighting against slavery — and for women's rights — in the 1840s.

Montague Street

Montague Street is the main commercial street of Brooklyn Heights.

A Heights sea captain in the Far East trade vanished with his vessel in Asia. Years later, locals maintained that the spectral captain was spotted walking along Montague Street at night, according to a New York Times article.

Brownstone house
One block south of the St. George Hotel

The St. George Hotel was once New York City's largest hotel and offered an indoor, salt-water swimming pool. Built in 1885, today apartments and a health club, the St. George Hotel was named after an 18th century tavern on Columbia Heights. It is one block south of the St. George Hotel where Mrs. Gwen Hinzie had her supernatural experiences. She contacted Hans Holzer, as related in Haunted America.

In 1946, when Hinzie was twenty-six years old, she lived for four months in two different "Heights" rooming houses (now many converted to cooperative apartments) and was aware of hauntings in both. She worked in the City (what many call Manhattan) as a secretary.

In the first house, she lived on the ground floor in a four-story building that needed work and had rats. Her apartment was off the furnace room and had a door that lead out to the side of the building. Her sole heat came from the furnace room itself.

Hinzie's encounters with the supernatural took place over a two week time period. She first heard the sobbing of a woman at night, countered by another woman speaking to the first which ceased the crying. The sobbing appeared to emanate from the other side of the wall in the apartment lived in by the only other tenant on that floor. When Hinzie inquired about the sobbing, the neighbor said she never heard it.

Late one night, Hinzie walked through the furnace room to her room and also through what appeared to be a shadow of black smoke. There was no smoke odor but the furnace was burning.

When Hinzie mentioned it to her landlady, she said the furnace was fine.

Another night, through the wall opening into her room from the furnace room, thick white mist materialized, appearing more like smoke than mist. Hinzie picked up something to disperse the "smoke" but when she turned, it disappeared.

Once during the day, thick white mist appeared before her eyes and vanished. A black mist appeared while her back was turned another time which scared her. Hinzie said aloud for 'it' to go away and many seconds passed until it finally vanished.

By then, Hinzie was convinced her room was haunted. But her landlady had nothing to say in response to her questions in regard to ghosts and only offered that if Hinzie was unhappy with her accomodations, she should find new rooms elsewhere. On December 1st, she relocated to another brownstone.

When Hinzie first came to the Heights, she was visiting friends and lived for awhile in their apartment. After a few days, she sometimes saw oddly dressed people on the street.

One was a woman in her twenties or a little older, tall and skinny, and looked to be about six months pregnant. She was attired in a long dress with full or three-quarter length sleeves and a bustle. The bodice was quite snug about the waist but still revealed her pregnancy. She stepped quickly across the street away from Hinzie.

When Hinzie came into her new boarding house, she saw the same woman in the doorway leading from the foyer to the hallway in the rear of the boarding house. The woman was facing the wall. When Hinzie unlocked the door, it startled the bustled woman who stared fearfully toward the door. The pregnant woman calmly walked through the wall and vanished.

And Hinzie never saw her again.

The Brooklyn Historical Society
129 Pierrepont Street at Clinton Street

Founded in 1863 originally as the Long Island Historical Society, in 1885 it changed its name to the Brooklyn Historical Society. In 1989, the museum opened on the first floor. As of this writing, the landmark 1881 building is undergoing a $5.7 million renovation and is scheduled to be reopened spring 2003.

But there are those not at all happy about the restoration.

In a *Brooklyn Bridge* magazine article, the society's public relations coordinator, John Showalter, stated that some fourth floor staff have noted that items are being moved when no one is there.

Spectral inhabitants, John and Mary (the deceased former custodian and his wife), are well-known for running the circa-1920s elevator late at night by an unseen hand. In that era, they lived on the fifth floor of the Society's headquarters. Occasionally, late-working researchers would hear Mary call to her husband. Since renovations, they have expanded on their antics.

Clara Lamers, former assistant librarian, noted window shades being pulled up and down on their own, along with hearing the elevator running, once again, on its own volition. Maybe the ghosts of the Brooklyn Historical Society will finally rest easy when all the commotion finally quits and they can once again settle down to their jobs as spectral custodians.

Cobble Hill

The name Cobble Hill harkens back to Revolutionary times when "Cobleshil" ascended where Court Street presently crosses Atlantic Avenue and Pacific Street. The Cobble Hill Historic District encompasses many late-nineteenth century brick and brownstone townhouses constructed largely by land speculators.

Atlantic Avenue and Court Street

The newspaper *Phoenix* relates a ghost story that took place at Atlantic Avenue and Court Street in the early 1800s.

A throng of neighborhood "young rogues" were having a spontaneous party in Cobble Hill when they realized all their brandy was imbibed. The closest place to get more was down near Fulton Ferry. To reach the brandy, they needed to travel past what was thought to be a haunted location by Atlantic Avenue and Court Street.

Master Boerum, of Boerum Hill and Boerum Place prominence, offered to get the needed spirits. But he never returned. When his drinking cohorts went in search of him, they found Master Boerum jabbering incoherently in the road. He remained in that state for three days and then passed away.

Locals maintained that he had seen the gruesome specter of a murdered man.

Atlantic Avenue Tunnel
c/o Brooklyn Historic Railway Association

Atlantic Avenue Tunnel (Entrance).

Robert Diamond, founder of the Brooklyn Historic Railway Association, discovered a subway tunnel, perhaps the first in Brooklyn, under Atlantic Avenue that traveled to the waterfront at Furman Street. With enough research, prodding, and help from the then Brooklyn Union Gas Co., he not only unearthed the tracks, but surmised there might be a locomotive engine hidden behind a wall.

The Long Island Railroad tunnel was constructed by the Long Island Railroad in 1844. But Atlantic Avenue was clogged with too much traffic for a train, and its pitch too steep for a steam locomotive. The tunnel was used as a rail line to a ferry across the river, then sealed up and forgotten. But tales were often told that, under a full moon, the steam whistle sound and the "chug" of a train could be heard under Atlantic Avenue.

Diamond learned that the tunnel ran for five blocks between Boerum Place and Columbia Street and was about thirty-five feet below Atlantic Avenue. Realtors who hoped Atlantic Avenue would become a "showplace" thoroughfare made deals with politicians to have the tunnel sealed, filled in, and paved over. To insure the legality of the closing, a law was passed forbidding the use of underground steam locomotives.

When Diamond was finally able to enter the tunnel, he discovered horse-shoe spikes, part of a whiskey jug, and a pair of high-button shoes. The tunnel was intact, offering brick walls and an arched ceiling of Roman architecture. Diamond's find garnered landmark status.

Diamond, who prints a newsletter and gives guided tours yearly or so of "the world oldest subway tunnel," is raising money to turn the tunnel into a museum that will have its own trolley connecting cultural sites from Grand Army Plaza to Fulton Landing.

(I took one of those tours in 1999, and it was quite an experience. The air is crystal clear. The tracks no longer remain, ripped up for use during the Civil War. You enter through a manhole cover at the corner of Court Street and Atlantic Avenue and descend a metal staircase into a tunnel that New York almost forgot about, if it was not for Robert Diamond).

The ghost of the Atlantic Avenue tunnel has to do with Irish laborers and an English fore-man. According to Diamond, Irish laborers worked six days a week, common in the 1800s, on the tunnel. They would take a break by scooping large mussels from the nearby Gowanus Canal (often called "Lavender Lake" now due to industrial pollution) and have a large bottle of beer to wash them down. Diamond found both mussel shells the size of small shoes, and the old beer bottles thrown about.

The English foreman of the work crew thought it would be a good idea if the Irish Catholic men worked Sunday also. As might be expected, the workmen did not cotton to that idea at all.

As a result, the Irish laborers apparently murdered the foreman, cut him up into little pieces and threw what remained of the foreman about the tunnel. When the police came to investigate the foreman's disappearance, the workers' reply was:

"We don't see him around here."

But apparently the Irish workers did. Afterwards, an eerie bluish-green light was seen float-ing about the tunnel. Could that also be the same ghost Master Boerum had encountered in his search for brandy?

300 block of Clinton Street

A one hundred year old private residence Clinton Street brownstone is thought to be haunted by the specter is a young girl.

Cesa Rist was the daughter of a doctor who owned the house. When she got pregnant by her boyfriend, her father attempted to abort the baby in their home but Cesa died during the operation. Cesa was interred in the Denver family plot, but it is thought her spirit wants her remains moved back to New York, to forever lie next to her sole lover.

Best True Ghost Stories fills in more details.

In the 1960s, two women in their early twenties rented the two top floors of the house that needed a thorough cleaning. When Sharon was vacuuming, the plug pulled itself out of the socket and fell to the floor.

During the next five months, they heard odd sounds throughout the house. When Sharon's younger brother visited, one night when they were listening to music and talking. The stereo went off that had been playing loud rock and roll. This was followed by the hallway light going out, along with the kitchen light. They thought a fuse had blown but it had not. When the brother went to get something to eat, he returned from the kitchen and reported it as cold as an icebox, but the rest of the room was toasty. Five radiators were blasting and all the windows were closed.

Another woman, Toby, moved in. One night, when all the girls had friends over, suddenly Toby had felt a chilly breeze pass by. The lights started to dim, and Toby saw the dial on the light dimmer switch move by itself.

Ghostly events usually took place around 11 P.M. when the girls and their friends were sitting around, talking. Cooking utensils went missing, clothing disappeared, windows opened, and garbage cans were overturned by invisible hands. They heard non-stop wailing in the living room, day and night, along with the sound of someone walking back and forth and stomping footfalls, like a woman's, sounding very angry. But invariably when the girls checked, they always found nothing.

Barbara repeatedly heard an indistinct whistling but not a recognizable tune. Whenever they had company past eleven, the specter would chase the company out of the house with her antics.

There were heavy shutters in the living room from floor to ceiling. Often, it seemed like the wind was coming through and the shutters would bang together as if a draft were disturbing them. Soon after, they heard footfalls, walking away from them, along with a disturbed feeling in the room.

Bruce, Toby's boyfriend, moved in. On a June night, Toby and her boyfriend were in bed, and Toby was looking at the wall. Suddenly, she saw a girl looking at her, but more like an outline of a girl or a shadow on the wall, with long hair in braids.

When Toby left the room, her boyfriend saw the handle of the bathroom door turn by itself and open. He dove under the covers until she returned. The following night, Toby got up to turn off the television, and saw the identical outline of the girl from the previous night, but thought the girl was smiling at her. Afterwards, she and her boyfriend parted but he gave no reason as to why.

She heard a voice calling:

"Toby," again and again. But no one was calling her in the house.

They had nicknamed the ghost "Hendrix" for Jimmy Hendrix, which Toby had shorted to "Henny." Toby asked aloud:

"Henny, did you call me?"

The voice replied:

"Calm down. Don't take it so hard, it will be all right."

It was a girl's voice, and it was 5 P.M.

Sharon moved out and Madeline moved in. Upon hearing the ghostly stories, the girls decided to conduct a séance. The ghost came through right away, saying her name was Cesa Rist. She got pregnant from her boyfriend, and died when her father performed an abortion on her. She yearned to have her remains interred next to her boyfriend's.

But no one could find any mention of Cesa Rist in the Hall of Records and so were unable to help her. Barbara explained to "Henny" that she must let go and to not be angry that they were in the house. As much as they wished, they could not help her be interred next to her boyfriend.

Barbara saw an ethereal form enter the room and stand near the couch. She made out the outline of the head and what appeared to be braids around the front of the chest of a girl about 5'4", weighing roughly 120 pounds.

The girls moved out, not renewing their lease. The house was bought by the father of an acquaintance of the girls, who, after moving in, found their kitchen flooded when they knew they had not left the water taps on.

Perhaps Henny did not like the new tenants or the fact that she was still not interred next to her love.

Boerum Hill

Boerum Hill is named for a Dutch farming family from Colonial times. From 1840-1870, middle-class business people constructed the three-and-four story Italianate and Greek Revival row houses that still stand today.

420 Dean Street

An 1892 *Brooklyn Daily Eagle* related the story of Mrs. Nicholas (Nelly) Siggone and her husband, a mounted patrolman of the then 10th Precinct, who lived at 420 Dean Street.

Since they moved downstairs from the third floor, laments, wails and other sounds were heard so much that their child grew ill as a result. They were quite irritated by the sounds all over the house that sometimes emanated from the ceiling. When she or her husband went to investigate, they heard the sounds upstairs. Wherever they ventured to find out the source, the ghost would turn up elsewhere.

The O'Donnells lived there before the Siggones. Nelly asked Mrs. O'Donnell why she did not let them know of the noises before they took the apartment. All O'Donnell said what that she thought they should leave altogether "and not downstairs, which is unlucky anyway."

One night it was so bad, Nelly called for her father, ex-Assemblymen Patrick Burns, via telegraph at his country estate, for her husband was on night duty. Burns stayed overnight.

At midnight, he felt a cold hand over his face. Burns automatically struck out but saw nothing. He heard a wail under the piano "that made his hair stand on end and sent cold sweat rolling down his back." For protection, he made the sign of the cross and peeked under the piano but saw nothing. Again, he fell asleep but woke to "the most unearthly groaning" under the sofa. He once again investigated but found nothing. The following night, he sat up with a bottle of rye, a pistol, and a "dirk."

Burns later paid a call on a Hoboken clergyman who counseled him to convince his daughter, her husband and son to leave the apartment, which they did, moving to 373 St. Marks Avenue. Nelly stated that she was happy to have vacated the ghostly premises and that her boy was much better, too, as a result.

[One of the most exhilarating experiences with a book such as *Ghosts of New York* is finding a site still intact. So much of the physical structure of New York has changed, but not 420 Dean Street, still there, well over one hundred years later.]

Carroll Gardens
100 President Street
Bordered by President, Columbia,
Hicks, and Carroll Streets

A *New York Times* headline of 1936 read: "1,000 in Brooklyn Seek Ghost on Roof."

The inhabitants of the three story tenement all heard the tale that a specter often frolicked up on the roof of the former furniture factory and some knew those who had seen the ghost.

The police first received a report of "unearthly doings" at 100 President Street two weeks prior to the running of the *Times* article. Word spread fast in the neighborhood. As a result, every evening, the throng who wanted a peek at a ghost had become so large that it caused the then Hamilton Avenue Precinct to dispatch six "of its best uniformed officers" to the site.

The crowd of almost 1,000 had to be coaxed by New York's Finest into going home. Around midnight, there were still roughly two hundred there, mulling over the ghostly reports.

The day before the *Times* article appeared, the Top Hatters, a social club for the young of the neighborhood, strung strong invisible wire a half foot above the surface of the roof. While they did not expect to catch the ghost, they said they wished to see it fall.

But the ghost, seeing what the youngsters were up to, failed to make an appearance.

CLINTON HILL - 136 Clinton Avenue

At #232 Clinton Avenue, Charles Pratt (for whom Pratt Institute is named), oil magnate and partner of John D. Rockefeller, built himself a mansion, along with four others, as wedding presents for his sons. Of those five, three remain. The area was considered the Fifth Avenue of Brooklyn at that time, or Millionaire's Row.

An 1878 *New York Times* ran the following story about 136 Clinton Avenue, its long headline announcing:

"The City of Phenomena: Ghosts in Brooklyn: Door-Bells Rung, Doors Rattled, and a Brick Thrown Through a Window-A Vain Search for Small Boys."

Edward F. Smith, his family and two boarders, R.B. Thomas and his wife, lived for more than two years at #136. One night in 1875, Smith's front doorbell rang. In those days when crime was low and peepholes not part of New York City doors, he went to answer it. But there was nobody there. Smith returned to the sitting-room [living room] and the bell rang again. Once again there was no one at the door.

The bell continued to peal numerous times that night. At the same time, the two doors of the house were kicked and rattled "with great vitriol," according to the article. A thorough investigation did not uncover anyone at the doors or any explanation why the doors should be rattled and banged and the doorbell rung. Ultimately, Smith resolved that it was "only the wind."

But the next night, the identical odd tappings and tollings were again heard. The shocked family thought it might be a haunting and the astonishing incidents persisted and eventually grew so repetitious that Smith thought it time to get to the bottom of the odd sounds.

The Smiths were most resolute in trying to unravel what was behind the happenings. A lookout was situated at each door, a guard set up in the yard. But it was to no avail – the sounds of doors clattering and pounding were just as furious and the bell tolled.

Smith, no believer in the supernatural or spiritualism (big at that time) and adamant about showing "the ladies" in the family that the bell was rung "by human agency," scattered a powder about the front steps to show footsteps leading up to the bell. But the bell continued to ring and no footprints were visible in the powder.

Police Captain McLaughlin of the then Fourth Precinct was called to investigate the situation. The Captain and Detective Price visited the house and were there but a few minutes when the same pounding and ringing ensued. The racket stopped at ten o'clock and the Officers departed, completely baffled.

The next Wednesday evening, the Captain stationed officers around the house, with directions to notice the most minute activity. The Captain and his detectives positioned themselves just inside the door, to open it once the bell was rung.

Soon enough, the bell rang furiously and heavy blows pounded on the door in rapid sequence.

The Captain flew out from behind the door and the officer on lookout outside saw – nothing. A large brick was tossed through the dining room window, shattering the glass and flying inside the room. The brick was thought to have been hurled from the pathway, although the officers were absolutely sure no one was there.

This was the most significant display yet made, as if the specter "wished to show its contempt for the Brooklyn Police," the Times reported. The following day, Detective Price scoured the house, from cellar to roof, to ferret out hidden wires "or other agencies by which human agency could produce the phenomena."

A Times reporter was dispatched to the site at night. As he made his way around the corner from Myrtle Avenue to Clinton Avenue, he saw a throng of several hundred men, women, and children standing in front of the "haunted" house, a lone officer futilely trying to get them to "move on."

Elbowing his way through the mob and hearing numerous tales of "stewart's ghosts," the reporter "dogged" the officer, made his way into the yard, and was soon at the door. He rang the bell and the door swiftly opened. In response to his questions of Thomas, Smith's boarder, the reporter was told that Smith was at home but was "protracted with nervousness" and could in no way be interrogated.

"Are the ghosts at work to-night?" inquired the reporter.

Thomas indicated that all was quiet on Clinton Avenue and that the police were not on lookout that night. Thomas swore he knew no worldly force was behind the ghostly phenomena which they had beheld for the last two weeks, but he was not prepared to say that Smith was thinking that it was "some evil spirit" who had a beef against a boarder of the house. Spiritualists were also in attendance, and asked if they could hold a séance that evening but were turned down.

Thomas did not want them in the house, stating the boarders of the house were "perfectly able" to handle any specters without the aid of spiritualists. Thomas stated:

"The whole thing in a nutshell is this. We have had the most mysterious sounds and actions about this house for a fortnight. We have tried our best to fathom the mystery, and can't. The police have tried and failed. We don't know what it is, but we do know that it is no earthly agency."

The Brooklyn Navy Yard
Main Entrance: 63 Flushing Avenue

Brooklyn Navy Yard (Cumberland St. Gate). *Courtesy of Martín Banker, Esq.*

The original Brooklyn Naval Yard commenced operations in 1781 when John Jackson and William Sheffield established a small shipyard on the shores of Wallabout Bay. The Yard, bought from Jackson in 1801 by the U.S. Navy for $40,000, grew into a vital base for servicing ships during the War of 1812.

A section of the Yard is the land marked Dry Dock #1 located on Dock Street at the foot of 3rd Street. Erected in 1851, it is the oldest granite-walled dry dock in the country and still operational.

The Brooklyn Naval Yard has quite a history. Famous ships built there include the battleship *Maine*, the *Arizona* sunk at Pearl Harbor and the battleship *Missouri*, where Japan surrendered, thus ending World War II. Work at the Yard reached its zenith in WWII.

The first United States steamship, the *Fulton* was built there in 1814-1815. The public swarmed to the launching of the "queer looking craft" but her captain and crew were not so enthusiastic for there were no skilled mechanics to operate her engines properly. She was kept at the Yard to receive and train seamen.

On June 4, 1829, the *Fulton* exploded, killing thirty-three, including three women. The cause was thought to be either negligence or retaliation on the part of a gunner's mate who also died. Barrels of gunpowder on board were used to fire the morning and evening guns. A rumor spread that the gunner had been whipped that morning (a practice brought out in Melville's *Billy Budd*, and, as a result, discontinued as a way of the sea), and had "thus made an end to his own and everybody else's miseries."

There was also a Naval Cemetery located at the Yard. In 1892, Naval Records showed that 1,187 people were interred there.

In recent times, locals have called for renewed opposition to the City's incinerator in the Yard by stating that the graves of American prisoners from the Revolution still lie under the "gritty piers and warehouses."

That area, Wallabout Bay, is the final resting place of the approximate 11,500 Continental Army men who perished on board appalling British prison ships in the river during the Revolution.

A *New York Times* story told of artist Nicholas Evans-Cato who has been painting the same vacant lot for over five years at Hudson Avenue and Front Street. But this site, some historians surmise, is also filled with patriots' bones. Evans-Cato, whose art has hung at the New York Historical Society and Pratt Institute, painted the triangle eight times prior to his learning its morbid history.

The triangle is up the hill from Wallabout Bay, a section of New York Harbor. During the Revolution, every morning, Continental Army prisoners collected corpses from the ships, where epidemics such as yellow fever and smallpox were widespread, and interred them in shallow graves along the shore.

In 1785, Congressmen Joseph P. Cook wrote of the inhumanity of "beholding a large number of human bones, some fragments of flesh not quite consumed, with many pieces of odd blankets, lying upon the shore." He petitioned Congress and was able to get the remains interred, but they kept surfacing.

In 1808, Tammany Society (which evolved into the notorious Tammany Hall,) erected a temporary memorial and vault neighboring the Yard. But no funds were collected for a lasting remembrance. The first wooden martyr's monument, noted in an 1828 property survey, which named as "Monument" the site where Evans-Cato has been painting.

By the 1830s, the memorial, a tiny wooden shack which held thirteen coffins of bones for each of the original colonies, was falling apart. In 1873, the remains were relocated to Fort Greene Park. Finally, in 1908, the Prison Ship Martyr's Monument, an impressive Doric column by McKim, Mead, and White, was erected. And the bones are still there today.

There are probably many ghosts in the Wallabout area from either the *Fulton* disaster or those who perished in the Revolutionary War. But the following story, from a September 1901 *Brooklyn Daily Eagle*, is thought to be about the ghost of Billy Hunt, a laborer who had drowned from a tug in the East River. The cumbersome *Eagle* headline, typical for its time, ran:

Prison Ship Martyrs' Monument.

Plaque, Prison Ship Martyrs' Monument.

"Ghost at the Navy Yard Startles the Marines, Corporal McNeal and Bates Have Seen It and Have Felt a Mysterious Influence, Whole Guard on the Hunt, A Mysterious Figures with its head Bandaged Up Is Pursued and Disappears."

Marines stationed in Cob Dock were sure that the phantom of Billy Hunt had ensconced himself at the "Jack Club" on the dock. Many were positive that they had felt Hunt's specter or had seen it within the past week of the *Eagle* report. The Marines had worked at the location for five years without feeling any similar occurrences. Not easily scared, the spirit unnerved the Marines.

The night before the *Eagle* story, the complete corps came together to search out the apparition.

It all stated on a Wednesday night when the specter first showed itself on Cob Dock. Corporal McNeal was on sentry duty at the time. In keeping with his duties, he was recording in the log book kept in the guard house (known at the "Jock Club"), near the ferry landing. It was here that Billy Hunt had slept for the past five years.

McNeal was about done with the log "when he felt his hand being drawn steadily away from his book." He attempted to pull away but a strange force proceeded to pull his arm up.

A voice from an unseen entity said:

"So! You intend to kill me."

The sentry quickly fainted and his fall woke the guards asleep in the guard house. It took them some time to bring McNeal to.

They all decided to keep what happened to themselves, afraid of the sneering that would no doubt follow hearing such a tale. And so, it was forgotten.

The apparition materialized next in a more hospitable way.

Corp. Bates was on sentry duty about midnight when an odd figure materialized, its head covered in cloth. The corporal confronted the form, but it gave chase. The specter began running, the corporal right on its heels, and the ghost raced onto the point leading to the dock where there was no escape to the mainland.

McNeal stated that when the figure reached about the middle of the dock, it vanished. "The figure disappeared so completely as it had melted away," McNeal stated.

The Corporal sounded the alarm at the guard house and a dozen men came out in search of the elusive shape. They were joined by Corporals McAffrey and Bates and Sergeant Mahoney. A complete search was begun. But it was discontinued after an hour and all returned to their quarters and to bed, but certainly not to sleep.

At about two o'clock, Bates, while logging the occurrence, had the identical ordeal that McNeal had experienced a few nights before. An invisible power pulled his hand away and no force could overthrow it. At that moment, there was a great rattling noise on the roof, "as if the building was being pelted with stones," he stated.

That was it — "even the bravest of the marines" all heard the din and the shouts of the Corporal and quickly left the "club house." They again made a thorough search which had the same outcome as the first and all declined to spend the rest of the night there. They dispersed about the yard, in twos or threes, or else went up to the barracks to wait until morning.

That morning, the "ghost affair" was the only conversation. The men, not superstitious, were sure that something uncommon was going on at the Yard. They decided to put on a double guard that night and try again to apprehend the specter.

The next day, the *Eagle* followed-up by returning to Cob Dock, its headline stating:

"Ghost Not Found Yet, But Some of the Marines are Certainly Justifying Their Ancient Reputation."

Many Marines roundly asserted they had seen, or heard, the ghost of Billy Hunt. The majority of them were astonished and extremely vexed that the story of the ghost of Hunt had gotten out.

Many daring people, including newspapermen, were at Cob Dock attempting to get some "clew"[sic] as to the strange ghostly business." Some asked authorization to spend the night on the dock to learn something of the matter first hand but this could not be granted.

One corporal stated that he had the same experiences and seen the same visions that many of the other young men had felt and seen. He also said he felt a strange pulling at his coat tail, as if some unseen hand were tugging him. A corporal maintained that the theory of someone hurling stones at the guard house would explain the din, but not the curious form. Many Marines were willing to swear that what they heard was positively true.

Was it the ghost of Billy Hunt, one of the many prisoners of war victims, the disgruntled *Fulton* seaman, or any of his comrades?

Bay Ridge

The Dutch settled this area, which originally included Bensonhurst and Borough Park, as the town of Nieuw Utrecht in 1662. Bay Ridge was rural until late in the nineteenth century, luring only an infrequent wealthy industrialist to the high ground overlooking the Narrows, a narrow body of water spanning from Brooklyn to Staten Island. Mostly Norwegian sailors and ship builders made their homes in the more middle class areas inland.

544 Bay Ridge Parkway
Upstairs apartment

Ghostly Register gives us the story of Ken and Linda Makuta's haunting of 544 Bay Ridge Parkway, a two-story row house.

The specters seemed to gather about Linda, who at the time of the story was a legal secretary staying at home to tend to her children, Justin and Lauren. Her husband, Kevin, worked in computers. Both were extremely psychic and, as such, the Makutas were perhaps able to draw ghosts to them.

The ghostly appearances started in their first apartment after Linda's grandfather, William J. Mahoney, a mounted policeman in the New York City Police Department, died on March 30, 1980.

Linda noted that her grandfather has been with them since he passed on. She and her grandpa were extremely close – she was his first grandchild.

Her parents were so uncomfortable about the spectral happenings they refused to baby sit in the haunted house. Neither would her sisters. Lights went on and off, doors slammed, and there was the sound of heavy footfalls. Linda grew too fearful to go home and would wait on the stoop for Kevin to return from work. Once she came home and heard music from the 1930s playing from inside their home. When she opened the door, the music stopped.

When home alone, Linda often heard someone else entering their home. Several times, the downstairs door would open and close and something would venture down the hall. Often she would hear a knock on the door and when she went to answer, there was no one there. The Makutas would hear heavy walking on the roof, sometimes running.

The first time they slept there, the Makutas heard three loud knocks on the bedroom wall which really shook them up and often heard what sounded like a man walking down the hall, shuffling his feet. One time, her son Justin inquired who was the old man in the hall and described what he looked like.

As related in an *Omni* Magazine article, eventually, the Makutas thought it time to contact the American Society for Psychical Research, a long-established and highly regarded association. They got in touch with Dr. Karlis Osis, retired, but then its chief investigator.

Osis visited the Makutas' first apartment, along with an associate, Donna McCormack, and well-known clairvoyant, Alex Tanous. The ASPR paid a call on the Makutas three times in both apartments, each time with another telepathic. In agreement with professional parapsychological methods, the psychics were kept "blind." They knew nothing of the case until they had made and reported their own feelings.

Tanous stated that the primary ghost was a man connected with Linda, especially her son, who saw the phantom and talked to him. When Justin was a baby, Linda used to hear a man talking who was not there and she knew it was her grandfather. The first time Linda saw him as a spirit, she was coming out of the bathroom with wash in her arms. A man was standing right in front of her, smiling. She kept on going and had a delayed reaction and said:

"My God, that was my grandfather!"

She had went through him.

At eleven o'clock on a Saturday, the Makutas noticed things were vanishing. They would walk away from a book on the table, and upon returning, it would be gone. Maybe for a week, or a month. At the time of their report, they had just gotten a pencil sharpener back that had been missing for a year.

That night, they played cards. Linda had put her cigarette in the ashtray to discard but when she went to pick it up, the cigarette was gone. Her friend Cathy crawled on the floor under the dining room table to look for it and Linda told her not to trouble herself. It was gone.

Linda believed it was her grandfather who used to take her cigarettes and did so maybe fifty times. Once a whole pack vanished, but mostly they just disappeared out of the ashtray. Sometimes, her grandpa put them out. In life, he never wanted her to smoke and would take the cigarettes away from her and snuff them out, saying nicotine was bad.

In that apartment, Linda lost her wedding ring. After they had moved into the new apartment about three months later, Linda was putting coffee mugs away in the closet. As she went to place the second mug in, there was her wedding ring, on the shelf.

There is another specter named Otto who was part of the other house, but had moved along with them. Linda believed that he lived there and sported a cigar smell. The Makutas have a lot of glass, and her grandfather tapped on it, like he was saying hello to them. He also rapped on the china closet or a desk.

The Makutas did not vacate their apartment due to the hauntings but because the people who owned the house needed the upstairs apartment for relatives. When the Makutas moved into their present apartment, it was still for six weeks before the same old haunting sounds started up again. They contacted the ASPR again, and Osis and McCormick came over, this time with a woman psychic who wished to remain anonymous.

The psychic told Linda that the spirits of a woman named Eileen had come with them from the other house and she was attempting to get in touch with Linda. Eileen was quite troubled and wanted Linda to call the police. Linda stated that she had once heard a woman very loudly and clearly call her name but when Linda would reply, she never got an answer.

Eileen wanted Linda to call the police and tell them that "they" had hit her on the head on the stairs. Eileen did not know she was dead and comes and goes.

The psychic also told Linda that her grandfather hoped she would stop reading so much, as Linda read constantly. He also relayed that he wanted her to stop being involved in the theatre, as she was very active in community theatre at that time. He instead wanted her to get a job, that "taking in wash would be good for a start." That had been a running joke between them. The psychic said that her grandfather was aware he was dead but was just watching out for everyone in the house.

In the first apartment, a local New York television station did a show on the hauntings, in the second, an Italian film crew. They came with Osis and McCormick of the ASPR, who also brought with them Brooklyn psychic Ann Rychlenski. At the beginning of the session, Ann, who was "blind," sat with Linda in her kitchen, having a cup of coffee.

Rychlenski said someone had just rubbed her cheek, and described a man who was Linda's grandfather and there was a woman specter at the top of the stairs. Linda was not shocked for her friend, Richie, had also seen her, as well as her husband. Linda believed the woman is connected to their house.

The ghost's name was Clarisse. Rychlenski stated that although Clarisse was well aware she has passed on, she still waits at the top of the stairs for a letter to come in the mail. There is also a child of about six with the woman and the child has been seen by Linda's husband and friends.

Linda stated that when Clarisse was there, they see light, "like flashbulbs going off-different colors." Clarisse was also accompanied by an extremely pungent floral fragrance. She was a tiny blonde-haired woman, attired in a gown and wearing a lot of jewelry. Clarisse appears young, but that does not necessarily mean she was young when she died. That is the way she appears as a specter.

Rychlenski stated that Clarisse was extremely loathe to give up her youth and that is the reason she was always decked out in her finery along with copious amounts of baubles. She gave the appearance of someone perpetually waiting for someone to take her to a dance. Sometimes Rychlenski heard a moaning in the hallway.

The Makutas also had a night visitor, a woman phantom who trailed Kevin home after seeing Linda in the musical *Godspell*. Linda had come out on stage to see how many people were in the audience and observed that the front row stage right had only a single person in it. Linda wondered why the rest of those tickets were not sold.

Following the show, the stage manager began to question Linda about the woman "who just glided in" and made herself comfortable in the front row. Linda knew, however, that no one could enter that way because of a fence they would have to scale first.

When Linda responded: "...[S]he glided in?"

The stage manager retorted that:

"...[T]he church is very old and there are people buried in the courtyard...from the 1700s and 1800s. Why wouldn't they have spirits here?"

The female specter wore a bluish print dress and was perhaps in her 60s with dyed blonde hair. Kevin, also in the audience, saw the theatre-going ghost, along with another member of the cast.

Linda went to the cast party and her husband decided to go home. When she returned, Kevin told her when he returned home and was watering the plants, he turned and saw the woman in the first row of the theatre watching him. As he continued to water the plants, the specter smiled. She was there for about ten minutes and disappeared.

Prior to the Makutas moving in, there were no known accounts of hauntings in the two locations. The ghosts appear as pitiful, roaming phantoms attached to the Makutas home for reasons of their own.

When Rychlenski was at the house, Linda offered her a fedora that her grandfather wore. Ann's psychic specialty is psychometry, gathering information from psychical objects. From handling the fedora, Rychlenski got the impression of an unrelated old man and a woman that appeared to "overlap" two distinct eras. Rychlenski beat her fist on the table and said to Linda that to the man you would want to say:

"Law and order, law and order."

Rychlenski twice felt a rap on the back of her head. She got the impression that whoever was communicating with her had difficulty displaying affection and that this was his way of doing so.

Indeed, that was Linda's grandfather's way. Rather than saying: "I love you," he would tap you on the side of the head and say:

"Get out of here, knucklehead."

Rychlenski picked up the feeling that he was estranged from his children in life, which Linda concurred with and that Linda was the only grandchild he felt close to, and he stayed around because of her children, to protect them. The psychic felt he had not had a childhood in life and, as a result, was very paternal in death.

In regard to the woman who waits at the top of the stairs, Rychlenski observed that her dress was flowing chiffon and she was weighed down with jewelry. She was a woman who was a senior but desperately wanted to appear about thirty-five and had a sorrowful way about her. Ann thought the woman had something to do with the house, and the phantom was in someway connected with the child.

Linda related that once they had a cast party in their house. A friend came over but was unsure as to which door was theirs and so he flicked his lighter on so he could make out the names on the bells.

The door slowly opened for him, a four hundred pound oak door. He said: "Thank you very much" and walked up the stairs. Also, the stereo went on by itself at that party.

The Makutas subsequently moved a few blocks away to another upstairs apartment in a row house.

69th Street Pier

The *Phoenix*, a local Brooklyn newspaper, ran the following story.

One fog-cloaked night, a New Utrecht doctor had to make a house call on Staten Island. But upon arriving at the 69th Street pier, there was no ferry running.

A "grizzled old captain who made irregular runs" showed up and offered to take the doctor across and wait for his return. The doctor made his rounds and returned to Brooklyn, thanking the captain for his effort.

The next morning, the doctor discovered that the captain had died two days before.

Midwood Old Vitagraph Studio
Avenue M and East 14th Street

The Old Vitagraph Studio opened in 1906 and many of the great silent stars, including Rudolph Valentino and Erich von Stroheim, reputedly passed through its gates. Today the studio is partially used for taping a National Broadcasting Company television soap opera.

Fatty Arbuckle, silent screen comic, was ruined at the height of his career when he was implicated in the death of a young starlet at a wild party which he had attended. Although he was exonerated of any wrongdoing, Arbuckle was unjustly finished in the movies as a result of the scandal.

An article in the *Phoenix* newspaper related that Fatty Arbuckle haunts the old studio, sadly reliving his glory days of the silent screen.

Fort Hamilton Avenue and 92nd Street

A *Brooklyn Daily Eagle* of 1900 featured the never-ending headline:

"The Ghost was a Woman who did not Pay Rent, For Hamilton Avenue Mystery Solved By Finding Her in Chimney, Only One Foot was Visible, For Weeks, Mrs. Barrett Had Disturbed a Whole Neighborhood and Puzzled Searching Policemen."

The specter, a woman of thirty-five, made herself known in the then empty house. According to neighbors, the phantom materialized about three times a week. One night she was in white and stood at an open window holding a lamp, and the following night, she was dressed in black. Neighbors said that when the ghost appeared, her groans were heard for some distance.

Mrs. Many, mother of patrolman Frank Many of the then Bergen Street station, lived opposite the haunted house in the same house with Patrolman Johnson of the then 71st Precinct and his wife. Mrs. Many saw the ghost at the window many times. She told her son Frank but he scoffed at the idea, paying no heed initially. But he did spend many nights attempting to get to the bottom of the ghostly doings, yet the specter was always one step ahead of the law.

Detective Martin White tried to uncover the mystery of the woman in white. For several nights he kept a lookout, but did not apprehend the woman. People in the area were very distressed over the haunted house that children would not venture past. Many tales were constantly told as to the possible identity of the ghost.

Every night, locals guarded the house. They were willing to swear that the ghost vacated the house in the night and yet the form in white or black materialized. The news of a real haunting of the old mansion in which Mr. Christenson, a rich man, had died in 1888 spread in the neighborhood. Many neighbors compared notes with the ghost of Old Drury said to haunt the old Town Hall.

The phantom was quiet for a spell and then appeared the night prior to the running of the story. When word got out, two hundred people surrounded the house for a peek at the apparition. The woman in white appeared at the window, mournfully wailed and vanished.

Park Slope

Park Slope is a neighborhood ascending from around the Gowanus Canal lowlands to the Prospect Park hills. One of its three locales is the North Slope, which features one of the United States' largest collection of Victorian architecture, choice brownstones built after the Civil War for the rich looking for an option to the City's Fifth Avenue.

The middle Slope has been working-class since it was created in the nineteenth century for workers on the Brooklyn docks and it is where we live now, in a limestone cooperative apartment that was once a boarding house.

Litchfield Villa
Prospect Park West
Between 4th and 5th Streets

Litchfield Villa. *Courtesy of Nancy S. Harvey, Asst. Counsel, City of NY, Parks & Recreation.*

Litchfield Villa is an Italiante mansion erected prior to the Civil War by lawyer/land-specular Edwin C. Litchfield. Litchfield lived with his wife, Grace Hill Hubbard, in the mansion, named Grace Hill for her. They lived there until Grace's death in 1882.

The Litchfields donated twenty-four acres of their land to the Park after the Civil War, but the land-hungry City wanted more, and ultimately grabbed the estate and home, renting it back to the family for $2,400 a year. Since 1883, the Villa has been headquarters of the City Department of Parks and Recreation Brooklyn division.

A *Brooklyn Bridge* Magazine article gives us the story of the ghosts of Litchfield Villa.

On a spring morning a few years back while working solo in the Parks Department's ground floor offices, Schools Program Manager for the Park, James Green, stated that he saw an attractive woman with an wellborn manner attired in a long black velvet dress with a high lace collar float through what where once the kitchen and storerooms of the mansion. She seemed to be well-acquainted with her surroundings.

Green believed that the phantom was Grace Hill Hubbard Litchfield.

The spirit appeared to approve of the Parks Department work. On two separate occasions, when Green had his arms full and could use a hand, the specter of Grace Hill Hubbard Litchfield opened a door for him.

PROSPECT PARK - The Scorcher

Prospect Park – The Scorcher.

Prospect Park was designed by Frederick Law Olmstead and Calvert Vaux, who first laid down Central Park. Many (especially us Brooklynites) think it their masterpiece.

A *Brooklyn Daily Eagle* of 1896 tells us the story of the Phantom Scorcher and Miss Anna Rosen.

With the invention of the bicycle, scorching, or bicycle speeding, was a great problem, especially in the new parks of the City of New York. In old newspapers, you would often read of speeding tickets being given out to scorchers.

Anna Rosen, of East 23rd Street near Avenue G in Flatbush, took a trip to what people then called New York – Manhattan prior to Brooklyn being incorporated into the City of New York. She returned home to Brooklyn at 9 P.M., "tired out from the long journey in the cars" [street-cars in those days before the subway].

Rosen thought she would retire just as soon as she arrived home. But when she enjoyed the glorious night from the veranda of her home, Rosen thought she might "take a spin through the park on [her] wheel" [in those days when it was quite common, and not dangerous, to bicycle in a City park at night]. Her parents were out and not expected home until eleven. Rosen assumed she would be back from her ride by then and had her "latch key."

Quickly, Rosen changed into her "bicycle costume," [usually knickers, which must have been quite hot on that August night]. Soon she "was spinning down Flatbush Avenue," turned into Fort Hamilton Avenue and entered the Park through the Ocean Avenue gates.

Scores of cyclists, men and women, had the same idea as Rosen that summer night. The main drive in the Park where the roadway runs parallel with Fort Hamilton Avenue was packed. Rosen, annoyed by the throngs and wishing for "solitary spinning, glided [her] machine" to the west drive, which led to the more isolated sections of the Park. Rosen soon came across the deserted roads and paths she wanted and was wheeling along the road on the top of the hill.

As Rosen peered from the road to the "inky blackness of the woods on both sides," her "heart fluttered." She worried that highwayman might ambush her and was soon enough "scorching to get back to the drive." Rosen turned onto a road running south, thinking it would lead her out of the Park in the quickest time.

Rosen saw the shadow of a form bent into that of a scorcher stealing up to her side. The scorcher gave her "heart gave a joyful thump" for she assumed "it was a wheel man of flesh and blood." Her nerves were just about shot by that point and she was heartened at the sight of human being. But the next second, Rosen got such a fright that she almost fell from her "wheel" as:

> "A frightful apparition hove into view. It was a phantom scorcher...clad in a flowing white robe, but...transparent and plainly revealed the skeleton underneath. The form was bent in a double curve and the place in the skull where the nose had been almost touched the handle bar, the end of which the skeleton hands held with a firm grip."

The apparition's bones clattered as he came alongside Rosen and sped ahead of her. Then it decreased his speed, to show that she could not get away from him by speeding up. "I felt the blood freezing in my veins," Rosen later stated to the *Eagle*. She pedaled like never before but the spectral scorcher maintained a vigil at her side, "apparently without an effort."

Rosen closed her eyes, not wanting to see it anymore, but the next moment opened them again, "for the specter, with all the fear it inspired, had an indescribable fascination."

She was led about the Park, "as if I had no will of my own," Rosen reported. Totally exhausted, she finally reached the Park gate through which she entered.

And the spectral scorcher vanished.

115 8th Avenue at Carroll Street
(Former Thomas Adams Jr. House)

The former Thomas Adams Jr. house was a mansion built in 1888 for the inventor of Chiclets chewing gum. The brownstone Romanesque house features an intricately carved entrance arch on Carroll Street. On the southwest corner of the intersection of 8th Avenue at Carroll Street stood Charles Feltman's mansion. Feltman, said to be the inventor of the hot dog, opened his Nathan's in Coney Island, which reaped him celebrity and wealth (and the good hot dogs we enjoy to this day).

Louis Singer, who has conducted historical, ethnic, and architectural tours of Brooklyn for over thirty years, told me in a telephone conversation that the Adams House was the first house in the City to have an elevator installed, a "sort of gilded bird cage contraception," according to the book *Brooklyn, People and Places, Past and Present*.

In 1894, the Adams family left Park Slope from May to October, the custom of the City's wealthy at that time to escape not only the City's heat but also the inevitable epidemics.

When they returned, they rang for the servants. But they did not respond. The family entered the house and rang for the elevator, but it did not come.

Apparently, when the family was away for the summer, the elevator became stuck between floors. The four servants, trapped inside, were found dead.

Eventually, the house was sold, broken up into apartments, and the elevator removed. But some apartments had bedroom alcoves in the former elevator shaft.

Since that time, Singer related that:

"The occupants of the building have had the most unusual dreams and heard screaming and crying and strange voices with Irish brogues, that wail out:

"Water-food-Mary, Mother of God, help us."

None of the tenants sleep in those bedroom alcoves anymore.
Could it be the Irish servants crying out into eternity for help?

Montauk Club
25 Eighth Avenue and Lincoln Place

The Montauk Club catered to Brooklyn's social, business,. and political elite in its heyday before World War I. Now it offers membership to a more average clientele. The structure is a varied design of Venetian Gothic and American Indian themes, honoring the Montauk Indians of eastern Long Island whose history is depicted in the terra-cotta frieze.

When the Club opened in 1891, membership was fixed at five hundred. Thousands were on the waiting list. In 1890, the Census Bureau noted that Park Slope had the highest per capita income in the country. Members of the Montauk Club were the zenith of Brooklyn society.

After World War II, membership markedly fell. Sections of the Club, like the bowling alley, were closed off. But from the elaborate mosaic tile lobby to the well-worn chairs in what were once the "gentlemen only card and billiard rooms," the Club continued to display the wealth of a lost era. There was a time when the club featured a private parlor and a separate entrance for women.

These days, the Montauk Club is much in demand by films. With membership holding steady once again, with private clubs shuttering throughout the city, today's members are pleased to endure.

And so probably is the deceased night watchman, sometimes seen at the Club, ever mindful of his duties, even after death, according to a *Brooklyn Bridge* magazine article.

The Old Stone House Historic Interpretive Center
(former site of the Vechte-Cortelyou House)
J.J. Byrne Park
Third Street between Fourth & Fifth Avenues

The former Vechte-Cortelyou House, constructed in 1699, was the site of intense combat during the Battle of Brooklyn. Walt Whitman recorded that the "slang name among the boys of Brooklyn" for the stone house was "the old iron nine" due to the wrought iron numbers on the gables, still there today, over three hundred years later. Over the years, this evolved into "the old iron nines."

The house was demolished in 1893, despite objections by locals. In 1935, to coincide with festivities commemorating the 200th anniversary of George Washington's birth, the Old Stone House was reconstructed several yards away from its original location, using many of the same stones believed to have been part of the original house. It was once the home to the Brooklyn Dodgers before the team moved to Ebbets Field in 1913.

Today, a replica of the 1699 house is situated in a playground on Fifth Avenue, (where we often bring our daughter Jade). The Old Stone House Interpretive Center includes a history of the house as well as a small-scale model of how it looked on that fateful day in 1776 when Maryland troops, in spite of the overwhelming numbers of British soldiers, attempted to defend the site, but lost.

American Brigadier General William Alexander's (British title Lord Stirling) men, surrounded on three sides, commenced charging the English troops that had taken over the Old Stone House at what was then known as Gowanus. Storming the house six times, seizing it twice, the "Maryland 400" sacrificed their lives in order so that the remaining American troops could wade through the Gowanus marshes to back up the fortifications that stretched through what is now Boerum Hill and Fort Greene.

When he dispatched his troops to face the British army at the house of Isaac Cortelyou, Gen. George Washington reportedly said:

"Good God, what brave fellows I must this day lose!"

The American army was decimated on that day, August 27, 1776.

Since that time, it has been said that the specters of many of these brave men still haunt the Park, including already mentioned Revolutionary War General Lord Howe, who walks with, "[M]easured tread and bothering no one in particular, according to a 1958 *New York World-Telegram*.

PROSPECT HEIGHTS - 499 Park Place

An E-Mail from Tina Skinner gives us the haunting of 499 Park Place.

Roommates Susan Gomersall and Richard Starno think their apartment was haunted by an irate "illiterate" poltergeist (a German compound of two words, "to rattle" and "spirit"). That might be the reason for the havoc this unseen visitor unleashed on their bookshelves. Starno had, upon waking, found that his books have been tossed from the shelves to the floor.

The single most astonishing discovery was when they found that all the books in their living room had been tossed from a shelf, the prefaces ripped out. Gomersall and Starno could not figure out how a vandal could get into their apartment, for both front and back doors were locked.

Bedford-Stuyvesant

New York City's largest black neighborhood, Bedford-Stuyvesant, was once two neighborhoods – Bedford on the west colonized by the Dutch in the seventeenth century and the Stuyvesant Heights area to the east, settled later. Bedford-Stuyvesant was initially farmland, followed by a suburb of freestanding frame houses, growing into an urban area with wealthy middle class brick and brownstone row houses.

Bedford always had a large black population with slaves on Dutch farms comprising twenty-five percent of the population in 1790. Between World War I and II, Jews, Italians, Irish, and West Indians began arriving in the neighborhood. After World War II, large numbers of African Americans created what is now known as "Bed-Stuy," the United States' second largest black community after Chicago's South Side.

There was once a slave burial ground located roughly at the intersection of Bedford and DeKalb Avenues. Maybe that accounts for the numerous ghostly sightings in this area.

East Broadway west of Nostrand Avenue

As of 2001, there were only four farms left in New York City, one in Brooklyn and three in Queens.

But it was quite a different story in 1896.

When this article came out in the *Brooklyn Daily Eagle* of that year, the area was acres of farm lands, "flat as a pancake," with only a few houses. One was an old two story frame house inhabited by Charles Norton and his wife.

While enlarging his cellar, Norton discovered the skeleton of a hand, one of the fingers sporting a ring. A murder had taken place "in this cheerful little cottage," as the *Eagle* reported.

In 1836, the house was lived in by Krug, a German, "a middle aged man, as big as a longshoreman and burly as a bear." While he consorted with many of the neighboring farmers, his wife and three daughters were "kept like prisoners." Many thought he was an escaped convict, now in Brooklyn under a false identity.

Late one evening, a traveler visited Krug's home and asked for directions to the "village inn." The newcomer apparently had just come from a long trip, for his horse was exhausted, and so was he.

"If you could give me a bed," said the man to Krug, "I wouldn't go any further tonight, and I'd pay you well for it."

Krug, in his surly manner, was about to let the man know that he maintained "no hostlery," but abruptly thought the better of it. He agreed to let the man have a room overnight. His horse was taken to the stable and Krug's wife made a meal for the visitor who was quite talkative, maybe too much for his own good. He boasted that he had enough gold pieces in his money belt to buy half a dozen fine farms.

Krug listened but said little. He soon bid his good nights to the lodger, crankily making it clear that he had given up his own bed to accommodate the man and would have to sleep in the hay loft as a result.

At 1 A.M., Mrs. Krug was stirred by a sound in the connecting room where the stranger slept. She listened, but all seemed still and so she returned to sleep.

In the morning, the Krug girls, who slept in the garret, rose and made breakfast at 6 A.M. Half an hour later, one rapped on the door of the stranger's room to announce that breakfast was served. But there was no response. At 7 A.M., she knocked again. Still no response. Krug, already at work in the field, walked up to the house and his eldest daughter said they could not rouse their guest.

Krug replied that the man had already gone, that he left early in the morning, saying he could not wait for breakfast.

Later, when Krug's daughter went into the man's room to make the bed, she was startled to see nothing but the bare bed. Sheets, pillows, and mattress were nowhere to be found. When she informed her father, he said:

"I burned the bedclothes, because the man told me he had just got over the yellow fever."

The next day, Mrs. Krug, shoving the vacant bedstead away from the wall, discovered a bloody hand, severed at the wrist.

She screamed and fainted. Her daughter raced into the room and also beheld the ghastly hand which silently affirmed a tale of murder, almost as if they had observed it with their own eyes.

It was later surmised that apparently the initial axe blow did not kill the man. He had reached his hand up, as though to thwart the blow, and his hand was sliced "clean" off by the second chop. The killer, in his great rush to rid the house of the corpse, bury it and burn the blood-soaked bedclothes and mattress, had forgotten about "the tell-tale hand which had fallen to the floor."

That night, Krug vanished, never to be seen again. As a result, two of his daughters lost their minds.

Since the skeleton hand was discovered, Norton's neighbors swore they witnessed the slain man's phantom "flitting about the scene of the crime." They claimed that the ghost will keep materializing every night until the hand is buried.

Norton, a fifty-year-old painter, was not very forthcoming when the reporter paid him a visit to this home. He did not like to talk about the hand, stating that his wife had "a nervous disposition." The tales of the specter and the murder that had taken place in their house exceedingly troubled her. But Mrs. Norton finally did join into the discussion.

She said:

"We haven't seen the ghost, but it wouldn't surprise me at all if this house was haunted. Everybody who has lived here since murder was done under this roof has had bad luck."

One man who lived in the house around 1856 ran out on his wife and children with another man's wife. A later resident was a thief, and when apprehended, a large cache of silverware was discovered secreted in the cellar. Another tenant committed suicide. Mrs. Norton said they had lived there for six years and had been plagued with nothing but sickness.

"I don't like to talk about these things – it sends a chill down my back," Mrs. Norton shook her head.

Norton, meanwhile, had also taken to digging in the cellar. As of the *Eagle* report, he had uncovered two rusty swords of the Revolutionary era and many pieces of coin.

929 Myrtle Avenue

This story appeared in *The New York Times* the same year as the Great Blizzard of 1888.

"Two of the tallest and biggest policemen" of the then Flushing Avenue station were on the lookout for ghosts the prior night of the *Times* report in the avowed haunted house at 929 Myrtle Avenue.

Tales had swirled about the house since the night of July 3 of that year. It was an amazing happenstance, since two days after Smith Tucker's family, residing on the third floor, were informed to leave the flat because they were not deemed proper occupants by the owner's agent Mr. Glenn.

Strange tappings were heard in the house that always commenced in the middle of the night. The tappings were on the outside doors of the other tenants' rooms and on the walls.

An additional peculiar display happened when Mrs. Tucker placed a lamp on a shelf just back of the door upon leaving the apartment. When she came back, the lamp had fallen to the floor and most of the oil had spilled out, but the chimney [the glass piece covering the wick] was not shattered. This was at once thought to be the work of the specters.

W.H. Pittman, a Myrtle Avenue [street] car driver who lodged with the family, maintained he saw the form of a female attired in mourning [clothes] with a white cord wrapped tightly about her neck. As a result, Pittman collapsed from the sight. Tales spread throughout the neighborhood that the house was haunted.

Miss Fannie Dickson, sister of Mrs. Tucker, believed the haunting. Dickson said her sister, Kate, was calling on her and almost "had a spasm" as a result of the supernatural noises in the house.

The Tuckers called in a spiritualist to visit the house and had a séance. The sounds of a guitar playing in the dark and other amazing additional incidents materialized.

STUYVESANT HEIGHTS - 281 Stuyvesant Avenue

A *Brooklyn Daily Eagle* of 1901 tells us:

"Ghost in a Flathouse Rang Electric Bells, Stuyvesant Heights Revels In Proud

Possession of a Genuine Haunted House, Griffins Frightened Away, School Principal and His Wife Say They Heard Hollow Groans and Creepy Steps on Stairs."

> "When door bells ring
> And no one waits...
> While chimneys growl
> In dismal tones,
> Be sure a ghost
> Is prowling near;
> His playful tricks
> Are what you hear."

From Spooks and Spirits at Home

A *Brooklyn Daily Eagle* of 1901 related the ghost story of 281 Stuyvesant Avenue, after first giving us this additional headline:

"...Stuyvesant Heights...has...an asphalt street where bashful maidens learn to wheel at night, so in the line of modern improvements and up to date attractions all it needed to make a residents' joy complete was a full fledged open plumbing, steam heated, gas range, haunted house."

Mr. and Mrs. Joseph Griffin lived on the first floor of the house at 281 Stuyvesant Avenue. Griffin, a school principal in Manhattan, married and signed a lease for the apartment he and his wife would reside in.

Immediately, a specter displayed his indignation at the incursion on his space. "A very daring spook," because No. 281 is next to Grace Presbyterian Church, some of the apartment's windows looking out at the stained glass panes of the church. Because the ghost's mischief so troubled residents, they regarded him "as an evil spirit."

The specter began his antics by ringing the "electric" bell in the vestibule precisely at 3 P.M. Initially, Griffin thought it the hoax of neighborhood children. But upon investigation, when Griffin came out into the vestibule and heard the bell ring on the inside, he found it was no youthful prank.

"The Stuyvesant spook" also emitted "hollow" wails, frightening footfalls on the steps and the sound of walking from room to room. The Griffins stayed as long as they could, not really being frightened but more irritated. And then they moved.

"Ghostly and flesh raising indeed was the appearance of the haunted house...," "the *Eagle* reported. "The only sounds to break the stillness of the neighborhood were...the rattle of grocers' carts on Hancock street and the bitter wails of a two year old resident."

The shades were drawn in the then supposedly empty apartment on the first floor. Both the second and third floor apartments were inhabited and the specter never made mischief for them. One young married woman related how the bells still continued to ring daily on the first floor, "and Stuyvesant Heights people needn't lose heart. They can feel confident that a real ghost is among them...", the *Eagle* reported.

The Griffins relocated to 602 Bedford Avenue and as of the *Eagle* article, there had been no stories to show that the specter tagged behind them to Williamsburg. The *Eagle* ended the account, stating:

"There is further cause for satisfaction among the Heights folk because it proves conclusively that the spook is a loyal resident of the Stuyvesant section."

Brownsville

Brownsville is named for Charles S. Brown who, in 1865, subdivided the remaining farmland of what would be Brownsville for housing. In 1887, several realtors built inexpensive housing and persuaded Jews to relocate from the Lower East Side, their departure accelerated by the building of the Fulton Street elevated line in 1889. Brownsville would later become the City's center of Jewish life.

By 1900, Brownsville was home to fifteen thousand sweatshop workers, a ghetto with no sidewalks or sewers, unpaved streets, and one lone public bathhouse. Notables who came out of Brownsville include comic Danny Kaye, composer Aaron Copland, and writer Sol Hurok.

Our Brownsville ghost story took place at Douglass Street near Howard Avenue.

Douglass Street near Howard Avenue

An 1896 *Brooklyn Daily Eagle* told of inhabitants by Atlantic Park, and primarily those in the area of the Italian neighborhood of Douglass Street near Howard Avenue, who were not getting much sleep for many "are out night hunting" for a specter first beheld and reported by a Brownsville woman who saw a "form in white."

The form in white was seen strutting the streets in the wee hours, so concluded an *Eagle* reporter who paid a call on many who lived in the area of the above named streets. Following the ghost's third appearance, at precisely the same time a group of young people were coming back from a picnic at Atlantic Park, the police were asked for help in locating the "unwelcome visitor." But up to the *Eagle* report, it was not successful.

Italians living in the area visited by the specter were reportedly very unsettled by the ghostly action. They staunchly believed that the apparition was a former neighbor accidentally killed and has "returned to earth," a dire sign, to be sure.

On May 18th, rag picker Catalino Curillo was killed in front of his house on Douglass Street by a trolley car. And this is the exact location where the specter had been sighted on his three visits. Italian residents maintain that the ghost is Curillo's phantom, that he materializes "with the bar and hook he had when killed." One man maintained that he saw the accident "repeated in visionary form."

The "ghetto class" of locals were "not resting as quietly" as they did two weeks prior to the visitations. The women were frightened, refusing to leave their homes at night. Many of the men, sometimes numbering fifty, were out every night watching for the arrival of the ghost.

A conductor on the Ralph Avenue trolley line, John Doppel, lived at the corner of Howard and Douglass. It is in front of his house the phantom is said to materialize. Mrs. Doppel said:

"My husband and I heard screams one night and the next day, we heard the ghost story. They say the white figure, whatever it was, started from in front of our gate and walked, or rather floated through the air up Howard Avenue and entered Mrs. Mullins' yard, disappearing into the grape arbor."

The first Brownsville woman to see the specter collapsed at the sight. The following day, she complained to the police and made inquiries about it at the house. The police were on the lookout all night in the Doppel's garden, after informing Mr. Doppel it was not wise to use his gun at night in the hopes of scaring away the ghost.

96 Rockaway Parkway
First Floor apartment

An article in a 1999 *New York Daily News* gives us the sad story of the "mummified tot."

A report indicated there was a tiny body in a closet and a missing twin girl who vanished more than twenty years ago when she was three. But at the time she went missing, there had been no police report filed.

It came out when a relative of the dead girl inquired of the child's twin brother, Andre Carmichael, then twenty-three, how his sister, Latanisha, was doing. Carmichael was not aware he even had a sister.

When he asked his mother, Madeline Carmichael, about his sister, she said she had four children then and did not have enough money to keep all of them, so she had sent one south. Unsatisfied, Andre asked an older sibling about it. It was then the family's grim secret came out and one called the police.

When the police arrived, Madeline Carmichael opened her door, believing Cold Case Squad Detectives Raymond Ferrari and Daniel D'Allasandro were there to look into a noise complaint called in by a neighbor. When the Detectives entered the apartment, the first thing they noticed was that the apartment reeked of mothballs.

When Detectives Ferrari and D'Allasandro entered the bedroom, they observed, almost hidden behind furniture, the door of a closet that been bolted and painted over several times.

They yanked open its door and inside found the closet packed with spent air fresheners and boxes of baking soda. A steel footlocker was also inside. As they worked to tear it open, Madeline Carmichael waited in the other room.

Once they got the trunk open, they found layers of plastic bags, wrapped about a second trunk. Inside the second trunk was "a skull, hair, some flesh" and "the outlines of a child," one Detective said.

They found the mummified remains of a girl.

Detectives said the little girl, Latanisha Carmichael, was slain in 1979 when the family resided on East 96th Street, Brooklyn. As the family moved around, so did the trunk and its gruesome holdings, "like so much family furniture," finally moving into the Rockaway Parkway apartment.

"It was one of the worst things I've seen as a police officer," D'Allassandro said. "It looked like a coffin. As soon as we saw that first plastic bag, we knew. It was...eerie."

After their macabre find, Madeline Carmichael was shaken and went into what seemed like a seizure. She collapsed, was given oxygen and taken by ambulance to Kings County Hospital, later charged with second-degree murder.

As Carmichael was being taken away, she cried:

"I just want the pain to stop, I just want the pain to stop."

Police had no clue that Latanisha was missing until the October, 1999 report. They came across her birth certificate and Social Security card in the apartment, as well as the same for her twin brother. But there were no photos of Latanisha.

Latanisha had been battered brutally prior to her death. After discovery of the remains, Carmichael's children were removed from the home due to abuse and placed in foster care. Madeline Carmichael, who had "an extensive medical history" but no prior police record, freely gave up her children.

Neighbor Madeline Ramos related that generally Carmichael was "very nice, very respectful, never bothered nobody."

For many of the months prior to the *Daily News* report, Ramos complained to the building superintendent about the sound of babies crying in the middle of the night.

But there were no children in the apartment above or below Carmichael's, Ramos said.

"I think her own child was haunting her," Ramos observed.

Madeline Carmichael was sentenced to fifteen years to life in prison. Prosecutors called for the maximum twenty-five years to life. But the Judge, taking into account that the defendant had terminal cancer and the family had forgiven her, believed that the maximum sentence would only sell papers, said Justice Anne Feldman.

Bensonhurst

In a four-block area off Bath Avenue, there is a small neighborhood of African Americans whose ancestors came with the "Underground Railroad" days of the Civil War, when a North Carolina horse trainer inhabited the area.

In 1887, one square mile of Bensonhurst was composed of nine farms, four held by members of the Benson family. When their holdings were broken up in 1889, Bensonhurst was opened to development. In early twentieth century, it was a resort area. Once mainly Italians and Jews, recent immigrants are from China and Russia.

8200 Bay Parkway

The January 25, 1952 *Brooklyn Daily Eagle* reported on a ghost story in Bensonhurst.
A "sober-talking sheet metal worker" stated that his apartment was seemingly haunted.
For two months, Frederick Garrison related, noises from unknown sources and blows struck

by unseen fists had almost reduced him to "nerve-wracking desperation" and placed his wife under the care of a doctor.

Every time his thirteen-year-old daughter, Virginia, came into the apartment, it was as though invisible heavy fists pounded the doors and hands struck the plaster walls and pulled over the venetian blinds slats. Each night when Virginia and her mother, Ruth, went to bed, dense thuds echoed from the headboard and the heavy bed frame.

Distraught and wishing to protect his family, Garrison finally sought professional help. He went to the Board of Health and related what was happening, asking for their aid. He assumed they might be helpful if the occurrences could be tracked to defective heating pipes or electrical currents traveling through his apartment from the X-ray machine under the television in the apartment above his, in those early days of television.

When he told of his troubles to the agency, they responded only with "sideways looks." Finally, he thought the *Eagle* might be able to help him and his family get to the bottom of the mystery and of the unseen hands which banged his forehead in his home.

Garrison provided the names of neighbors who had also been witnesses to the curious events and their statements backed up those of the Garrison family. Wife of the building's superintendent, Ms. Viola Ciabattari, had investigated the apartment and also heard the noises.

Neither she nor her husband could provide a reason for the peculiar slamming and pounding which seemed to trail Virginia from each room.

Neighbor George Eiskamp of 2160 85th Street joined Garrison in experiments to try to find the source of the sounds. Garrison went into his bathroom and rapped out a rhythm while Eiskamp, stationed by the bed, would hear taps that echoed the Garrison's rhythm, but only louder.

The first night they heard the knocking, it completely ruined the Garrisons' sleep. Four policemen, who also heard the sounds, explored the site but could find no source for the sounds.

When the knocking on the bed headboard made sleep impossible, Ruth moved her head to the foot of the bed, whereupon the pounding just followed her there.

At first, she and Virginia thought they might make a game of it. In bed, they would utter four words. They would then hear four imitation knocks from the headboard. One night, Mrs. Garrison shushed Virginia quickly. The bed responded with a long sound like a wire brush being pulled across just above their heads. That was enough for Ruth.

The night before the *Eagle* report, its reporter kept a late vigil in the apartment with the family. After Ruth and Virginia retired, there was a quick, heavy whack and Ruth and Virginia raced into the living room.

Garrison and the reporter followed Virginia into the room where she and her mother again resumed their posts on the bed. It was quiet until something unseen struck the wooden headboard again. But when the lights were switched on, the knockings did not come.

The Garrisons were not afraid of the sounds but only wanted a good sleep. They were unaware their troubles were similar to what psychical researchers call "poltergeists." Such occurrences usually center on a girl in her earliest teens as the center of the happenings.

Garrison's wife and daughter were almost growing used to being stuck by unseen light blows on the head, like a small whack, or an electrical shock.

Virginia was the least upset by the hauntings. They scared her initially, but then she grew accustomed to them. Apparently, the "playful ghosts" never followed her out of the apartment.

Mapleton

65th Street and 18th Avenue
Border of Bensonhurst and Borough Park

A *Brooklyn Daily Eagle* of 1894 related this story of Mapleton.

At about 1:20 A.M. on August 10th, the last train (when trolleys were called trains and did not run all night) was coming up from Coney Island on the Sea Beach Road. It was behind its time and the conductor was trying to make it up. As the train passed Twentieth Avenue in Mapleton, it started to slow down and ultimately came to a dead stop. This was peculiar, for the 1 A.M. train from Coney Island never stopped there normally.

But Nineteenth and Twentieth Avenues was where Margaret Barning shot herself, a stone marking the location. And from what the locals said, this was the "ghost base of operations."

The phantom was tall and "shadowlike," roughly the size of a woman, and wore a white, sheer veil, its arms enveloped in puffed sleeves. It squatted, flashed eyes of fire and was as large as a tree but grew smaller as you gazed upon it. It moaned in a forsaken and hopeless way, floated and evaporated into a transparent white "nothing."

Engineer Mallen, Firemen C. Van Pelt, and Conductor Puttys were manning the train which halted. Superintendent of the road, Richard Larke, was traveling in the engine [car].

Larke related to the *Eagle* reporter that they had just passed Woodlawn, the only station between Coney Island and Mapleton, without stopping and had rounded the turn, when Firemen V. Can Pelt pulled Larke's coat sleeve and pointed over to the left of the track. Larke saw:

> "...[W]what seemed to be a tall, white figure [which] seemed motionless at first...standing or appeared to be standing, just where the suicide occurred....[t]wo seconds later...it began moving over toward the railroad track...slowly at first, waving its long, draped arms...it motioned to us, gesticulating as one would do trying to stop a train."

Engineer Mallen saw the specter, began to blow his whistle and put on the brakes but "it" did not get out of the way, although it was careful to avoid the light of the head lamp. As the train stopped, the specter glided off the track toward the woods, motioning as if someone should follow. It then vanished into the woods.

The passengers did not understand why the train stopped in an open field. Many saw the phantom which created a great disturbance. Some ran from the cars when the train came to a halt, and it took those manning the train to convince them to re-board.

Larke continued:

> "...[A]s sure I'm alive, I saw what I've represented to you. The train stopped to prevent the possibility of running over anything."

Aside from Larke, the engineer also saw the apparition, along with John Meyers of Coney Island's Palace Cafe, McGuiness, one of John Y. McKane's policemen, flag men James Scott, George Mills, John Luyden, Homer Denae, William McAuley, a Sea Beach brakeman who lived on 24th Street, George McCormack of the Sea Beach place, Miss L.C. Oliver, a telegraph operator and Sophie Stewart, a "colored woman," and a young woman who ran the soda fountain at Feltman's [later Nathan's].

An *Eagle* reporter interviewed Jere Lott, who lived at 65th Street and 18th Avenue, roughly as close to the location of where the specter was seen than as any other local. Lott concurred that he, too, had seen the phantom.

Was Margaret Barning trying to tell them something about her death and why she shot herself, if she had, indeed, done so?

Sheepshead Bay

Sheepshead Bay derived its name either because its shape resembled a sheep's head or because sheepshead, a black-banded fish with sheep-like teeth, once thrived in its water. Sheepshead Bay was a quiet fishing village before the land boom of 1877 and the opening of a race track that attracted Diamond Jim Brady and Lillian Russell, among other notables.

Wyckoff-Bennett House
1669 East 22nd Street and Kings Highway

One of the last Dutch colonial farmhouses still surviving in Brooklyn, the Wyckoff-Bennett House was erected in 1766 for Henry (Hendrick) and Abraham Wyckoff. During the Revolutionary War, soldiers quartered there scratched their names: "Toepfer Capt of Reg de Ditfurth" and "Mbach Lieutenant v Hessen Hanau Artilerie," on two panes of glass in the farmhouse.

In 1835, the house was acquired by William Bennett. The final Bennett to live in the house was Gertrude Ryder Bennett, author of the books, *Living in a Landmark* and *Turning Back the Clock* about her life in the Wyckoff-Bennett House. After her passing in 1982, the house was

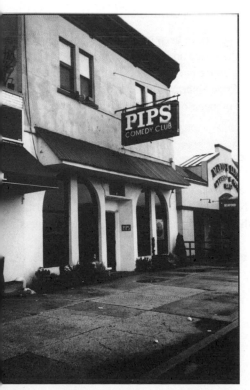

bought by Annette and Stuart Mont. Except for necessary modern conveniences, the house retains much of its original furniture, clothing and artifacts of the Bennett and Wyckoff families.

According to a *Brooklyn Bridge* magazine article, the Monts stated that the house was "organic." Throughout the house, generations of Wyckoffs and Bennetts could be sensed. Footfalls on the steps were routinely heard. Gertrude Ryder Bennett experienced events in the house that made her "think twice" about the presence of supernatural boarders.

Pips Comedy Club
2005 Emmons Avenue

Pips Comedy Club. *Courtesy of John Garvey, Co-Owner.*

The oldest comedy club in America, Pips was founded by the legendary George Schultz in 1962. Following his death in 1989, Pips struggled for many years, as a result of inferior acts and unoriginal management. It started its comeback with Mike Palmero in 1995, which brought back some of Schultz' "wacky magic," which launched the careers of comics Rodney Dangerfield, Robert Klein, Elayne Boozler, and Jerry Seinfeld.

In 1998, local Sheepshead Bay brothers John and Ray Garvey, along with Dominic Bruno, took over Pips. They opened with "Saturday Night Live's" Colin Quinn, another native Brooklynite who got his big break at Pips to headline a grand reopening for the sold out show. Since that time, Pips has featured the best comics around to a sell-out crowd most weekends.

Many believe that the ghost of George Shultz is back at Pips and appreciates the good times again, according to a story in *The New York Daily News*.

Music sometimes starts to play from speakers when it is not turned on. Doors slam, footfalls are heard from the empty apartment above and the television turns itself on to a great blare, the screen choked with "electronic snow, as if from another dimension." It then quickly shuts off. Sometimes, a ghostly giggle is heard, "like an imprint from the past."

Ray Garvey stated that his hair stood straight out on the back of his neck the week of September 12, 1999. He was cleaning up alone and leaned the mop against the bar. "[The mop] fell over backwards like on a spring." Garvey reported. When he washed out a glass and placed it on the bar and turned to put beer in the refrigerator, quickly, he heard a rattle from behind him. When he turned, there was ice in the glass. But it was when the toilet flushed by itself, he knew that something was going on at Pips.

Waitress Debbie Schmidt found a lone tabletop candle curiously aflame that should have been put out the night before. The wax was fresh, as if the candle had just been lit. When she turned, another table candle across the room burst into flame, (something also known to happen at Ye Waverly Inn, already mentioned).

Initially, Waitress Schmidt thought the candle might have been burning all night. But that could not be for both had fresh, unmelted wax and there was no one in yet to light them.

Ray was slightly jarred when the odd happenings started in October, 1999, but now thinks the ghost is a friendly one. And he maintains it is George Shultz, returned after ten years.

One time, Ray was there alone. Two bricks just plopped off the wall behind the stage and Ray simply shrugged and said:

"Hey, how you doing, George? Wanna beer?"

Pips had an impressive first year, and comics always played Pips due to the name George Schultz imparted on the venerated comedy club. Now that Schultz is back, even if in ghostly form, John Garvey said he would lay money that the new and improved Pips will "give the next Dangerfield and Seinfeld their starts."

John feels there is someone unseen standing by the back door and he does not like to go upstairs alone. The week prior to the *News* article, a comic was on stage. Out of nowhere, the "Blues Brothers" music belted out of the speakers. Maybe specter George "was having a good laugh with John Belushi from the other side."

John believes that the spirit George Schultz has come back to Pips to enjoy the laughs once again.

Coney Island

Coney Island Boardwalk.

The Dutch called the island "Konijn Eiland" (Rabbit Island), presumably because of their great abundance on the island. Its history as a resort began with the Coney Island Hotel (1829) at Sea Gate, had its ups in the Dreamland and Luna Park days, its downs after the closing of Steeplechase, but forever perseveres, in an abbreviated fashion.

[I enjoyed Coney Island in the 1950s-60s as a young girl with my family and still look forward to it, now with Glenn and Jade, for an afternoon of fun, rides, and hot dogs.]

The Brooklyn Historical Society provided this un-cited story from their scrapbook clippings. It dates from the late 1800s, and in the customary long-headline of the time, announced:

> "The Old Road Houses, Changes Which Have Taken Place in Thirty Years, The Recollections of Mr. Peter Ravenhall — The Haunted House, Hicks Post, the Old Toll gate, and Their Associates, Some Interesting Reminiscences."

Peter Ravenhall, the then famous tycoon of the Coney Island Boulevard, was on the veranda of his road house and gazed with satisfaction over the green, flat stretches of woods and fields that extended all the way to the ocean on one side, the horizon on the other.

It was a brisk morning for business. There were [horse]races in the afternoon and the flow of vehicles past his home was akin to a "moving procession."

Ravenhall observed, to an elderly stableman leaning against the doorpost beside him, that it was very different from thirty years prior. The stableman concurred and Ravenhall noted that there was not even a road there then.

"All wild, boss," the stableman observed.

"Old plank road had all the business," Ravenhall responded.

The old plank road had been transformed into a dirt road and the old road houses that were so merry and wild were converted to dwelling houses, "just the same as men brace up and reform when they feel old that there's no fun in being bad any longer." All the gents who owned and frequented those establishments were long gone, too, and the road that used to be the most active in the country "is as lonely as a tom cat in a garret."

Half a dozen young men collected about Peter and asked about the old road.

Pat McCarthy's, McCarthy's Hill, was the first place you came to in those days. It stood where the reservoir was then by the entrance to the Old Coney Island road [now Shell Road]. McCarthy's was an old farmhouse and he was a short man with only one leg. Opposite his place was...

"The haunted house," the stable man added, enthusiastically.

"Aye, the haunted house...[t]he country folks were afraid of it..."

Coney Island Boardwalk toward West Brighton

An 1893 New York Times gives us this final Brooklyn entry:

"Ghost of Alcoholic Spirits: Coney Island's Alleged Apparition Investigated: Fred Bader and Dr. Ward Say They Have Seen It, and that When Pursued It Floated Away..."

Police Sergeant "Billy" Von Fricken, Dr. Ward, Fred Bader and Frank Yokel swore they saw a specter the day before the running of this story and, "...so far as the Police Sergeant and the Colonel are concerned, that they saw."

Two of the gents beheld the meandering ghost spirit and tried to grab her arm "in the customary endearing manner of the "Bowery" [a street in Coney Island].

Dr. Ward reported that he saw, "...[A] white object walking toward West Brighton."

He chased it and ran along the beach nearly half a mile before he caught up with it. Ward tried to seize it, but his hands "seemed to pass through it as though a shadow, and then it ascended into the air about ten feet and turning, floated rapidly along toward Norton's Point [a section then full of crime, now called Sea Gate, a gated community.]

Sometimes referred to as "Bader's Bogy," the "wandering spirit" is thought to be Margaret Sinclair, murdered daughter of a fisherman. Coney Island authorities, without a moment's notice, stated that the specter seen by Bader and Ward to be the same as the ghost of the late Sinclair.

Chapter XX

Queens

The Rockaway Indians were the first settlers of Queens, followed by the Dutch in 1635 after Governor Kieft bought title to the land from the Indians. In 1898, Queens County elected to join Greater New York. Queens is the largest borough in the City of New York.

Astoria

Astoria, upon its incorporation as a town, was so named in 1839, although there was great resistance to the name "Astoria" by those locals not enamored with John Jacob Astor. Astoria came into its own as a suburb after steam ferry crossings to Manhattan began. In the 1840s, Astoria was the apex of a successful shipping business.

Kaufman Astoria Studios (1919) utilized actors such as Paul Robeson, Gloria Swanson, the Marx Brothers, and Rudolf Valentino before Hollywood became the place to make movies. The Astoria Motion Picture and Television Foundation eventually gained title to that property where it now operates the American Museum of a Moving Image, devoted to the history and art of movies.

Steinway, situated to the east of Astoria, was created by William Steinway, piano manufacturer in 1872, who included in his company town a park, library, ball fields and kindergarten, some of its row housing still standing at this time.

Today Astoria boasts the greatest concentration of Greek-Americans in the City of New York.

George Templeton Strong, already mentioned, noted in his diary the second of two haunted incidents in the City of New York in the mid-1800s. On August 30, 1859, he wrote of a friend named Graham, who reported meeting an Astoria ghost.

This story was told by the petrified inhabitants, who reported marching noises — upstairs and down, all night long. It would stop any time a tenant peered out to the foyer to investigate. Two large, unpleasant, seemingly unyielding bulldogs were let loose on the stairs at night. As soon as the bedroom door opened, the dogs flew in, tails between their legs. They dove under the bed, and raced from the house the following day. No one could convince them to return or the tenants, who fled right along with them.

A *New York Times* of 1934 had another Astoria ghost tale, with the long title:

"Gold Ghost Walks in Astoria House: Psychic Expert Called to Old Frame House, Unable to Explain Garratings and Attacks: Treasure Pit in Cellar; Man and Woman Continue Dismal Search After Rooms are Routed by 'Spirit.'"

This took place in a frame house dating back to the 1830s. Director of the American Psychical Research Institute Hereward Carrington related the tale.

In 1932, an Italian man came to his office. The man had sold a prosperous beauty parlor to purchase the house in question in Astoria and he told Carrington he had information that a cache of gold was secreted under the house. An eighty year old Irishwoman was in cahoots with the man. They planned to let rooms in the house to underwrite the household costs while the man continued with his basement digging.

They soon discovered, however, that no boarder would stay very long. One tenant, a woman, woke one night in the upstairs bedroom. According to the *Times* article, "something had caught her by the throat." When the light was switched on, her neck showed fingerprints.

Carrington looked into the tale and came across records to back it up. He also found out that, in the same room, the "garroting ghost" had called on the first owner of the building and strangled his daughter-in-law. The old Irish woman, "free of the superstitions of her people," attempted to come up with new tenants, but the random visit of the poltergeist chased them all away.

Deep in the cellar, the former beauty parlor man continued with his digging. When Carrington and his wife visited the site, the digger had already been looking for the treasure for more than two years, resulting in a pit twenty feet deep and ten feet wide. But he found no gold.

One afternoon, the old Irish woman was walking out of her bedroom on the lower floor of the building with her large German shepherd proceeding ahead of her. Something hoisted the dog several feet from the floor and the woman watched in horror as his great legs contorted at a weird angle as if unseen hands were bending them.

The shepherd fell, whimpering, both legs broken. Six weeks later, in the same location, invisible hands elevated the woman and dropped her, which broke her left leg and arm. She was restricted to her bed for a long time as a result, which Carrington stated could be corroborated by records of these injuries.

One night, as the man was asleep, something woke him. Seated on his bed was a shape, somewhat shadowy. He realized from its voice that it was the spirit of the woman who had been killed.

"Do not be afraid of me," it said. "Go on with your digging. There will be no rest for me until you find what you seek."

This took place prior to Carrington and his wife ever visiting the house. The Carringtons said they would finally come when the man and Irishwoman requested their presence, which soon happened, for they could not make a living without tenants. They hoped that the Carringtons, with their knowledge of the supernatural, might be able to help rid them of their distressing callers.

The Carringtons visited the house three times. Each time, they were accompanied by a medium who had no prior information as to the circumstances of the house. Each of the mediums, upon arrival, became instantly aware of the paranormal entity. They were able to describe the large pit in the basement without ever visiting it.

Nothing that transpired during the visits of the Carringtons showed that the powers behind the antics that vexed the household were of human origin. They were at a loss to explain the occurrences.

At twilight one night, a reporter called on the house. Described as an ideal place for a ghost story, the building sagged and was weather-beaten, much in need of paint, the porch warped, and loose boards creaked as you walked upon them. The bell rang out "deep and hollow somewhere inside."

The door opened to the reporter about two inches wide. A gray elderly face peered out in the shadows, somewhat obscured by tangled gray hair. A large German shepherd growled threateningly behind the old woman's skirt.

When the reporter stated that he had come from the Carringtons, the door opened slightly and he was allowed into a dark hall. There were no lights burning at all. He was conducted into the front room, where furniture, curiously shaped and distorted in shadows, appeared to crowd in upon him and the woman.

"For the love of God," she pleaded, "don't use this story. The world is filled with wicked people. Don't use my name. Don't, if you are a Christian gentleman, even mention the name of this street," the woman implored the reporter.

And he respected her wishes, to sooth her troubled soul.

Flushing

Vlissingen, a Dutch town from where many of its first colonists relocated to the new world from, was later renamed Flushing and chartered in 1643.

The Quakers have long been hailed as one of the creators of religious freedom in the United States, dating back to their seventeenth century struggles with Peter Stuyvesant, who wished to suppress them, along with many other religious groups, except of course his denomination, the Dutch Reformed Church.

The Department of Parks held up a $4.2 million restoration of the Everette P. Martins Field playground after it was discovered that the tiny park served as the "Colored Cemetery of Flushing" for much of the 1800s. A 1936 *Long Island Press* article told of how workers digging the park's wading pool unearthed "bones galore" and rare pennies, one worth $17, that had covered the eyes of the dead. The article noted there was no way to identify the graves, "so the digging continued."

Bowne House
Southeast corner of Bowne Street at 37th Avenue

The oldest structure in Queens (1661) and one of the oldest in the State of New York, the Bowne House was a well-known stop for fleeing slaves on the Underground Railroad. The House was lived in by nine generations of Bownes until 1945 when it opened as a museum.

In the kitchen of the house, Quaker convert John Bowne permitted clandestine gatherings of the group whose unconventional creed, fervor, and seemingly unusual way of worship ("quaking") attracted the ire of conservatives, especially Governor Peter Stuyvesant, who loathed the sect.

Stuyvesant fined Bowne and deported him to Holland where Bowne made his case with the Dutch West India Company. Company administrators, always looking at the bottom line, thought bringing Dutch immigration to an under-populated colony was of more financial value than the religious conformity that Stuyvesant forever strived for. As a result, they told Stuyvesant to temper his ways, the earliest legal test of religious tolerance in the United States.

In the garden of the Bowne House, the plaque engraving of the Flushing Remonstrance (a response by the Flushing people to Stuyvesant's edict of 1657 that the Dutch Reformed Church was the sole allowed religion in the colony), was once displayed. It is now housed inside the Kingsland Homestead (which we will read about soon).

The National Directory of Haunted Places states that the Bowne House is ghosted by an unseen entity. The almost 350-year old house is thought to be home to a Colonial ghost, which the Bowne House's Education Director has called "friendly or positive."

The Kingsland Homestead
143-35 37th Avenue
37th Street west of Parsons Boulevard
Present headquarters of the Queens Historical Society

Kingsland Homestead. *Courtesy of Stanley Cogan, President, Queens Historical Society.*

Weeping Tree offspring, in back of Kingsland Homestead. *Courtesy of Stanley Cogan, President, Queens Historical Society.*

The Kingsland Homestead was built in the 1780s by Charles Doughty and named for British sea captain Joseph King, who wed Doughty's daughter. The Kings' daughter married Lindly Murray (of Murray Hill) and their descendants lived at the Homestead, a stop on the Underground Railroad, until the 1920s.

The Dutch-style house was relocated from its original site to make room for a subway line in the 1920s, and again moved to its present location in 1968. The second oldest house in Flushing, the Kingsland Homestead sits on land that was once held by Samuel Parsons, who planted a Weeping Beech tree there in 1847.

More than 150 years later, the Weeping Beech tree's cuttings have grown their own Weeping Beeches, bestowing on the original Weeping Beech the title of "Mother of American Weeping Beeches."

The ninety-foot span of the original Weeping Beech is sadly no more, being cut down a few years ago. A memorial service was held on the site to honor the memory of the venerable old tree.

New York City Ghost Stories describes how volunteers and visitors have described thudding noises at different locations in the house. In all instances, those who heard the noises were alone in the Homestead when they took place. The most modern tales of the hauntings of Kingsland consist of two ghosts, one young, the other old.

An historical society spokeswoman stated that a few people who have worked or done research at the society archives have heard the sad sound of a baby sobbing.

Another specter is much more threatening.

The historical society archives hold the statements of three Murray family members who related their encounters with the ghost in the garret of Kingsland.

In 1878, H.G. Murray wrote a seven-page account about the ghosts of Kingsland, thirty years after it took place, to Mrs. Ford.

It related that Mrs. Ford's attorney husband died, leaving her little money. As such, Ford was forced to take in cleaning and mending jobs to support herself. Luckily, the Murrays had a great deal of work for her. As such, it seemed logical that she would live in their house but the only vacant room was a garret. The room was broken into two chambers, one filled with family mementos, the other a guest bedroom which was given to Ford.

It was on Ford's first night in the house that she met the ghost of Kingsland.

Ford was having trouble sleeping and it did not help that the town clock tolled each hour on the hour. At midnight, the ghost made its entrance. Ford heard nothing, but felt something moving in the direction of her door. Choking with fear, she was too paralyzed to scream for help (as I have often felt in nightmares, as I am sure have many others). The town clock tolled the first stroke of midnight and there was not a sound from outside her door. The second stroke, a sound was heard from outside her door. As the final bell tolled for midnight, Ford heard three prolonged distinct raps on her room door. A hushed moaning voice cried:

"Let me in. For God's sake let me in!"

That was followed by a long cry of torment and despair. Ford fainted as a result. The next thing she recalled was daylight and she raced downstairs for aid and solace. When she told her tale to the Murray family, they stated that none of them ever had a supernatural experience in the Homestead, and neither was there anything passed down in the family history as to ghostly happenings. She calmed down, thinking it all a nightmare, and fretfully went about her day.

The next night, Ford again retired to her garret room. In the middle of the night, the Murrays woke to a dreadful shriek and a crash. They fast made their way to the attic, the source of the commotion, to find Ford trembling at the foot of the stairs. Crying and wailing, she pleaded pitifully to be taken home.

She told them that once again, at the first stroke of midnight on the town clock, Ford felt that outside her door was the prolonged movement of — something. At the second stroke, her door creaked somewhat, "as if something had softly pressed against it."

On the third toll of the midnight bell, distinct and prolonged, came three raps with the cry:

"Let me in. For God's sake let me in!"

Again, this was followed by an extended moan of torment and despair. Ford flew out of her bed and raced from her room to the Murrays. She was finally quieted down and told that would be her final night in that bedroom.

The Murrays made a thorough search — of the stairwell, the storage room, and garret bedroom. But there was nothing amiss. Property values being what they were back then (and still are), it was better thought to keep the matter under wraps by the family.

H.G. Murray, eighteen years old, challenged Ford to sleep once again in the attic bedroom, that he would stand guard at the foot of the attic stairs with the door ajar until quarter after twelve. If Murray heard nothing, Ford would concur she was the victim of a dream or delusion. Ford agreed to his plan. H.G. made himself comfortable at the foot of the attic stairs, sitting in a chair next to a table, and by lamplight read a book.

The first stroke of midnight tolled from the town clock. H.G. heard nothing from the attic, but, according to his account:

> "...[T]he roots of my hair stiffened, every muscle in my body locked rigid, and a cold chill ran down my spine."

He heard the second bell toll and knew he was not alone.

The final toll of the town bell barely pealed when, on the bedroom door up the stairs, boomed three distinct raps and a pitiful cry:

> "Let me in. For God's sake, let me in!

This cry was again ended by a prolonged moan of despair. H.G., with a scream of both fright and boldness, raced wildly up the steps. He saw, drifting across the attic, a large white shape, blurred in the night. But when he searched he found nothing.

All the commotion woke H.G.'s parents who raced to the source of the disturbance and again found Ford shaking in bed. The women of the house dressed and helped her downstairs where their carriage was ready to take her home.

For weeks after, Ford lay in bed, fearing being left alone. Finally, she felt herself but swore to never visit the Murray house again.

When I visited the Kingsland Homestead, a volunteer told me of a former volunteer.

> "She felt a peaceful presence at the homestead that was both protective and reassuring."

And then there is the story of the slide projector.

"About five years ago, a slide show was being prepared for visitors," the volunteer related. "But when the visitors arrived, the other volunteer and I could not get the projector to work. One of the volunteers went upstairs to see if the caretaker could help. Suddenly, inexplicably, the projector went on by itself."

(The ghost of?) Kingsland Homestead. *Courtesy of Stanley Cogan, President, Queens Historical Society.*

Flushing Friends Meeting House
137-16 Northern Boulevard between Main and Union Streets

Flushing Friends Meeting House. *Courtesy of Linda Shirley, Flushing Friends Meeting.*

Friend's Meeting House welcome sign. *Courtesy of Linda Shirley, Flushing Friends Meeting.*

The Flushing Friends Meeting House is the oldest house of worship in New York City. It has been continuously used by the Society of Friends since 1694, except from 1776 to 1783 when the British turned it into a prison, a hay storehouse, and a hospital. Iron stoves were not installed until 1760 and central heating in 1965.

A *New York Herald-Tribune* of 1884 provided the story of the ghost of the Meeting House.

Flushing (in what was then considered Long Island) was in a great uproar over the purported arrival of a specter in the center of town. It was first seen about a week prior to the *Herald-Tribune* report at 1 A.M., coming out of the Old Quaker Meeting House.

The Chief of Police and a reporter rushed over to the Meeting House. As they approached, the chief clearly watched as a curious shadow vanished into the house.

They neared the Flushing Friends Meeting House carefully, only to discover that the door and windows were well secured. By that time, their search party numbered ten. One of the party peered through the key-hole of the front floor and quickly fainted away.

When he came to he said:

"...I saw three big men dressed in white and with swords hanging by their sides...they were close together, and one...seemed to be explaining something to the other two. Then they commenced to dance and I ran away..."

On the following Friday night, another village young man who had not heard of the phantom story was passing the Meeting House and saw the ghost. E. Enbank, then eighty years old and one of the leading members of the church, lived in the rear of the Meeting House. His youngest son, about sixty years, gave his report of the specter as follows.

When he was a boy in the 1830s, he recalled there was a phantom in the Meeting House. He pointed out, where the Meeting House stood at that time, was a Revolutionary War burial ground and there were over four hundred Hessian soldiers interred there. The headstones in the small graveyard were unmarked until 1848, in accordance with the Quaker belief that death is the great equalizer.

Lawrence Street

A 1901 *Brooklyn Daily Eagle* headline reported in a typical elongated headline of its day:

"Queer Doings Nightly Around a Flushing House, Weird Noises, Clanging Bells, Flying Stones, Knocks and Explosions Disturb Mrs. Bogert...There Are Ghost Symptoms, However, And Those Who Believe in the Uncanny Are Nodding Wisely."

The *Eagle* noted that it had been some time since Flushing had a ghost featured in their paper, for, in olden times,

"...[G]hosts used to turn up every month or so, especially in the summer..."

Ringing bells, hurtling rocks, blasts, and "night noises of a weird kind" were heard emanating from the Lawrence Street house. Several people thought there was something extraordinary about the exhibition which Mrs. L. Bogert swore happened each night at her "handsome residence."

For six weeks, Bogert said she had been eyewitness to odd and startling happenings at her home, which included strange footfalls on the piazza, great raps on the door, and the whacking of stones on the roof. Croaking voices had been heard in her house, and the ringing of her bell, so intense that it was ripped out of the door casing.

Bogert was a fearless woman, the *Eagle* reported, but still she had to summon the police many times as a result of the hauntings. Her husband, John Bogert, owner of washing machine shops, was on the west coast when the unrest took place. Bogert related that since her husband was away, she had to take matters into her own hands.

One night, she was unsettled by the arrival of two strange men. She went for her husband's revolver, having used firearms since a girl and reportedly "a good shot." She stood in the front hall, aiming her husband's revolver, ready to shoot if they tried to break in the door.

Another night, something tried to break in through the back doors and frightened the servants by tossing stones, then tried to force the front door with a fence rail. Bogert went to the window, took precise aim at the closest of the interlopers and let off with three shots.

After Bogert summoned the police, detectives stayed one night in the house to try to get to the bottom of the hauntings. The sounds persisted in spite of their presence but no one was sighted or caught.

Another night, the unseen tormentors tried to set the house on fire. The police, still unable to nab the dangerous offenders, pressed Bogert to seek help from the Deputy Chief and Commissioner York. Consequently, she received improved protection, but the sounds persisted and stones were hurled at them each time they went to a window, which broke the glass. Bogert was also regularly troubled by what sounded like a blast that woke her every night.

As a result of all the commotion, Bogert had grown into a fascinating topic of discussion in Flushing. Great compassion was voiced for her by the neighbors, but many of the men were somewhat troubled by Bogert's statement:

That she aimed to shoot the first man she could get her eyes on pestering her home.

The former North Prince Street Police Station

A *Brooklyn Daily Eagle* of 1902 scared the wits out of Queens residents with the headline:

"Flushing had a Ghost that Frightens Coppers."

Patrolman Hanniman first night's sleep in the then new station house was not at all a restful one – he felt quite anxious, his sleep troubled. He heard odd sounds all night, making him quite jittery. The next morning when he was relieved, he related his experiences to his sergeant and asked to be reassigned, balking at staying in the building one second more, and was transferred to Brooklyn.

A search was made for the cause of the "grewsome"[sic] events that befell Patrolman Hanniman. Patrolman McKenna discovered that water dripping from a leaky ladder on a tin roof might be the source of the problem. But when the leak was stopped, the strange sounds continued.

One of the policeman thought that the sounds were like the laments of a woman in dreadful suffering, and it was claimed that a white robed form of a tall young woman had been seen tracking through the halls in the "shadowy moonlight."

Gabriel Winters built the house that became the North Prince Street police. When it was still the Winters' residence, the youngest daughter, Miss Winters, was found dead in her room under questionable circumstances. Some say she committed suicide, others maintain that she was murdered.

In any event, no one ever solved either mystery – the cause of Miss Winters' death or the haunting of the station house.

GLENDALE - The Woods Inn Saloon

Located at a dead end of 73rd Street near the railroad tracks, the Woods Inn Saloon is bordered east by the Lutheran All Saints Cemetery. A perfect location for a ghost story.

Poltergeist Mr. Dare is said to ramble through the halls of this old saloon in central Queens. According to a *New York Times* article, the Woods Inn Saloon resembles a barn because its windows are always closed.

When Dare makes his appearance, the door inexplicably flies open, a whiskey bottle falls off the bar or a wallet goes missing. Dare drops by infrequently, and most nights the Saloon is filled with regulars whom Dare never annoys.

Regular Jimmy Soran stated that Dare does not disturb the patrons of the Woods Inn Saloon and looks like a hazy film or a caped gent. Soran further related that Dare does not impart a ghostly chill or a rotting odor.

Many locals believe Dare died upstairs while in the throes of passion with a woman of "questionable virtue." Others maintain he was an old rummy who succumbed to tuberculosis in a rented room. Still others think Dare drank himself to death at the Woods Inn Saloon, and there are those who hold firm to the belief that Dare is a homeless spirit whose grave nearby in Lutheran All Saints Cemetery was removed to make room for a fresh body.

One of the oldest saloons in Queens, the bar is hand-carved mahogany from Germany's Black Forest, placed there in 1854, embellished with a lion's head and gargoyles, and had has five mirrors and five supports joined in a counterclockwise swirl, save the middle, which goes clockwise, the signature of the artist who carved it.

The Woods Inn has been a hotel and a brothel. Its apex was in 1868 when the railroads came through and ironworkers came in on the Long Island Rail Road Montauk line. Farmers would ride up on horseback and tie up their steeds outside. The hitching posts were stolen in 1985 and the rail line discontinued in 1998 due to a lack of customers.

Manager Debbie McBride noted that the same names have been regulars for years, for generations.

Including Mr. Dare.

Rockaway Beach
Fair View Avenue

"Here's your fine clams
As white as snow
On Rockaway these clam do grow!"

—A clam-seller singing his wares
in the streets of Lower Manhattan
Mid-1800s

The Rockaways are a peninsula spanning Jamaica Bay. Their remoteness made them a restricted summer retreat until the railroads in 1868 finally brought in the general population.

The house on Fair View Ave was erected in 1894 at a cost of $12,000.

A *Brooklyn Daily Eagle* of 1896 reported that prior inhabitants who lived in Augustus Gustersin's large, four-story double flat[apartment] house stated that it was haunted, corroborated by the J. Weller family.

They had relocated from Brooklyn to the Fair View Avenue address. Just as quickly as they had moved in, they moved out, stating that no money in the world "would induce them to spend another night in the house."

Weller told an *Eagle* reporter that he was happy to escape with his life for "he both saw and heard the uncanny visitor." The ghost looked like an elderly gent and wailed pitifully. Weller recalled the wraith's footfalls that would always end with the terrible sound of a man falling down a flight of stairs, which Weller noted was "accompanied by shrieks that made my hair stand on end."

A complete probe was conducted, but nothing was discovered as to the reason for the haunting or any mishandling of the furniture.

The owner did report that an elderly man named Quinley did live in those rooms, fell downstairs, and died as a result. It was after his internment that the eerie sounds began in the house which was filled with tenants, who soon relocated and were replaced by new renters. Some stayed a month, others two weeks and a few but one night.

When the *Eagle* report ran, the house was empty. Gustersin was trying to rent the flats for almost any amount named but he found no takers.

☯taten Island

Henry Hudson visited what would be Staten Island in 1609 and named it "Staaten Eylandt," in honor of the States General, the government of the Netherlands. In the following years, the Dutch tried repeatedly to colonize the Island, but contentious Indians, enraged by the repeated incursions with and by the colonists, struck at the settlements. In 1661, a group of French and Dutch farmers created the first lasting colony, present day Old Town, near what is now Fort Wadsworth.

In 1776, 30,000 British soldiers and Hessian soldiers of fortune upset the farming tranquility of the Island, which soon evolved into a large military camp from which the British staged assaults on Long Island. Staten Island is thought to be where the final shot of the Revolutionary War was fired from.

In 1829, Cornelius Vanderbilt, born by Stapleton, created a regular ferry service to Manhattan, his initial stride toward becoming Staten Island's, and eventually, the nation's richest man.

In the mid-1800s, Staten Island bloomed as a seaside resort. Herman Melville was a visitor along with Frederick Law Olmstead, who tried farming before finding fame as the architect of both Central and Prospect Parks. During the Draft Riots, already mentioned, abolitionist Horace Greeley was hidden from enraged mobs by his friend George W. Curtis, whose house stands today in West Brighton.

TOMPKINSVILLE - Monroe Avenue

A Tompkinsville ghost was mentioned in an October 4, 1873 *New York Times*.

Tompkinsville had a specter that had been haunting an unidentified home on Monroe Avenue. It not only scared away the tenant but also terrified the neighbors. The phantom enjoyed banging on a window to attract the attention of passers-by and quickly vanishing.

The *Times* report ended with the observation that:

"There is danger it will cause the depopulation of the neighborhood."

563 Henderson Avenue

In a *New York Daily News* article, Hans Holzer wrote of the ghost of 563 Henderson Avenue.

When Carol Packer resided at 563 Henderson Avenue, it was common for objects to fall from tables or move on their own volition. Once, a freshly baked apple pie flew out of the pantry.

Packer's two nieces knew that there was something amiss about the old Victorian house. The day her aunt moved out, Carolyn Westbo recalled that quite suddenly, a great sense of hopelessness enveloped her. Westbo wanted to wring her hands and was extremely distressed. The feelings were fleeting, but she had the clear impression of a woman who was quite upset. Westbo felt something or someone pressing against the right side of her head.

She saw a mist in the large downstairs dining room. Its form was somewhat tall and thin, without a face, and appeared a bit worn. "But I did see hands wringing," Westbo reported.

The same day, Carolyn's sister Betsy had a similar ordeal. She felt the presence of someone sobbing, and Betsy wanted to sob right along with her, as if someone were next to her asking:

"What's going to happen to me?"

When they related to their aunt their curious feelings, Packer said she had noted the misty form when alone in the house.

Another owner, Mariam Goez, had similar experiences. Her silver spoons vanished one by one, later discovered secreted about the house. Irene Nelson, her daughter, was sitting in the kitchen when screws began falling from the table on their own, one by one. Nelson got up and the table collapsed, one of its legs coming off by itself.

Another time, Nelson awoke at 4 A.M., opened her eyes and discovered she was unable to close them again. She felt goose bumps all over her body and was aware of an intense cold.

Nelson sensed a presence in the room. She heard an odd noise, seemingly coming from the outside as if someone was sweeping the sidewalk. This kept up for roughly ten minutes. Nelson could only lay there, unable to move and totally petrified.

Packer and her nieces did research on the house's history and the only discovery out of the ordinary was that a woman had dropped dead on the porch.

Hans Holzer and clairvoyant Sybil Leek were contacted to learn whom the specter was and why it still walked the earth. Leek had no prior history of the house or its occupants, and, upon arriving at the house, waited in another room while Holzer questioned Packer and her nieces.

When Leek came into the room, she appeared unusually agitated.

She was standing by the refrigerator and the kitchen door opened about two inches. Leek did not want anyone to think she was opening the door to eavesdrop on the conversation between Holzer and the women he interviewed. There was a presence in the room with Leek, who said she could easily have gone into trance at that time, but resisted the urge due to her never entering trances without Holzer's presence.

Leek was scared, which she seldom was.

Soon enough, a dull voice came through Leek and Holzer asked the name of the spirit.

"Anne Meredith," was the response, uttered with breathing difficulties. Holzer asked if the house belonged to her.

"Yes...I want to get in. I live here I want to be let in!...I...have...heart trouble...I can't get up the steps. Can't get to the door...door must be opened!"

The specter did not know she had passed on. She swore it was 1955 and that her son and mother waited for her in the house. Holzer attempted to tell her that she was dead but the ghost did not want to hear of it.

Holzer tried another course. He stated that the door was being opened for her, and Holzer took her "by the hand" to prove that someone else lived there now. The phantom was astounded, and even more so when informed by Holzer as to what year it was.

"Where is my mother?" The shade demanded.

Holzer said she too had passed away and the ghost of Anne Meredith finally understood. Holzer mentioned that her mother was waiting for her outside the house.

"May I come back sometime?" the ghost inquired in a frail tone.

Holzer told her she could but it was time for her to join her mother. As the phantom slowly wafted away, Leek came back to her own body. Prior to awakening, tears fell from her eyes.

Alice Austen Cottage ("Clear Comfort")
2 Hylan Blvd.

Alice Austen House. Photo: Albert Balossi. *Courtesy of Carl Rutberg, Exec. Dir.*

The original sections of the historically land marked Alice Austen Cottage gingerbread house date back to the late seventeenth century, the last alterations being made in 1844.

"Clear Comfort" was home to photographer Alice Austen from 1866 to 1952. When her father abandoned Austen's family when she was two, they moved to "Clear Comfort" with her grandparents, where she grew up when Staten Island was a famous resort. Austen was forced to leave her beloved Clear Comfort due to illness and poverty at age seventy.

It was not until Austen, a pioneer in photo realism, was near death, that her contributions to the art of photography were finally recognized. Oliver Jensen, then Editor-in-Chief of *American Heritage*, tracked her down to the poorhouse. Using the proceeds from an article about her remarkable career published in a 1951 *Life* magazine, Jensen enabled Austen to live in a private nursing home for the last months of her life.

The Staten Island Historical Society has some 3,500-4000 glass negatives wherein Austen depicted in great detail the world around her from 1880-1930.

(Of all the sites I visited for *Ghosts of New York City*, the Alice Austen Cottage and grounds are perhaps the loveliest. They offer a spectacular view of the Verranzano Narrows Bridge and New York harbor, and the scent of the garden's flowers bring to mind a more genteel time. Additionally, it is one of three sites – the others being the Morris Jumel Mansion and the Poe House – that offer an audiovisual tape to detail not only the backgrounds of the sites but especially the personalities that make them so interesting.) It also includes a ghost story.

The ghost story of the Alice Austen House is that of a British soldier quartered there during the Revolution. On stormy nights, neighbors have reported hearing his boots pacing woefully back and forth on the old wooden floors. It was reported that he hung himself in the House over an unrequited love and has apparently never left the Alice Austen House.

Crawley Mansion

Ghosts in American Houses gives us the specter of the Crawley Mansion.

The owner of this Victorian mansion was slain by a "vengeful" specter in 1870. Mrs. Dartway Crawley lived alone in the mansion after her husband joined in the California gold rush. Her maiden name, Magda Hamilton, was well known to New Yorkers in those days, for she was a police informant who cracked an infamous "smugglers doll" diamond gang.

One of those indicted was Franchon Moncare, a young French girl who pretended to be the child of Ada Danworth. The innocent-appearing Franchon, clutching her fragile china "dolly" that held $250,000 in jewels, sailed right by customs. Moncare and Danworth lived together in a handsome mansion on Staten Island and worked with Boss Tweed's cronies in a string of robberies and smuggling jobs.

When Mrs. Dartway Crawley was still Magda Hamilton, she joined Moncare and together schemed to fleece a Chicago millionaire. Apparently successful, Hamilton was accepted into the gang. But she turned on the gang, married, and she and her new husband purchased the old mansion.

One night, after Moncare died in prison, the tiny French woman's specter materialized in the now Mrs. Crawley's bedroom, rammed a china doll down her throat and suffocated her.

Moncare's phantom was still seen on the grounds almost one hundred years later. New York Harbor authorities have had dozens of accounts from witnesses in passing boats of a spectral form on the widow's walk on top of the old Crawley mansion.

RICHMONDTOWN - Historic Richmondtown
441 Clarke Avenue

Richmondtown was founded about 1690 when it was "Cocclestown," perhaps due to the oysters and clams fished from nearby waters. The name further evolved into "Cuckoldstown" and was changed to Richmondtown by the end of the Revolution.

During the Revolutionary War, Staten Island was held by the British. As a result, a few of the Richmondtown structures were demolished. In 1729, Richmondtown became the seat of the county government. During the 1830s, Staten Island grew into a suburban resort from the City, hosting new industries as well as a new civic center erected in Richmondtown.

In 1898, when Staten Island became a borough of the City of New York, St. George was named seat of its government, which essentially halted development of Richmondtown, but insured its status as an historic site in the future. Food Editor Jackie Plant, already mentioned with the Old Merchant's House Museum, had a supernatural experience at Historic Richmondtown.

The Kruser-Finley House

Kruser-Finley House, Historic Richmondtown. *Courtesy of Maxine Friedman, Chief Curator, Historic Richmondtown.*

Located next door to the Basketmaker's House across Richmond Road is the Dutch and Flemish influenced Kruser-Finley House. Built in 1790, with an addition in 1820 along with a shop erected between 1850-1860, legends holds that the house, which was relocated from Egbertville (near the intersection of Richmond and Rockland Avenues), was owned by a cooper. Today's shop, outfitted to depict the day-to-day life of a saddle, trunk, and harness maker, has craft demonstrations, when Historic Richmondtown's budget allows.

In 1985, Jackie and her future husband Bob Plant were visiting Historic Richmondtown. It was a beautiful autumn day and the foliage was in full blazing glory. As it is now, the house was not open to the public. But because it was such a glorious day and the light just right, Bob wanted to take a picture of Jackie in front of the Kruser-Finley House.

Jackie positioned herself at the front door and Bob went to shoot. But Jackie balked.

"I can't stand here," she protested.

"But the lighting is perfect," Bob implored.

"I can't. There's an angry man behind me," said Plant, who rushed away fast.

She stated that, although she could not see him, she got the feeling of an enraged man standing behind her. Bob, who saw the fear in her, did not push the photo.

We do not know who the angry man of the Kruser-Finley House is, but perhaps he was sore that, when Jackie and Bob visited in 1985, the house was closed due to budgetary constraints. Or perhaps he was "the man of the [Kruser-Finley] house," who takes umbrage with the fact that the house had been moved from its original site, and forever keeps letting those who visit know of his eternal dissatisfaction with the new location.

The Polly Bodine House
Richmond Avenue

The *New York Times* has an article about "The Witch of Staten Island."

As of October, 2000, what is known as the Polly Bodine House was enveloped in gray vinyl siding, a Perkins™ restaurant and Wendy's™ across the street, the Dr. Martin Luther King Jr. Expressway nearby.

In her day, Polly Bodine was as notorious as Lizzie Borden. P.T. Barnum called her "the Witch of Staten Island." This old house, more than 150 years ago, was where Polly Bodine lived with her parents.

In 1843, Staten Island was a rustic seafaring and agrarian home of 10,000 who resided in villages. Christmas night, two boys coming home from a skating party saw smoke billowing from a Richmond Road house which stood near the Bodine House, roughly where the Perkins™ parking lot now stands. The Bodine House belonged to Polly's brother, schooner captain George Houseman, away at sea. His young wife, Emeline, and their twenty-month-old daughter, Ann Eliza, were home alone.

Neighbors hurried to the burning house but no one could find Emeline and the baby. Initially, rescuers thought they had visited relatives or friends for the holidays, until something was found in the kitchen near a burnt basket of pumpkins and onions.

It was Emeline's body.

Court papers detailed Emeline's body's condition in gruesome particulars. The back part of her head was extremely burned, the brain roasted by the extreme heat. Both bones of the left forearm were broken.

The remains of baby Ann Eliza, found nearby, were in even worse condition.

Authorities fast pieced together a spine-tingling scenario. Someone had slain both so viciously, that their bones were smashed and skulls broken, then set the house afire to mask their dreadful deeds. A few days later, there was a suspect.

It was Polly Bodine.

Bodine, however, was close to her sister-in-law, and many times stayed overnight to help with baby Ann Eliza. When robbery was suggested as the likely reason for the murders, many scratched their heads. Polly had money and the amount taken was small, indeed.

Polly, though, did lead a rather unconventional life for a nineteenth-century New York woman. She was separated from her husband and was having an affair with New York apothecary (pharmacist) George Waite. She had abortions when public feeling was turning away from this formerly approved form of birth control, just two years prior to New York making abortion a crime.

History professor Amy Gilman Srebnick of Montclair State University stated that because abortion was such a hot topic at that time, Bodine's history definitely would have influenced how she was seen in her community. Many Staten Islanders thought her "a fallen woman," and, as such, open to all kinds of conjecture.

Bodine's actions at the time of the killings only heightened questions as to her involvement. Early on the morning of Dec. 26th, when Polly said she was in Manhattan seeing Waite, a chambermaid observed Bodine on a ferryboat leaving Staten Island, guzzling gin and munching a slice of pie, appearing tired and apprehensive.

Polly was also seen in a pawnshop on lower Broadway sporting a hooded cape and a green veil, pawning objects from the victims' house. Still others recollected Bodine stumbling about the streets of Manhattan in a stupor.

Bodine was arrested on New Year's Eve. Three days after, she had a premature birth, a stillborn boy, another bastard, locals whispered amongst themselves.

In June, she first appeared before the Richmond County Court. The new penny press newspapers like The Herald, The Sun, and The Evening Post gobbled up every morsel about the case. The trial was the talk of the City, and anything even remotely related to the case was retold in special editions of the presses. The Bodine case had everything: illicit sex, avarice, and butchery. "There cannot be a doubt as to the guilt of the wretched woman," The Post proclaimed.

Even Edgar Allen Poe got involved, filing a report on the eve of the trial for a Pennsylvania newspaper. An article in the New York Herald related that Poe stated:

"This woman may, possibly, escape, [f]or they managed these matters wretchedly in New York."

Poe was correct, for the first trial ended in a hung jury. One juror refused to convict on the grounds that he did not have "circumstantial evidence in the fourth degree."

In a bid to find an impartial jury (double jeopardy not yet part of jurisprudence), the second trial took place in Manhattan, rendering it a more sensational event than the first trial. Women, specifically, appeared enthralled by Bodine. The Herald commented on the crowds "of highly fashionable female spectators, giving the courtroom all the appearance of some of our fashionable theatres."

P.T. Barnum upped the ante of the tumult with a wax depiction of Bodine in his museum a few blocks from the courtroom. He depicted her as a toothless "witch" of seventy, (in spite of her being thirty-five,) barbarically chopping away at her victims.

Bodine was convicted but the verdict overturned.

Her third and last trial was in Newburgh, New York. Bodine's attorneys adeptly discredited the testimony of numerous significant witnesses. After more than two years in jail, Bodine was found not guilty.

Upon hearing the final verdict, Bodine simply said to her lawyer:

"Can't I sue Barnum now?"

But the press could not get enough of Polly Bodine. In 1846, a New York publisher circulated a wild pamphlet depicting Bodine as a vampire and "woman of ill repute, possessing an undying enmity to the human race, an insatiable thirst for blood, following murder as a calling."

Bodine, meanwhile, moved back to Staten Island and lived there in increasing anonymity until eighty-two. When she died, her heirs were two grown children.

But the killer was never found and the public never quite gave up the idea that it was Bodine. But if it was her, what was the motive and why the savagery of the deeds? If not her, then who?

Marguerite Rivas, local poet and an adjunct professor, College of Staten Island, has written about Bodine in her poetry, along with other Staten Island notables. Rivas speculated that Bodine was somehow connected with the crime, even if she did not actually commit the murders herself.

"I think she probably did it, or at least had something to do with it, Rivas noted. "That's what my gut tells me."

For inspiration, Rivas often pays a call on the small cemetery where Emeline and Ann Eliza lie interred together. Their headstone is situated at the border of an active four-lane road, in the shadow of a big shopping center.

A tiny woodland somewhat thrives across the street from Polly's old house. According to the *Times* article, locals have seen a hazy specter in gray skulking through the woods at night.

Perhaps the "hazy specter" has information as to who committed those dreadful slayings almost 160 years ago.

Tottenville

Tottenville is located at the southernmost point of Staten Island, originally settled as a fishing village. (And it was of no great surprise, that when I got off Staten Island Rapid Transit at the Tottenville stop, the first thing I noticed was the smell of salt in the air, everywhere.)

At one time, Tottenville's byways were paved with oyster shells and it is no wonder. For when I walked the beach in front of the Conference House, I found oyster shells the size of my hand. To this day, Main Street sometimes gives a glimpse of how it looked in the nineteenth century, with gingerbread houses that showed the skill of local craftsmen.

Conference House
7455 Hylan Boulevard

The Conference House. *Courtesy of Mrs. Madalen A. Bertolini, Pres., The Conference House Assoc.*

The Conference House plaque. *Courtesy of Mrs. Madalen A. Bertolini, Pres., The Conference House Assoc.*

The historical land marked Conference House was built around 1687 and is located on the southernmost point of New York State.

British sea captain Christopher Billopp, a violent man who served in the British Navy, erected the then Bentley Manor overlooking Raritan Bay with an eye toward British architecture. For many years, Bentley Manor was thought to be the most exceptional structure on Staten Island, with 1,600 acres of prime land.

Legend has it that Billopp is the reason for Staten Island's being part of New York as opposed to New Jersey. In 1664, when the British invaded New Amsterdam (then New York City), the Lords of Berkeley and Carteret, landholders of New Jersey, claimed the island was theirs.

To resolve the claim, the Duke of York proclaimed he would give Staten Island to that province whose citizen could circumnavigate Staten Island in less than one day. The competition was won for New York by Billopp.

On September 11, 1776, Benjamin Franklin, John Adams, and Edward Rutledge met with British commander Lord Howe at his home to work out a peace plan in the Revolutionary War. The house where the historic meeting took place was Bentley Manor.

The British were in control of New York, Long Island, and Staten Island. Due to his victories against the colonists, Howe believed that the crushing of the War for Independence was simply a matter of weeks.

According to Hans Holzer's The Spirits of '76, Howe, wishing to prevent additional casualties and also make it easier on himself, proposed a peace conference be held to see if an "honorable peace" could be agreed upon. The United States Congress received his communiqué about the "peace plan" with mixed feelings, for they had just finished battling out their own differences of opinion in regard to the signing of the Declaration of Independence.

The three legislators traveled by horse to Perth Amboy, New Jersey where they were met at the Jersey shore by a barge staffed by British soldiers to safely transport them across the bay. For all the cordiality and politeness displayed by Lord Howe, the sight of British soldiers in full battle dress lined up along the road was somewhat off-putting to the legislators.

Afterwards, John Adams described the soldiers as:

"[L]ooking as fierce as ten furies, and making all the grimaces and gestures and motions of their muskets, with bayonets fixed, which, I suppose, military etiquette requires, but which we neither understood nor regarded."

Lord Howe explained his plan for a settlement, stating that it was hopeless for the Americans to continue with the War, that the British were willing to put on the table a "peace with honor" plan. But the sticking point was that any settlement would keep the colonies under British rule.

Benjamin Franklin then told Lord Howe that the Declaration of Independence had already been signed on July 4, 1776, and that we would never again agree to British rule. The conference broke up, strengthening the resolve of the Continental Congress to see the war of independence to its very end, and the colonies won their independence.

The Billopps were fervent Tories. Captain Billopp's grandson, also named Christopher and born in the manor, resided there until War's end when he relocated to New Brunswick, Canada, along with many other Tories who were no longer welcome in the newly independent colonies.

Slowly, Bentley Manor began falling apart. In the early twentieth century, it was a factory making rat poison. Plans for rescuing the manor house finally began in 1926 when the Conference House Association was created to refurbish and oversee the restoration at the old Bentley Manor.

There was once a tunnel from the basement vault to the water's edge in the Conference House utilized as a means of escape from Indian attacks. This secret tunnel could also be used to acquire supplies by the sea route without being observed from land. A former Indian burial site was discovered in 1895 near Billopp Avenue where six skeletal remains were discovered.

Curious happenings have been witnessed at the historic House for over 150 years.

Since the 1850s, odd mumbling and wailing sounds, along with the shrieks of a young girl, have been heard. Legend has it that an enraged Captain Billopp killed a servant girl on the large, winding staircase. Mediums have depicted Billopp's specter as a large man wearing a fur coat, black trousers and high boots. Local lore holds that Billopp had thrown over his fiancée who later died of a broken heart in the house.

As a result, queer sounds, including mumblings, sighs, groans, and entreaties of an unseen voice were said to have been heard in the house from the 1850s. According to the old Staten Island newspaper *Transcript*, the incidents were heard by workmen involved in the restoration of the house after it became a museum.

In 1962, Hans Holzer first heard of the Conference House and its ghostly reputation and paid a visit that year with medium Ethel Johnson Meyers and two of her friends, Rose de Simone and Pearl Winder, which he wrote about in *The Spirits of '76*. Meyers, as is customary when using a medium, was not privy to any of the details of the haunting. But before they arrived at the Conference House, she offered her sense of where they were heading to.

Meyers related that the house was white, the ground floor divided into two rooms, the east room containing a brown table and eight chairs. The room to the west of the entrance was the larger of the two and that silverware was displayed there.

When they reached the house, Holzer compared the set-up of the house to Meyers' initial impressions. They were correct, except for the number of chairs, one of which was removed for repair.

"Butler," Meyers muttered as they came into the house. The estate next to Bentley was that of the Butlers who most likely had visited the Conference House often. Meyers was drawn to the second story room, left of the staircase, where she sat on the floor.

Slowly getting a psychic fix on the Conference House, Meyers spoke of a woman, Jane, whom she depicted as rotund, white haired, and attired in a dark green dress with a fringed shawl. Meyers also described a "presence," a specter of a large man wearing a fur hat, skin coat, high boots, a brass-buckled belt, and black trousers.

"I feel boats around him, nets, sailing boats, and...a broad foreign accent," Meyers stated.

She "saw" him in a four-masted square-rigger ship and mentioned the initial "T." Was it Tory Billopp?

"I feel as if I am being dragged somewhere by Indians," Meyers cried out. "There is violence, and somebody dies on a pyre of wood. Two men, one white, one Indian; and on two sticks nearby are their scalps."

Meyers had picked up the remains of great unrest in pre-colonial days.

When they went into the cellar, Meyers stated that six people had been interred near the front wall during the Revolutionary War, all British soldiers. There were eight more buried elsewhere on the grounds, and Meyers had the impression that the basement was used as a hospital during a skirmish.

Later research authenticated that Billopp family members had been buried on the grounds by the road and British soldiers could have been interred there also, due to the numerous battles that took place around the house from July, 1776 to the end of the year.

Again Holzer and Meyers returned to the house's upper part. Abruptly, Meyers turned white and grasped the handrail to the winding staircase. For a second, she appeared frozen. Returning to the present, she slowly walked down the stairs and indicated an area by the second story landing.

"A woman was killed here with a crooked knife!" she said.

Did Meyers pick up Billopp and his jilted fiancée? But Billopp did not kill her. It was passed down that she had died of a broken heart. Then custodian Mrs. Earley was quizzed by Holzer about any murder that could have taken place in the house. Earley responded that Billopp once, in a rage, killed a female slave on that precise spot on the stairs.

Holzer asked Ingrid Beckman, whom he had worked with for many years, to serve as a medium for a November 25, 1972 visit to the Conference House. All Beckman knew about the house was what Medium Meyers picked up in the 1962 visit. Holzer asked her to visit the House alone.

To evade tourists, Beckman came to the House prior to the 1 P.M. opening time. Beckman walked about the grounds close to the House and felt a presence as if the place were "alive." Beckman went up to the front porch and had a feeling of melancholy and dread, of a perilous state.

As Beckman sat on the front porch of the House waiting for opening time, she had the awareness of someone watching her.

"I felt as if someone knew I was there...and I especially felt this coming from the window above the hallway..."

At opening time, Beckman first went to the basement, assuring the guide that she would be fine alone. Looking around, she felt directed to a small archway.

The area "made her literally jump," and she was plagued by heavy chills. Beckman picked up that something dreadful had taken place by the fireplace and simultaneously at the tunnel entrance.

"The tunnel entrance is particularly terrorizing...[it] caused me chills all the way up to my neck."

The Conference House, door to basement. *Courtesy of Mrs. Madalen A. Bertolini, Pres., The Conference House Assoc.*

When she walked upstairs to the upper landing, Beckman went to the bedroom at the left. At its entrance, Beckman heard a sound, like a knock.

"The hallway upstairs felt terrible," Beckman explained.

She turned and looked down the stairs, and almost became dizzy. Beckman picked up that someone had been pushed down or hurt on them. To insure she was really feeling this, Beckman went up and down those stairs many times. Each time, the feeling was identical. She concluded that the window, which had drawn her attention while waiting outside, was just outside the haunted stairwell. Beckman,

"...[G]ot the impression of a slave woman, especially in the upstairs bedroom...there was [also] a disturbance around the table downstairs."

But she did not believe the two were connected. Beckman picked up that the woman was connected with the upstairs bedroom, the stairway and perhaps the tunnel entrance.

When Holzer inquired as to when the disturbances dated back to, Beckman replied the 1770s, prior to the Revolution. She added that there was still something unsettled at the Conference House with a woman, but also maybe a man – the commotion at the table had something to do with a man. Perhaps he was shot, or abducted from that room and dragged through the tunnel.

Billopp was twice abducted by Yankee irregulars from the Jersey shore. Gabriel Disosway, in his 1846 story of the Manor of Bentley, related that Colonel Billopp, at the time a military leader, was vigilantly watched and twice seized from his house by armed bands from New Jersey and made a prisoner.

In January, 1973, Beckman paid another call to the Conference House and this time spoke to the caretaker. She reported hearing heavy footfalls upstairs every so often, sounding like those of a man in heavy boots with spurs. Also, on the anniversary of "the murder," the caretaker saw a man running up the stairs toward a girl waiting on the first landing.

The caretaker reported that the girl was beheaded. In addition, the caretaker related that in the summer of 1972, as she was dusting the room to the left of the ground floor, she put her hand "right through" a British soldier.

That same summer, her daughter from South Carolina visited and stayed upstairs in the haunted rooms. That night, she heard an unseen man's laugh, followed by a woman's laugh, and then a shriek. The caretaker reported that this occurs at regular intervals.

The final account of the haunting of the Conference House has to do with a grandmother and her granddaughter, Margaret.

While her grandmother was speaking with the guide downstairs, the young girl walked up the stairs alone. In one upstairs parlor, she saw a man in a corner chair. Assuming he was another guide, when she questioned him about the room, he quickly vanished. She had not heard him leave and would have, given the squeaky floorboards.

A second later, he reappeared, and she repeated her question. He answered her in a measured, precise tone that appeared to emanate from far away. Her questions answered, it was his turn, and he asked her about herself and ended with just one more question:

"What is General Washington doing now about the British?"

Margaret was startled. Although young, she knew that George Washington was dead for a long time. Delicately, she told him about Washington's demise, and that Harry Truman was now president and the year was 1951. The man appeared startled and sat down. As Margaret gazed "in fascinated horror," he slowly vanished.

Chapter XXII

The Subway

The New York City subway system has been in the business of transporting millions of people for one hundred years. In that time, there have been subway accidents, suicides, and murders. A whole underworld of homeless people live in many of the stations, sleeping each night only inches away from the tons of steel that rumble along the dangerous third rails. Some simply roll over in the night, to be hit by a train.

Writers from Thomas Wolfe, in his "Death the Proud Brother" from *Death to Morning*, to Ben Hecht have written about the subway and the dead. There is no doubt given all the life, and death, that occurs underground, there are many ghost stories in the subway system alone. Subway workers would sometimes place crosses on the tunnel wall to mark the spot where someone died.

The following story is from Ben Hecht, entitled "The Ogling Corpse" from his book, *1001 Afternoons in New York*:

A dead man on the subway sat with his eyes riveted on a woman passenger. Not aware that he was dead, but insulted by what she viewed as his disgusting leering, the got up and slapped the man's face, not knowing he was in the fixed stare of the dead.

His corpse hurled out of his seat "and much hysteria ensues."

The identity of the woman who punched out the cadaver was never learned, nor was the identify of the cadaver for that matter, or "the subway guard" who witnessed the entire event. Hecht observed that there were readily available to a good reporter scores of citizens who heard the tale from a neighbor whose aunt or uncle were on the train when it all happened.

(From my experience, the Metropolitan Transportation Authority, which oversees the subway and bus system of the City of New York, is extremely tight mouthed about any ghost stories. But, they always trickle out, sometimes turning into fictional accounts, such as in the film *Ghost*, and both *Ghostbusters* movies.)

The book *Subway City* mentions *Ghostbusters II*, following a brief introduction to New York City's [almost] first subway system:

Alfred Ely Beach introduced his concept of transporting people via a pneumatic railway in an 1867 exhibition held in Armory Hall on 14th Street. After a cycle of highs and lows where Beach attempted to raise funds toward the completion of his pneumatic railway under Broadway and Murray Streets in Manhattan, by 1870, 312 feet of tunnel was completed. But the Depression of 1873 finally put an end to Beach's dream. The tunnel was turned into a shooting gallery.

When the Broadway Mass Transit (BMT) subway line was being built, astonished workmen came across Beach's tunnel.

In *Ghostbuster's II*, actor Dan Aykroyd uncovers "ectoplasmic slime" coursing through an underground tunnel labeled "Pneumatic Transit System."

"I can't believe it!" the Ghostbuster cries out, "It's still here!"

Chapter XXIII

Ghosts without a Home

This is a category born out of necessity. There are so many ghost stories in the City of New York, the City forever altering its face, either by changing street names or addresses, demolishing structures or building over them, that these ghosts no longer have a house, flat, or apartment to call their own.

But they once did.

Lower East Side
374 Pearl Street

This area was once located at the banks of the East River, the shoreline later being extended. Pearl Street is so named for the "opalescent" sea shells that glistened on its shoreline. Herman Melville, already mentioned, was born at #6 Pearl Street in 1819.

This story of 374 Pearl Street comes from a *New York Chronicle* article.

According to a *New York Daily News* article of 1997, the population of New York in the early 1700s consisted of 4,848 whites and 970 blacks, most of them slaves.

In 1741, a white preacher, John Hughson, was sentenced to hang for inciting slaves to riot. Hughson was hanged from a gallows built on the southeast border of Henry Rutger's farm, an area now covered by 374 Pearl Street, one of the Alfred E. Smith Houses (projects).

Hughson's body was left hanging as a warning to other slave sympathizers. According to eyewitness reports, the display was so frightening that the site was averted for months afterward.

For years to come, many whispered that John Hughson's wraith would not quit the area, frightening all who crossed his path.

GREENWICH VILLAGE - 106 West 3rd Street
at Sullivan Street

Sullivan Street is named for Brigadier General John B. Sullivan, promoted by George Washington to battle the Iroquois. A letter to the *New York Times* by Michael Alcamo stated that Sullivan perhaps did more to crush the Indian way of life in New York than anyone else in colonial times. At the end of the Revolutionary War, he was a major general.

But perhaps Sullivan paid for his dastardly deeds after death.

When Sullivan passed away, he was so mired in debt that his creditors put into place an ordinance that allowed them to place a lien on his cadaver by confiscating it until his bills were settled. As a result, to get Sullivan's body back, his friends ultimately paid off his debts.

The Cafe Bizarre (1950s-1984) was once located at this site and it was quite a happening place. Beatniks, Bohemians, and hippies made it their home away from home.

What has been described as a gent from colonial times in a *New York Times* article has been sighted in a corner where the old artists' hangout and a colonial-stable once stood. Many employees and customers of the Cafe saw the phantom of a young man with piercing black eyes and a short beard, attired in a ruffled white shirt.

Many believe that the ghost is none other than Aaron Burr, who got around not only in life, but is still doing so in death. Up to the 1830s, the structure was a portion of Burr's stables.

Burr was thought to be calling for his only child, Theodosia, who vanished at sea.

Or could it be the ghost of John Sullivan still trying to atone for the wrongs he did to the Indians or rectify his financial problems, even after death?

132 Waverly Place

Waverly Place was named for the Sir Walter Scott novel in 1833.

A *New York Daily News* article tells us that in the 1980s, the top floor apartment was once home to writer Paul Rudnick.

Rudnick swore it was haunted by John Barrymore's spirit, Barrymore once living in that same top floor. The apartment was the scene for Rudnick's play, *I Hate Hamlet*, about an actor who resided in an apartment ghosted by John Barrymore, noted actor, alcoholic and womanizer.

African Grove Theatre
Formerly located at the corner of Mercer & Bleecker

Quiche Lloyd-Kemble's letter mentioned the haunting of the *African Grove Theatre*.

Founded in 1821, the *African Grove Theatre*, the first black theatre in America, was said to be haunted. The spectral occurrences were so bothersome that after awhile, they were part of the reason for its closing.

27 Jane Street
(Former Francis House)

#27 Jane Street was mainly a wooden house from the pre-Revolutionary days. It is named for John Francis, Alexander Hamilton's doctor, who treated him, but to no avail after his fatal duel with Aaron Burr. Hamilton died a few days later across the street at home at #80, a house that also no longer exists.

Aaron Burr's try for the presidency in 1800 and his run for Governor of New York four years later were thwarted by his powerful arch-foe, Alexander Hamilton. The two men's contempt for one another came to a head on July 4, 1804 when they faced each other in a pistol duel in Weehawken, New Jersey (dueling having been outlawed in New York City at that time).

Hans Holzer's *Great American Ghost Stories* tells of Jean Karsavina who lived at #27 since 1939.

Since first moving in, Karsavina heard footfalls, squeaking stairs, the opening and closing of doors, and an unseen hand flushing a toilet. One time, the toilet chain (the old "crapper" chain for early toilets) was swinging, and there was no one around who could have caused that.

"I suppose a toilet that flushes would be a novelty to someone from the eighteenth century," she said in a short newspaper report of June, 1957.

Karsavina has also seen a cloudy form. The upstairs tenant related that one night, "a man in eighteenth-century clothes, with his hair in a queue" strolled into her room, took a peek at her and strolled right out again.

Holzer and trance medium Mrs. Ethel Meyers paid a call on #27 Jane Street in March 1960. In customary fashion, Meyers knew nothing of the occurences prior to the visit. Upon their arrival, she was placed in a trance by Holzer.

Meyers, while still "in waking condition," saw a "shadow" of a elderly gent with a wide face and "bulbous nose"; a woman wearing a black shawl whose name Meyers thought was Deborah; white lilies covering an altar; a bridal couple; a tiny coffin adorned with flowers; and a very elderly woman lying in a coffin lavishly decorated, relatives, including a young boy and girl, peering into that open coffin. Meyers caught the name, "Mrs. Paterson," and the girl's as "Miss Lucy."

Meyers also "saw" a vacant coffin, people crying, speaking, and walking about. The American flag was draped on top of the coffin, usually an honor reserved for war veterans. It contained "a man's hat, shoes with silver buckles, and gold epaulets." Meyers picked up that the man's lungs were full of liquid and he had died with a "pain in his side."

In semi-trance, Meyers related that she "saw" a party of men in a small boat on the water, a man in white pants and a blue coat with blood splashed over the pants. There were two boats and it was twilight.

Shifting evidently to a different time, Meyers picked up that something took place in the cellar and that "they" attempted to divert notice to what took place downstairs. There, a woman was being detained by two uniformed men in short jackets and round hats with wide brims and pistols. Screaming, the woman is forced back harshly, men are marching in step, someone concealed had to be abandoned, and an elderly man in a nightshirt and red socks was pulled out of the house into the snow.

Meyers was psychically lead in the direction of the rear of the house, where someone died in childbirth. She added that this kind of death took place several times in the house. Police were called and the name Henry Oliver or Oliver Henry came to her.

After returning to consciousness, Meyers said there was a cold spot in the middle of the downstairs room. Meyers "saw" the form of a lean gent, well-built, over common height, wearing white trousers, black boots, dark blue coat with tails, and white lace in front. He was connected with George Washington and Lafayette, whose faces come to her also. She picked up that Washington possibly had been in the house and that the man she "saw" was also a general wearing epaulets.

The elderly woman and the children she saw earlier were associated with this. There was a battle in a boat and Meyers picked up the name, "W. Lawrence." She had a good feeling about the long-past owner of the house, that he sheltered many people, like immigrants.

Shoes and coats were stocked here, Meyers reported, characteristic of a military post. Food was dispensed and the name "Bradley" was picked up. Meyers "saw" an elderly man playing a cornet, and two men wearing white trousers were "seen" at a long table hunched over papers, a crystal chandelier above them.

Following the séance, Karsavina stated that the premises was once owned by Hamilton's physician. Until 1825, #27 was held by a doctor who was the physician for the Metropolitan Opera. The cornet player could very well have been one of his patients. Before the Revolution, the building might have been operated as headquarters for an "underground railroad" around 1730.

"Lawrence" may refer to George Washington's portrait by Lawrence which hung over the fireplace. Holzer located "T. Lawrence, M.D. at 146 Greenwich Street in *Elliot's Improved Directory of New York* 1812), a "Widow Patterson" is listed by Longworth (1803) at 177 William Street, and William Lawrence, druggist, at 80 John Street."

Charles Burr Todd's *Story of New York* related that Oliver Wolcott and John L. Lawrence were two of Hamilton's pallbearers. The white trousered man was "the perfect image of Hamilton," and the many coffins and women dying in childbirth were sadly in keeping with a doctor's residence, at that time.

Alexander Hamilton's ghost apparently kept to the house of the doctor who attempted to save his life, but could not. Hamilton is also reported to have visited other town houses on Jane Street and is fascinated by today's appliances.

UNION SQUARE

The old Union Square Theatre
Formerly located at 14th Street between
4th Avenue and Broadway

Located at the former center of the City's first theatre districts, the old Union Square Theatre (not to be confused with the present theatre of the same name) stood on an empty lot at 14th Street between Fourth Avenue and Broadway.

Quiche Lloyd-Kemble's letter stated that it was said to be haunted by the ghost of George M. Cohen who wrote "Give My Regards to Broadway," "Over There," and "I'm a Yankee Doodle Dandy."

EAST SIDE - 226 Fifth Avenue

226 Fifth Avenue is most likely the most extensive probe Hans Holzer ever undertook, as noted in *America's Haunted Houses*. Holzer took part in seventeen separate sessions in five months studying this haunting.

Holzer "found" this ghost through *The New York Daily News* of July 1953. Danton Walker, a Broadway columnist at that time, ran the following:

"One for the books: an explorer, advertising his Fifth Avenue Studio for sub-let, includes among the attractions 'attic dark room with ghost.'..."

The top apartment of 226 Fifth Avenue was a duplex, owned by Captain Hassolt Davis, an explorer, who spent much of his time overseas. During Holzer's probe in 1953, the building was closed for renovation. Davis was unnerved by the ghost and wanted to get to the bottom of the hauntings. Holzer was given an introduction to Davis by the late Danton Walker.

Holzer discovered through extensive search, a Confederate officer, a hero, crossed Confederate lines in the middle of the Civil War to be with his friend, General Samuel Edward McGowan of McGowan's Brigade.

Medium Ethel Johnson Meyers provided certain details. The general's love, French Creole Mignon Guychone, had become involved with another man, Walter. Walter surprised McGowan and Guychone, finding them locked in an ardent embrace.   Enraged, he choked McGowan to death.

To avoid being charged with murder, Walter hung McGowan's body from the rafters in the small attic to appear a suicide, suggesting it was McGowan, who found Walter and Guychone passionately kissing, could not take the betrayal and strung himself up.

The most compelling request of the specter, upon communication with the medium, was to show the world his death was not a suicide but murder, and he did so through Ethel Johnson Meyers. Holzer, through trance medium Meyers, helped move along General Samuel Edward McGowan to a sphere where he finally attained peace.

The old Metropolitan Opera House
Originally located on Broadway and 39th Street

The Metropolitan Opera was created by a party of "new" capitalists: the Goulds, Whitneys, J.P. Morgan, and Vanderbilts, who were refused boxes at the Academy of Music on 14th Street due to the "old ruling class" holding claim to them all, not wishing to give way to the "Nouveau Riche."

Built in 1883, the first Metropolitan Opera House included an auditorium whose deep Diamond Horseshoe offered box holders a bird's-eye-view of each other but not of the singers, with roughly seven hundred seats having a partial or totally blocked view of the stage. But for the elite society that frequented the opera, that was all they wanted, to see and be seen (and even better if they also saw the opera in the process). In spite of its physical limitations, the house remained open until 1966, when it then moved uptown.

The annoying specter of Madame Frances Alda, wife of director Giulio GattiCasazza, had been seen sighted sitting in the center seats. She was attired in a silk dress and ridicules singers, specifically young sopranos. When anyone tried to find out who she was, Alda vanished.

One story about her annoying actions was said to have taken place in 1955, as related in *I Believe in Ghosts*.

Early in the season, a woman who customarily attended the opera with a friend instead went to a matinee alone. As a result, she turned in the extra ticket to the box office. As she sat down, she realized her friend's seat was already taken by a large woman in a silk dress.

During the first act, the silk dressed-woman fidgeted in her seat, often checked her program, and grumbled aloud about what she thought were inadequate performances. Most irritating, she repeatedly hit the arm of the increasingly aggravated woman next to her. "Flat, flat, flat!" she stage-whispered when a specific aria irritated her.

Irritated, the woman was fed up with the insufferable silk-dressed woman. She stormed up the aisle at intermission and related her tale of woe to the manager, even displaying black-and-blue marks on her arm where the large woman had pressed it. The manager dispatched an usher to the seat of the silk-dressed woman to warn her to desist in her actions.

The baffled young man came back and reported that the seat was empty. In fact, the seat was empty for the entire first act, stated the other opera-goers seated close by.

Brooklyn Melrose Hall

A *Phoenix* newspaper and an 1895 *Brooklyn Daily Eagle* give us the ghost of Melrose Hall, quite a famous story in its day.

Melrose Hall was originally situated on Bedford Avenue between Clarkson and Winthrop Streets. Melrose Hall was considered once one of Brooklyn's most frightening haunted sites until it was torn down in 1890.

Dating back to 1749, Melrose Hall was on a grand estate and the ornate home of Revolutionary War Tory Col. William Axtell.

During the Revolution, Axtell was host to British officers. Melrose Hall, like other massive homesteads, was transformed into a jail, its dungeons holding patriot prisoners.

For many years following the War, travelers on the lonely road at night would hear an anguished moaning and tell of beholding a spectral young woman floating through the house. It was also related that years after, the bones of a woman patriot prisoner were found in the dungeon of Melrose Hall.

The story was that Tory Axtell took advantage of "the fair Alva," his future sister-in-law, and afterwards locked her in a secret upstairs room, where she slowly starved to death. One night when local Tories were partying at Melrose Hall, the emaciated ghost made an appearance. She was later reported floating from window to window.

24th Precinct Station House

An 1894 *Brooklyn Daily Eagle* was the source for the haunting of then 24th Precinct Station House dormitory. The ghost was first discovered by Patrolman Daniel York.

The following night, the apparition again appeared, this time seen by Patrolmen Shea and York. Two nights later, Patrolmen Tucker and Ryan said they distinctly saw the phantom.

About three years prior to the *Eagle* report, a girl, Lizzie Rose, was arrested for intoxication. She was placed in a cell, but died before morning.

Many of the officers were convinced that the ghost was the apparition of the unfortunate Lizzie.

Queens - Flushing
153 Madison Street

A 1927 *New York Times* headline read:

"Ghostly Pianist Arouses Flushing: Sad, Classical Music Issues Nightly From Attic of Deserted Dwelling."

The inhabitants in the area of 153 Madison Street were reported ready to go to the authorities concerning the strange character of the "rambling old vacant house," reported to be tenanted by a phantom musician who played an unseen piano in the dusty garret.

The last show of the ghostly visitor was said to have occurred on Christmas night. Music was heard emanating from the upper floors of the building. There were also reports of forms skulking in the darkness of a tall hedge and calling out to those who passed by. The phantom recitals happened only at night and were heard by those rushing past the run-down building.

The music was said to be classical, but with a sad refrain. The structure, formerly owned by Mrs. Adele Newell, was sold three years prior when she relocated. Newell maintained that, in her occupancy, there were no curious exhibitions.

A pallid light was said to illuminate the garret while the music played, which kept up periodically through the night. The display was thought to be only what "a real artist" could produce.

The look of the old house gave the appearance of what formal ideas of a haunted house looked like. Its doors hung wide and swayed on creaking hinges. Contorted trees and piles of trash rose from a lawn encased in snarled yellow grass. The house drooped in a weary manner. Even the soot-encased windows appeared to be withholding something. Neighborhood children avoided it, at all costs.

The rooms were empty save for strewn trash. The garret also was unfurnished. There was no piano in sight, but come New Year's Eve, it was believed several of the locals would rally together in "comforting groups waiting for the concert."

Long Island City
Jackson Avenue off Dutch Kills Road

An 1874 *New York Times* announced:

"Long Island City has a new sensation: this time is it a "haunted" house.

In 1874, the Daly family leased the Jackson Avenue structure in question for a modest fee.

They were advised that there would be other "dwellers" besides themselves in the building. That did not sway them. They stated that, "they were not afraid of ghosts, or even the 'old boy' himself."

They resided there quietly for roughly one week, when, one Monday evening, after they went to sleep, muffled moans were sharply heard. Worrying that someone might be freezing from the frigid temperatures, Daly got out of bed and stepped into the hall. The moans appeared to emanate from the kitchen.

Daly went there, when, to his amazement, the sound was then heard in the parlor. When he went to investigate the parlor, the sound now came from the cellar. Astonished, Daly inspected the building thoroughly, thinking he would eventually unravel the cause for the mystery sound. But after a fruitless search, he decided to "give up the ghost" and return to bed. Briefly afterward, he heard a sound as though a heavy body was tumbling down the stairs.

The next day, Mrs. Daly vowed that the crockery in the cupboard was thrown down and smashed, and said the outside door was unopened. One Daly child was so completely scared "that it was thrown into violent convulsions and has since died," according to the *Times*. The following Tuesday night, the same scenario took place again with slight differences.

At midnight, shouts of, "Murder! Murder!" were heard throughout the house, frightening the entire family. Neighbors were summoned and the building inspected thoroughly but nothing was found. Finally, the Dalys moved out, stating that no, they were not afraid, but that "it was impossible to sleep in such a racket!"

Stapleton Enterprise Variety Theatre

An 1883 *New York Times* ran the headline:

"A Very Rude Ghost: The Flaming Apparition Which Deluded Some Strictly Sober Firemen."

Ex-Deputy Sheriff Tom Brown was said to have seen a specter in his Tom Brown's Theater. Brown indicated to the *Times* reporter who visited the site the curtains across the stage where he beheld the ghost.

Brown took a group of friends to the [Arthur] Kill, north of Prince's Bay, including James Donaldson of the London Theatre, Alderman Thomas Foley, and Detective O'Mally of Staten Island. The New Yorkers [Manhattanites] had missed the last boat back to New York and were forced to stay overnight in the Enterprise Variety Theatre.

Between 1 and 2 A.M., blankets and robes for bedding were spread on the floor and the gents tucked in for the night. At 3 A.M., Andy McGinnis shouted out:

"Howly Mowee! A ghow-est!"

When he turned to get a better position, which faced the stage, he saw there an apparition "in ghostly habidments."

That had every man on his feet. Brown stated that the specter stood in stage center, motioning as if giving a speech "but not a word did it utter." Brown ventured toward the stage, but within five feet of it, the spirit moved slowly off to the right and vanished. There was no door from the building on that side and so the men surmised that the apparition dissolved "into thin air."

A second later, there was a commotion behind the stage. The men, terrified, raced back and in so doing, fell over chairs. All scrammed for the door and they stood trembling in the street until dawn.

Brown's friends did not believe the story. As a result, Brown made the following affidavit:

"Thomas Brown, being duly sworn, says that on the night of October 2, 1883, he and a number of New York friends...were disturbed by...a ghastly specter...who broke the furniture...the apparition seemed to be in flames and in great pains...said deponent, was sober at the time...and...now firmly believes that the ...ghost [was] of the wife-murderer Rheinhardt...his prisoner prior to his execution, that he is confirmed in said belief by the fact that when he stuck at said apparition his hand encountered no substance."

"I believe they said they saw a ghost," said the beat policeman, "with much caution."

Chapter XXIV

Cemeteries

It is only appropriate that we end our collection with ghost stories of New York City cemeteries. Some think it is impossible for a haunting to take place in a cemetery as the energy left by death is sometimes retained at the site of death.

But how many of us would venture, willingly, through a cemetery at night?

According to a *New York Times* article, the City's land has been altered repeatedly many times since the first arrival of the Dutch for the purposes of burial. The Dutch blanketed over Indian vestiges, the British, Dutch vestiges. Farms flattened forests, tenements bulldozed farms. Cemeteries, sadly, are not always protected and sometimes only looked upon as just more valuable real estate in the City of New York.

Chatham Square First Shearith Israel Graveyard
New Bowery at Chatham Square

First Shearith Israel Graveyard.
Photo: Joyce Gold History Tours.

A *New York Times* article, along with the *Blue Guide New York*, gives us much information about the First Shearith Israel Graveyard.

The First Shearith Israel Graveyard, the oldest existing cemetery of the City's first Jewish congregation ("Remant of Israel"), was first requested in a petition of 1655, but rejected because no Jews had died yet. It was finally bought in 1682 (presumably a Jew had died). The First Shearith Israel's oldest gravestone is from 1682 or 1683 and is that of Benjamin Bueno de Mesquita. The First Shearith Israel Graveyard was used until 1805 or 1828.

During the Revolution, Gen. Charles Lee hid guns in what was then called "the Jew Burying Ground" to aid in the City's safekeeping. Eighteen Revolutionary War soldiers and patriots are interred here, including Gershom Mendes Seixas, minister of the congregation, who took the Torah scrolls for safekeeping to Stratford, Connecticut in the midst of the British occupation. As the congregants relocated uptown as the City developed, Shearith founded two other cemeteries, one at West 11th Street, the other at West 21st Street.

Joyce Gold of *Joyce Gold History Tours of New York* took the startling accompanying picture of the First Shearith Israel Graveyard. Gold indicated that the luminous form in the photograph was not seen through the lens when the picture was taken, but showed up after being developed, hovering near a tombstone.

In an article in the *New York Daily News*, she stated:

"I was on a tour there and just decided to take a picture of a tombstone. When I developed the slides I noticed a blur, and it wasn't until a year later that I realized the blur had a very definite shape that I didn't see when I took the shot."

Gold said that after seeing the mysterious print, she researched the grave site and discovered that the woman buried there was Richa Levy, who lived in New York during the Revolution. Levy was from a family of thirteen and died at age eighteen.

Trinity Church Graveyard
Broadway and Wall Street

Trinity Church Graveyard. *Courtesy of John Allen, Dir. – Parish Communications.*

Trinity Church. *Courtesy of John Allen, Dir. – Parish Communications.*

Astonishingly, both Trinity Church and St. Paul's Chapel withstood the destruction of the nearby World Trade Center.

The cemeteries of both churches also sustained little if any structural injuries, only the coating of tombstones with the ash that fell from the towers, and already has been cleaned up.

A *New York Times* article tells us that the north part of Trinity Church's yard covers the location of the "new Burial place without the Towne," a Dutch site from 1675. The first church on this site was built in 1698, but was destroyed by fire. Its replacement, built in 1790, was damaged by heavy snowfall. The present structure went up in 1846.

Trinity Church is the first Protestant Episcopal church established in New York City. For years the spire, at a height of 280 feet above the steps, served as a landmark. During British occupation, Trinity Church served British officers as their own house of worship.

Captain William Kidd was one of the most active and charitable parishioners of the church in 1698, and Queen Elizabeth II paid a call in 1976.

In the cemetery, the Martyr's Monument, a tall memorial to American patriots who died while imprisoned by the British in New York, stands near the Broadway and Thomas Street corner. By the iron railing along Broadway on a sunken granite stone is carved the name, Charlotte Temple. Charlotte, said to have been the granddaughter of the Earl of Derby, eloped with an English officer, who brought her to America and abandoned her after the birth of her child.

A popular novelist of the day (1791), Sarah Haswell Rowson, used her story in *Charlotte Temple*, one of the most widely read novels in the English language.

At noon, the cemetery is an oasis for the office workers of the financial district. During their lunch hours, they sun themselves on the benches along the paths while eating lunch, or on the steps and railing of the porticos.

Included in the notables buried in the churchyard are Alexander Hamilton (who is reported to haunt the cemetery) and Robert Fulton.

The graveyards of Trinity Church and nearby St. Paul's Chapel are the settings for numerous ghost stories.

New York City Ghost Stories tells us of the "cackling" of Adam Allyn in the Trinity Church Graveyard.

Allyn is entombed in section north-three. His tombstone, according to the official church brochure, features a "unique and intriguing epitaph." It is only marked, "Comedian," Allyn's profession. He passed away en route to a show but has apparently never stopped performing. His spirit snickers as visitors to the cemetery walk by.

A tomb with an unusual array of inhabitants just off the Broadway entrance holds the remains of War of 1812 naval officer Capt. James Lawrence ("Don't Give Up the Ship!"), Mrs. Lawrence, and Lt. Augustus C. Ludlow, second in command to Capt. Lawrence on the frigate *Chesapeake*. Perhaps due to the highly unorthodox situation, or reasons known only to Ludlow, he has been said to appear and tell war tales to anyone who might listen.

St. Paul's Chapel
Fulton Street and Broadway
Graveyard at Vesey Street and Broadway

St. Paul's Chapel. *Courtesy of John Allen, Dir. – Parish Communications.*

The oldest church in the City, the Episcopal St. Paul's Chapel was built in 1766. Trinity Church is its parent church.

On the Chapel's interior's north side is a painting of the United States coat of arms, marking George Washington's pew. On the south side, Governor Clinton's pew is indicated by the arms of New York State. Trinity Church is the location of the service following George Washington's inauguration as President.

For more than thirty years, the World Trade Center framed the steeple of St. Paul's Chapel. Now, following the terrorist annihilation of the World Trade Center, you can see past St. Paul's to the World Financial Center.

The front railings of St. Paul's were festooned with memorials to those who lost their lives, and thanks to the living who all helped out in the rescue and recovery efforts. The Chapel became a supply station and haven for the rescue – later recovery – workers, where they could rest, pray, and reflect.

A *New York Times* article reported that St. Paul's closed in order for a hazardous materials clean-up to take place to get the Chapel up and running fully again for not only its congregation, but also the general population. St. Paul's is once again reopened to the general public. The scuff marks on the back of pews have not been covered over, however, to honor the rescue and recovery workers who took solace, and very often slept in their work boots, in those hallowed pews.

St. Paul's Chapel Graveyard. *Courtesy of John Allen, Dir. — Parish Communications.*

Metropolitan Museum of Art conservationists and students cleaned and mended damaged gravestones and memorials of its cemetery, some of which date back to the 1600s.

New York City Ghost Stories tells us about the ghost of George Frederick Cooke in St. Paul's graveyard.

George Frederick Cooke was the first major British actor to perform in the United States. Cooke was most notable for his Park Lane Theatre performance of "Richard III" wherein 2,000 patrons clamored to see the famous Cooke.

Cooke was an artist but no businessman. As such, his debts mounted until he saw no way out, except one.

A trailblazer in organ donation, Cooke sold his own head, while still alive, to a Philadelphia medical school, so his escalating medical bills could someday be paid. After his death, people whispered that his flesh was peeled from his skull, and that his skull was later used in productions of "Hamlet."

Cooke is interred headless in the churchyard. His small specter is reported searching the graveyard in vain, forever looking for his lost head.

QUEENS - Long Island City
Calvary Cemetery

A *Brooklyn Daily Eagle* of 1900 garnered great interest with the story:

"Policemen See Things, A Blood Curdling Ghost Story From Long Island City."

It was related that on a night in 1900, a white hearse pulled by snow white horses raced through a side gate of Calvary Cemetery at midnight. A clock tolled the hour when the steeds bolted out, swung through the gate and raced down the road at a wild gallop.

Two uniform policemen were stationed by the Calvary Cemetery gate. Thinking something was amiss, one officer started to take off after the frenzied steeds.

"Come back! Come back!" hollered his fellow officer, but only to himself. "Don't you see that it is a ghostly turnout?"

The other man scoffed at the fear of his comrade but never got over the sight of those ghostly horses.

Those same officers were at the identical posts the following midnight. Again, a hearse and four white horses barreled out of the gate at a spirited pace and raced down the road just like the previous night.

As a result, the two officers were so shaken up it was almost impossible for them to resume normal duty. When relieved in the early morning, they were overjoyed to escape the ghostly doings of the Cemetery and return to the police station of "Fourth Street, this city."

The account related by the officers was that the graveyard gate was always bolted at night, which apparently did not stop the supernatural steeds in their nightly trek. They glided right through the closed gate like thick white mist and were down the road before the frightened observer had a chance to get a look at them.

The police account was that there was an invisible energy holding the observer to the site, rendering it impossible to follow the ghostly steeds on their nightly ride.

Maspeth Lutheran and Mount Olivet Cemeteries
Near Maspeth and Fresh Pond

This story comes from an 1884 *New York Times.*

Gloomy swamps, stagnant marshes, and dense vegetation at one time lay between the Lutheran and Mount Olivet Cemeteries, in what was then considered Long Island. There, a ghost,

"...[S]quatted himself, much to the annoyance and alarm of the residents of that quiet neighborhood."

One Thursday afternoon, women and girls were noiselessly collecting peas for the evening dinner on the farm of Mr. W.H. Ring, which was situated nearby Mount Olivet Cemetery and flanked by Newtown Road.

Screams were suddenly heard from the cemetery. With a burst of compassion and inquisitiveness, the pea pickers abandoned their pails and headed in the direction of the screams. They followed the screams to the edge of a pool, where it dwindled away into a empty groan. The women raced to Ring's farmhouse and related the tale to him and were so petrified, they refused to resume with their work.

Ring believed them and escorted the women and girls to the town constable, Henry Bosch. He had heard tales of the strange voice and an accompanying presence, depicted as a "tall man, six feet in height and perfectly nude."

Like something out of the Wild West, Bosch quickly gathered a posse. Accompanied by ten "able-bodied citizens," he put out to resolve the mystery, "leaving the trembling and admiring women behind."

The sun was barely going down when the posse reached the boundaries of the Cemetery. At the fence, one man stated he had forgotten to take a bag of flour home to his wife and if the other gents would pardon him, he was heading home to do just that. Without the flour there would be no supper. Secondly, night was coming. While he was unafraid, he did not cotton to the idea of traipsing about a graveyard at night.

The other men seconded his feelings about being in a graveyard late at night and returned to Bosch's house. There, they were greeted by a great throng, including Barbara Emerine, who swore she, too, had seen the specter often, that he was "tall and thin, always dressed in white, and that he brandished a huge carving knife."

Soon the grave digger joined in as well as stonecutter John Devon. Both were thought to be "honorable men." The posse was now fifty and set out just before midnight, with fifty shotguns, heading to Mount Olivet Cemetery.

When they arrived at the site in question, they too heard the mysterious cry and moved toward it. As hard as they tried, the wails kept its distance from them. The posse trampled through the mud for about a mile, until reaching the Lutheran Cemetery, where the strange voice stopped and was heard no more.

The following night, the brave constable again assembled a posse, and followed the voice, with the identical results as the prior night, which sent the men home baffled and scared.

Those who heard the unearthly cries between the two Cemeteries grew in number. Doors were prudently bolted, "and prayers more often said then ever before, even in that moral community."

The source for the cries of the Lutheran and Mount Olivet Cemeteries was never found.

Staten Island Emerson Hill Cemetery

The neighborhood was named for William Emerson, Richmond County judge and brother of Ralph Waldo Emerson. William Emerson kept a summer home, "The Snuggery," on today's Emerson Hill where he welcomed his brother and employed Henry David Thoreau briefly in 1843 to tutor his son.

According to *New York City Ghost Stories*, in late summer 1921, a "tombstone-toting, trolley-chasing" specter sent locals and police into a "tizzy." The tale focused around the old Emerson Hill Cemetery.

Trolley motorman John Haynes swore he had two encounters with the spirit in the sparsely-settled neighborhood. The first time was at twilight one day when, as his trolley rumbled by the graveyard, he saw a spectral object float through the Cemetery wall. He said it was toting a tombstone on its back.

On an early Friday morning in August, when Haynes turned his one-man car from Clove

Road onto Oak Street, he saw the ghost again. Haynes said the "misty and sad-looking" specter come into the front door of the vehicle, roamed through the car, and exited through a closed window.

Haynes screamed, which caused more than a dozen young men to come running from a nearby hillside.

He told the young men of the ghost and they took off in fast pursuit of the specter. All this commotion resulted in officials of nearby St. Simon's Church calling the police, who entered into the fray.

Neighbors hung up amulets and talismans to keep the specter from their doors, while nosy visitors crowded to the Cemetery hoping to see the "tombstone-toting ghost of Emerson Hill."

BROOKLYN - SUNSET PARK - Green-Wood Cemetery
Fifth to McDonald Avenues and 20th to 37th Streets

Green-Wood Cemetery. Courtesy of Kenneth A. Taylor, VP – Operations.

The famous Green-Wood Cemetery opened in 1840 and soon became *the* place to take a picnic or a leisurely stroll in. A milestone in internment customs, (which up until that time were relegated to family plots and churchyards), Green-Wood Cemetery fast became a stylish expedition for Victorian strollers who fancied "taking fresh air in a funereal setting."

Among those interred there are Lola Montez, Samuel F.B. Morse, "Boss Tweed," Henry Ward Beecher, and Peter Cooper. The Cemetery is fascinating not only for those interred here but also for its Victorian tombstones. To commemorate the unique lives and deaths of those laid to rest, the tombstones include steamboats going to their watery graves, smashed railroad cars, fire hydrants, children's beds and chairs without an occupant, and troupes of angels kneeling, standing or overcome with sorrow.

A *Brooklyn Daily Eagle* of 1893 related the story of the ghost of Green-Wood Cemetery.

Parfitt and Fergerson were on their way to Brooklyn on a Bath Beach and West End train from Bensonhurst (Brooklyn was not yet incorporated, and so each section was a city unto itself). It was twilight, April 17th and the sun had set.

As their train approached Green-Wood Cemetery, they saw a light emanating from the Cemetery about one hundred yards from them, higher than the tree tops.

The train followed the side of the Cemetery fence for over a mile. All the while, the light followed alongside. Fergerson saw it first, called Parfitt's attention to it, and they mentioned it to the five women in their party who saw it also.

It was not a reflection from a lamp on the train. The seven witnesses even cupped their hands to the side of their faces and peered out the train windows to insure being mislead by a light reflection. They later described what they saw as roughly the size of a football or a human head. Sparks of fire shot backward from it like hair.

In an article in a 1996 *Brooklyn Bridge* magazine, Green-Wood Cemetery tour guide John Cashman related tales he heard when he worked at the cemetery as a young lad.

The old grave diggers told him about the specter of a little child who left her hand prints in the iron fences, and the woman whose hair turned white after she was accidentally locked in a mausoleum overnight.

EAST FLATBUSH - Holy Cross Cemetery
Brooklyn and Tilden Avenue

Our final story is "The Man in the Gray Overcoat," courtesy of *Fate* Magazine.

It was a hot, sticky Sunday in 1910. Every Sunday, the family of Louise Pantozzi-LeClaire had to keep their Sunday best on after mass and head right to the Cemetery to visit their grandmother's grave.

While Louise's mother prayed at her mother's grave in Italian, Louise wandered around. The Cemetery was empty. She stumbled over to a mausoleum and sat down on its bench of stone and noticed the graves there were much older than where her grandmother was interred and that the grass had not been trimmed for quite some time.

Immediately, she felt a odd feeling of cold "as if someone had placed a piece of ice down the back of her dress." Her heart raced and she saw an eerie refection in a pool of nearby water. She suspected it was one of her brothers playing tricks.

Suddenly, standing before Louise, was a man well over six feet tall. His face was ashen with white lips and deep sunken eyes and was dressed in "winter fashion," all in gray.

Louise wanted to cry out and backed up. The man moved toward her. His eyes, "black as the night," seemed to look right through her.

"Do you see me?" His voice came out in an unearthly echo.

"Y-yes I do!" she cried.

The man moved closer and said:

"When you see me, run!"

The man stepped back and vanished.

Louise just sat there, stunned. Finally she ran, screaming for her mother. For what seemed like an eternity, on legs that felt like they could not move, Louise heard her mother calling out. She ran to her fast.

"Where were you Louise? Answer me!" she pleaded in her broken English.

"Mama, there was a man! He was horrible-looking. All in gray! And Mama, he disappeared right before my eyes!"

Her mother saw her tears, pulled her closer, and placed her hands on her shoulders. Her mother crossed herself and Louise's sisters and brothers all drew closer to her.

They walked along while their mother called out in both Italian and English for the stranger to show himself, but no one answered. Their mother pulled them close as she hurried them along.

Louise asked, tugging at her mother's skirts:

"Mama, do you think it was...a ghost?"

Her mother gave no reply.

And they never again returned to Holy Cross Cemetery.

Bibliography

Adams, Charles J. III. *New York City Ghost Stories: Chilling, True Encounters with the Supernatural in the World's Most Exciting - and Haunted - City*. Reading, Pennsylvania: Exeter House Books, 1996, ISBN 1-880683-09-1.

Alcamo, Michael. Letters to the Editor. "The Mixed Reputation of Sullivan Street's Namesake," *New York Times*, June 12, 1994, City Section, page 17.

Anbinder, Tyler. *Five Points: The 19th-Century New York City Neighborhood That Invented Tap Dance, Stole Elections, and Became the World's Most Notorious Slum*, New York: copyright 2001 by Tyler G. Ambinder. Reprinted with permission of The Free Press, an imprint of Simon & Schuster Trade Publishing Group.

Asimov, Eric. "Jinx? What Jinx? Restaurateurs Defy Bad Traffic Flow and Bad Karma. Sometimes the Force Is With Them," *New York Times*, April 6, 1997.

Bahrampour, Tara. "Celebrating a Sea of Faith, Still at the Full," *New York Times*, February 25, 2001, City section.

Becker, Maki and Singleton, Don. "Mummified tot found," *New York Daily News*, November 7, 1999, © *New York Daily News*, L.P., reprinted with permission.

Bell, Bill. "Slave revolt scarred N.Y.," *New York Daily News*, December 14, 1997.

Berger, Leslie. "Exclusive Key Club Renews Its Membership," *New York Times*, August 13, 2000.

Berger, Meyer. "About New York: Haunted-House Party Plans a Macabre Menu," *New York Daily News*, March 5, 1956.

Berger, Meyer. "About New York: Quest for Haunted Houses Here Finds Ghosts Shun Metropolis of Steel and Concrete," *New York Daily News*, February 29, 1956.

Berman, Connie and Katz, Susan. "Here's a ghostly guidebook to New York: Listing some haunts, spooks, spectres and apparitions and places where they get together for rapping sessions," *New York Daily News*, 17 February 1974.

Blue Guide New York, Federal Writers Project. New York: Random House, 1939, Reprinted, New York: Pantheon Press, 1982.

Boland, Ed., Jr. "Spirit Hot Spot," F.Y.I., *New York Times*, City section, page 2, 27 October, 2002. Copyright @ 2002, The New York Times Co. Reprinted by permission.

Botkin, B.A. *New York City Folklore: Legends, Tall Tales, Anecdotes, Stories, Sagas, Heroes and Characters, Customs, Traditions and Sayings*, New York: Random House, 1956, from Wellman. Manly Wade. *Look Behind You! Ghost, Demons and Haunted Houses of the Metropolitan Area*, New York City: from Researches of the Federal Writers' Project, Manuscripts of the Federal Writers' Project of the Work Progress Administration, 1938.

Bridge Cafe brochure.

Brooklyn Daily Eagle. "Flushing has a ghost that frightens Coppers, the police Headquarters in the Village Declared to be Haunted It is a feminine Ghost, Patrolman Hanniman's Experience. One Night in the House Caused Him to Seek a Transfer to Brooklyn," October 3, 1902.

Brooklyn Daily Eagle. "Ghost in a Flathouse Rang Electric Bells, Stuyvesant Heights Revels In Proud Possession of a Genuine Haunted House, Griffins Frightened Away, School Principal and His Wife Say They Heard Hollow Groans and Creepy Steps on Stairs," October 23, 1901.

Brooklyn Daily Eagle. "Ghost Not Found Yet, But Some of the Marines are Certainly Justifying Their Ancient Reputation," September 24, 1901.

Brooklyn Daily Eagle. "Ghost at the Navy Yard Startles the Marines, Corporal McNeal and Bates Have Seen It and Have Felt a Mysterious Influence, Whole Guard on the Hunt, A Mysterious Figure with its head Bandages Up Is Pursued and Disappears," September 23, 1901.

Brooklyn Daily Eagle. "Queer Doings Nightly Around a Flushing House," Weird Noises, Clanging Bell, Flying Stones,

Knocks and Explosions Disturb Mrs. Bogert, he Thinks it Isn't Ghosts, There Are Ghost Symptoms, However, And Those Who Believe in the Uncanny Are Nodding Wisely," April 1, 1901.

Brooklyn Daily Eagle. "The Ghost was a Woman who did not Pay Rent, For Hamilton Avenue Mystery Solved By Finding Her in Chimney, Only One Foot was Visible, For Weeks, Mrs. Barrett Had Disturbed a While Neighborhood and Puzzled Searching Policemen," August 29, 1900.

Brooklyn Daily Eagle. "Policemen See Things, A Blood Curdling Ghost Story From Long Island City," January 21, 1900.

Brooklyn Daily Eagle. "Miss Anna Rosen Frightened by Phantom Scorcher," August 21, 1896.

Brooklyn Daily Eagle. "News From the Suburbs: The Police looking for an Italian Rag Picker's Ghost: Tat appears in Brownsville: It frightens returning Picnickers and has caused Sleeplessness and Excitement in that Neighborhood," June 2, 1896.

Brooklyn Daily Eagle. "News From the Suburbs: Another Ghost Said to be Walking in Flatbush: Looking for his Loose hand: Charles Norton Finds the Member When Digging in His Cellar and His Wife Thinks the House is Haunted," April 20, 1896.

Brooklyn Daily Eagle. "Latest Long Island News, A Brooklyn Family's Experience With a Rockaway Spook, They Moved out in a Hurry, Property Deserted by Tenants on Account of Continued Uncanny Visitations and Unearthly Noises," January 8, 1896.

Brooklyn Daily Eagle. "The Ghost of Melrose Hall," October 13, 1895.

Brooklyn Daily Eagle. "Haunts the Station House: This Ghost May be The Shade of Lizzie Rose," December 10, 1894.

Brooklyn Daily Eagle. "Mr. Parfitt's Ghost Story," April 23, 1893.

Brooklyn Daily Eagle. "Ghosts in Dean Street," January 10, 1892.

Brooklyn Historical Society Library Scrapbook, Volume 83, "The Old Road Houses, Changes Which Have Taken Place in Thirty Yrs., The Recollections of Mr. Peter Ravenhall-The Haunted House, Hicks Post, the Old Toll gate and Their Associates, Some Interesting Reminiscences." undated (approximately late 1800's).

Brooks, Michael W. Subway City: Riding the Trains, Reading New York, New Brunswick, New Jersey: Rutgers University Press, 1997.

Burrows, Edwin G. & Wallace, Mike. Gotham: A History of New York City to 1895, New York: Oxford University Press, 1999.

Chayefsky, Paddy. Television Plays, New York: Simon and Shuster, 1955.

Chevalier, George. "Sail of the Century: Success and Sad Fate of Henry Hudson Vivified at Maritime Museum," Woodstock, New York: Woodstock Times, November 25, 1992, quoting Johnson, Donald S., Charting the Sea of Darkness, New York: International Marine/McGraw Hill, 1992.

Cleaves, Henderson. "No Kidd-ing, Boro's Specters Are a Paine," New York World-Telegram, March 24, 1958.

Clyne, Patricia Edwards. Hudson Valley Tales and Trails, Woodstock, New York: Overlook Press, 1990.

Cohen, Daniel. Encyclopedia of Ghosts. New York: Dorset Books, 1984.

Cohen, Joyce. "A Long Sense of History, and a Private Park, New York Times, August 29, 1999.

Copquin, Claudia Gryvatz. "Names of New York: Barrow Street," Newsday, May 25, 2000.

Cronin, Anne. "The Ghosts of Graveyards," New York Times, Metro section, May 23, 1993.

Custen, George F. "Yes! It's Him! Whaddya Mean, Never Heard of Him?" New York Times, City section, September 3, 2000.

Daly, Michael. "Some brass tacks of slavery revealed," New York Daily News, December 7, 1997.

Delaney, Edmund T. and Lockwood, Charles. Greenwich Village: A Photographic Guide. New York: Dover Publications, Inc., 1980.

De Voe, Thomas F. The Market Book, Containing a Historical Account of the Public Markets in the Cities of New York Boston Philadelphia and Brooklyn with a brief description of every Article of Human Food sold therein, The Introduction of Cattle in America and Notices of Many Remarkable Specimens. Burt Franklin: New York. Reprinted 1969 in two volumes, Vol. I.

Diehl, Lorraine. "The intentional tourist," New York Daily News, December 9, 2001, Lifeline section.

Donovan, Aaron. "Isolated Brooklyn Area Starts to Awaken," New York Times, Real Estate section, June 10, 2001.

Dowd, Maureen. "Is New York Too Scary Even for its Ghosts," New York Times, October 31, 1985.

Dunlap, David W. "Near Ground Zero, Unbowed Spires," New York Times, Real Estate section, September 30, 2001.

Dunning, Jennifer. "Meredith Monk Looks Into Roosevelt Island's Past," New York Times, September 22, 1994.

Dupont, Inge and Mayo, Hope. Morgan Library Ghost Stories. New York: Fordham University Press, 1990.

Ferris, Marc. "Dwellings in the past," Brooklyn, New York: Brooklyn Bridge Magazine.

Fischler, Stan. Uptown, Downtown. New York: Hawthorne Books, 1976.

Fodor, Joe. "Anonymous beginnings," Brooklyn, New York: Brooklyn Bridge Magazine, May 1997.

Fodor, Joe. "History Moves on," Brooklyn, New York: Brooklyn Bridge Magazine, March, 1997.

Fodor, Joe. "Hunting for ghosts in the 'hood: They're spectral, they're dead, and they're hauntingly familiar." Brooklyn, New York: *Brooklyn Bridge* Magazine, October, 1996.

Fodor, Joe. "Kings County Almanac: Washington Schlepped here." Brooklyn, New York: *Brooklyn Bridge* Magazine, August, 1996.

Fodor, Joe. "Open for interpretation," Brooklyn, New York: *Brooklyn Bridge* Magazine, October, 1996.

Glueck, Grace and Gardner, Paul. *Brooklyn: People and Places, Past and Present*, New York: Harry N. Abrams, Inc. Publishers, 1991.

Gordon, David. "Whatever Else Changes in Brooklyn, the Traditional Ghosts Remain," *New York Times*, Brooklyn – Queens – Long Island section, May 18, 1975.

Gray, Christopher. "A Block that Offers the Quintessence of NoHo," *New York Times*, January 17, 1999. Copyright 2002 by the *New York Times* Co. Reprinted by permission.

Gray, Christopher. "Cornerstone Building on a Block of Artists' Studios," *New York Times*, Real Estate section, May 14, 2000.

Gray, Christopher. "Fixture on the Block May Face an Upstart Neighbor," *New York Times*, Real Estate section, December 30, 2001.

Gray, Christopher. "For Rent: 3-Floor House, 9 1/2 Ft. Wide, $6,000 a Month," *New York Times*, Real Estate section, November 10, 1996.

Gray, Christopher. "Poe's Last Home, 1810's Cottage That's a Museum," *New York Times*, Long Island Real Estate section, March 18, 2001.

Gray, Christopher. "Preserving a Ruin on Roosevelt Island Proves Costly," *New York Times*, September 22, 1996.

Gray, Christopher. "A Residence With a View, Even Without the Mayor," *New York Times*, Real Estate section, May 26, 2002.

Gray, Christopher. "Street of Lush Gardens and Architectural Coherence," *New York Times*, July 6, 1997.

Grimes, William. "A Gang of Ghosts, Ready to Rumble," *New York Daily News*, October 29, 1993.

"A Guide to Guides: All you Need to Know," *New York Times*, January 21, 1996.

Guiterman, Arthur. *Ballads of Old New York*, New York: E.P. Dutton & Co. Inc. 1939.

Hamill, Denis. "Ghost story comes with a punch line." *New York Daily News*, September 19, 1999, © *New York Daily News* L.P., reprinted with permission.

Hamill, Denis. "3 Haunting Tales." *New York Daily News*, October 30, 1994." © *New York Daily News* L.P. reprinted with permission."

Hammerstein, Oscar Andy. "Call It the Hammerstein," *New York Daily News*, Letters, Week in Review section, March 25, 1995.

Hanscom, Leslie. "Still Mystified By Weird Noises After 2 Months," *Brooklyn Daily Eagle*, January 25 & 27, 1952.

Harney, John. "Streets full of lovers," *New York Daily News*, Spotlight section, February 18, 1996.

Hauck, Dennis William. *The National Directory of Haunted Places*. Sacramento, California: Athanor Press, 1994.

Haviland, J.C. "More Ghosts Walk the Hudson Valley." *Kingston (New York) Daily Freeman*, October 26, 1983.

Hays, Constance L. "Life Above the High Notes," *New York Times*, City section, January 5, 1997.

Hays, Tom. "Mom gets 25-life in death of mummy-tot," Brooklyn, New York: *Brooklyn Paper*, November 6, 2000.

Hecht, Ben. "The Ogling Corpse," from *1001 Afternoons in New York*, New York: Viking Press, 1941 from Botkin, B.A., *New York City Folklore*, New York: Random House, 1956.

Heiman, J.D. "Tales from the Urman Crypt: Legendary Whoppers about Gotham's Buildings, Subways, Hotels and Bridges run Ghastly and Ghostly Gambit," *New York Daily News*, September 13, 1998.

From Hans Holzer's *America's Haunted Houses: Public and Private*, © 1991, Stamford, Connecticut: Longmeadow Press.

From Hans Holzer's *Best True Ghost Stories*, ©1983, Englewood Cliffs, New Jersey: Prentice Hall.

From Hans Holzer's *Ghost Hunter*, ©1963, New York: The Bobbs-Merrill Company, Inc.

From Hans Holzer's "The Ghost of Gay Street and Other Gotham Chillers," *New York Daily News* Magazine, October 26, 1986, reprinted with permission.

From Hans Holzer's *Great American Ghost Stories*, ©1990, New York: Dorset Press.

From Hans Holzer's *Haunted America*, ©1993, New York: Barnes & Noble Books.

Holzer, Hans. *The Spirits of '76: A Psychic Inquiry into the American Revolution*, ©1976, New York: Bobbs-Merrill Company, Inc.

Hopkins, M. Daly. "Ten Years with a ghost," *Fate* Magazine, 1954.

Horowitz, Larry. "Where the stars shine." *New York Daily News*, January 9, 1994, quoting *New York City Starwalks*. New York: Street Martin's Press, 1993.

Huggett, Richard. *Supernatural on Stage: Ghosts of the Theatre*, New York: Taplinger Publishing Co., 1975.

Innaurato, Albert. "Notes on Madama Butterfly." *Metropolitan Opera Stage Bill*, New York, April 1997.

Jones, Charisse, "Bringing Slavery's Long Shadow to the Light," *New York Times*, April 2, 1995.

Kennedy, X.J. "The Man Who Hitched the Reindeer To Santa Claus's Sleigh," *New York Times*, Book Review, December 3, 1993.

Kinetz, Erika. "A Patch of Dirt With a Haunting Past," *New York Times*, November 4, 2001.

Kirby, David. "Old House's Future Debated," *New York Times*, City section, January 11, 1998.

Kornblutt, Anne E. "New York Haunts," *New York Daily News*, Spotlight section, October 15, 1995.

Krajicek, David J. "Woman down the Well," *New York Daily News*, January 7, 2001.

Lanigan Schmidt, Therese. *Ghostly Beacons: Haunted Lighthouses of North America*, Atglen, Pennsylvania: Schiffer Publishing, Ltd., 2000.

Lanigan-Schmidt, Therese. *Ghosts of the Catskills and Beyond*, 1994, unpublished manuscript.

LeDuff, Charlie. "Bending Elbows: The Living and a Ghost, All Preserved in Whiskey," *New York Times*, June 11, 2000.

Lee, Denny. "A Deal Could Give a Tower's Neighbor 2 More Centuries, *New York Times*, City section, March 11, 2001.

Lee, Denny. "The Fall of the House of Poe (Unless Scholars Prevail), *New York Times*, City section, July 2, 2000.

Legend of the Storm Ship.

Leyda, Jay. *The Melville Log: A Documentary Life of Herman Melville 1819-1891*, Volume One. New York: Harcourt, Brace and Company, 1951.

Lipkin, Lisa. "Gasp! City's Ghosts Evoked," *New York Times*, October 30, 1994.

Lippincott, E.E. "Unsavory Past, Great Design and a Makeover Looms," *New York Times*, March 3, 2002.

McCullough, David W. *Brooklyn...And How It Got That Way*. New York: The Dial Press, 1983.

McNamara, Joseph. "Deadly Draft," *New York Daily News*, March 19, 1995.

Melville, Herman. *Moby Dick*, New York: Bantam Books, 1981; Layda Jay. *The Melville Log: A Documentary Life of Herman Melville 1819-1981*, Volume One, New York: Harcourt Brace, and Company, 1951.

Merchant's House Museum Newsletter, April/Summer 1995, Spring 2001.

Millner, Denene. "Once on this island," *New York Times*, Lifeline section, January 30, 2000.

Molyneux, Michael. "Joined in Romance, and Scandal," *New York Daily News*, February 11, 1996.

Murphy, Robert T. "Shadowy Spectre of Fear," *Phoenix*, October 26, 1978.

Myers, Arthur. *The Ghostly Register*. New York: The McGraw-Hill Companies, reprinted with permission, © 1986.

Myers, Arthur. *The Ghosts of the Rich and Famous*. Chicago, Illinois: Contemporary Books, 1988.

Nevins, Allan and Thomas, Milton Halsey, eds. *The Diary of George Templeton Strong*, New York: The Macmillan Co.

New York Chronicle, "Other Assorted Ghosts," Vol. 2 Number 2, 1987, *Memorial History of New York*.

New York City Guide: Federal Writers' Project (WPA), Random House, New York, 1939, Reprint, New York: Pantheon, 1982.

New York Daily News. Lifeline, July 18, 1999.

New York Herald Tribune, "News From the Suburbs, Long Island Sees Another Ghost," April 20, 1884.

New York Times. "City Haunts: A Ghostly Guide," October 29, 1995, © 2001 by the *New York Times Co*. Reprinted by permission.

New York Times. "A Night for Ghosts, Real and Unreal," October 30, 1986, ©1986 by the *New York Times Co*. Reprinted by permission.

New York Times. "1,000 in Brooklyn Seek Ghost on Roof," August 14, 1936.

New York Times. "Yorkville's Ghost is Crowded Out," July 30, 1936; "Banshee Turns Up in 86th Street Flat: Former Tenant of Place Now Vacant Insists it Is Haunted by a Woman in White: $10,000 Doubter Is Told, Skeptic With Money to Back Hip Opinion Will Visit House-Hopes for the Worst," July 28, 1936, ©2002 by the *New York Times Co*. Reprinted with permission.

New York Times."Gold Ghost Walks in Astoria House: Psychic Expert, Called to Old Frame House, Unable to Explain Garratings and Attacks: Treasure Pit in Cellar; Man and Woman Continue Dismal Search After Rooms are Routed by "Spirit," November 21, 1934.

New York Times. "Ghostly Pianist Arouses Flushing: Sad, Classical Music Issues Nightly From Attic of Deserted Dwelling," December 31, 1927.

New York Times. "The Ghost Decline to Walk: Hundred Waited for Him and were much Disappointed at his Absence," August 20, 1894.

New York Times."Ghost or Alcoholic Spirits: Coney Island's Alleged Apparition Investigated: Fred Bader and Dr. Ward Say They Have Seen It, and that When Pursued It Floated Away on the Air-Many Other Residents Did Not See the Ghost." August 29, 1893.

New York Times. "A Ghost at the Battery: Policemen and Boatmen Ready to Swear they Saw a Spook," December 2, 1892.

New York Times. "Ghosts in Myrtle Avenue: Stalwart Policemen on duty in a Haunted House," July 16, 1888.

New York Times. "Following an Elusive Voice: Posses of Men Hunting in Vain a Ghost on Long Island," July 27, 1884.

New York Times. "A Very Rude Ghost: The Flaming Apparition Which Deluded Some Strictly Sober Firemen," October 11, 1883.

New York Times. "The Fourteenth-Street Ghosts: No Clue Discovered Yet to the Invaders of Mrs. Carr's House," June 25, 1881.

New York Times. "Two Spectral Lodgers: Ghosts in a Fourteenth-Street Boarding-House: Boarders Frightened away and Servants in Terror-What Persons who have seen the Phantoms say; and"Officer Quinn's Spectre," June 24, 1881.

New York Times. "The City of Phenomena: Ghosts in Brooklyn: Door-Bells Ring, Doors Rattled, and a Brick Thrown Through a Window-A Vain Search for Small Boys," December 21, 1878.

New York Times. "A Ghost in Long Island City," January 29, 1874.

New York Times. "Staten Island," October 4, 1873.

New York Times, Editorial, 1872.

New York Times. "Raising A Ghost: True History of the Twenty-seventh-street Goblin," September 18, 1870.

Norman, Michael and Scott, Beth. Historic Haunted America. New York: Tom Doherty Associates Books, 1995.

Norris, Kathleen. "Too Long at the Fair," Poets & Writers Magazine, September/October 1995.

Norwich, William. "House of Mirth: When Benjamin Sonnenberg lived here, it was party central," New York Times Magazine, May 16, 2000.

O'Regan, Michael. "Dead Men walking," New York Daily News, January 28, 1996.

Oser, Alan S. ""New Landlord, Old Tenants, Hard Questions, New York Times, Real Estate Section, February 27, 2000.

Poets & Writers Magazine, March/April 1995.

Poniewozik, James. "Stages of Development," Book review of Ghost Light by Frank Rich, Time Magazine, October 30, 2000.

Rasenberger, Jim. "The Witch of Staten Island," New York Times, October 29, 2000.

Rattray, Jeannette Edward. Perils of the Port of New York: Maritime Disasters from Sandy Hook to Execution Rocks," New York: Dodd, Mead & Company, 1973.

Regan, Michael P. "Dead Men Walking," New York Daily News, January 28, 1996, Spotlight.

Regan, Michael P. "Life and loves of a B'way hellraiser," New York Daily News, April 14, 1996.

Reidel, Michael. "James Dean's walk on the West Side," New York Daily News., Spotlight section, September 24, 1995.

Reynolds, James. Ghosts in American Houses, New York: Bonanza Books, 1955.

Riccio, Dolores, Bingham, Joan. Haunted Houses USA, New York: Pocket Books, 1989.

Richmond, Clergyman J.F. New York and Its Institutions, 1869.

Riedel, Michael. "A Walk On The Wild Side: New guidebook maps out the red-hot gossip about the rich, famous & infamous of Greenwich Village," New York Daily News, June 11, 1995, excerpting Greenwich Village, by John Gilman and Robert Heide.

Rhode, David. "A New Life for an Old Club," New York Times, March 16, 1997.

Rostler, Suzanne. "Disney tries Deuce dance," New York Daily News, September 25, 1994.

Roura, Phil. New York Daily News, September 13, 1998. Extra section.

Rutenberg, James. "Curtain Up!" New York Daily News, July 30, 1995.

Schwartzman, Paul. "Central Park's vanished black settlement," New York Daily News, January 19, 1997.

Senning, Judith A., as told to by her maternal grandmother, Pantozzi-LeClaire, Louise, "True Mystic Experiences: The Man in the Gray Overcoat," Fate Magazine, November, 1985,

Sheinman, Allen J. "Other Assorted Ghosts," The New York Chronicle, No. 2, Number 2, 1987.

Shelton, William Henry. The Jumel Mansion, New York: Houghton Mifflin, 1916.

Singleton, Don. "It's the best haunt in town," New York Daily News, October 31, 1993.

Spisak, Maureen. "My Proof of Survival: A Knock at the Door." Fate Magazine, December 1990.

Spooks and Spirits at Home

Stafford, Sam. Sidewalks of New York. Walking Tours

Steinhauer, Jennifer. "Watery Spring Street," New York Times, F.Y.I. Column, January 9, 1994.

Steinhauer, Jennifer. "A Worn Gracie Mansion Awaits Its Face-Lift," Metro section, New York Times, April 28, 2002.

Stevens, Kimberly. "Inn's Ghost Liked Smoke, but Fire?" New York Daily News, February 2, 1997. Copyright c 2002. New York Times Co. Reprinted by permission.

Sweeney, Matthew. "Plymouth gets nod as 'Grand Central' of Underground RR," The Brooklyn Paper, October 10-16, 1997.

Tawa, Renee. "'Twas his poem - or 'twasn't it?" Los Angeles Times, December 22, 2000.

Thrush, Glenn. "The Fireman's Legs and Other Ghost Stories." Downtown Express, New York, May 22, 1991.

Ultan, Lloyd. The Beautiful Bronx (1920-1950), written in collaboration with the Bronx Historical Society, New York:

Harmony Books, 1979.

Vaughan, Causewell. "A ghost of a chance for you." *New York Daily News*, October 26, 1980.

Vidal, Gore. *Burr, A Novel*. New York: Bantam Books, 1976.

von Pressentin Wright, Carol. *Blue Guide New York*. New York: W.W. Norton & Co., Inc., 1991.

Wakin, Daniel J. "Huddled Masses of City Statuary Face Eviction," *New York Times*, City Section, October 15, 2000.

Walker, Danton. *I Believe in Ghosts*. New York: Taplinger Publishing Co., 1956.

Walker, Danton. *New York Daily News*, July 1953.

Wolfe, Thomas. *From Death to Morning*. New York: Charles Scribner's Sons, 1970.

Zagat Survey 1997 New York City Restaurants, New York: Zagat LLC, 1997.

Websites

"Shadowlands Haunted Places Index - New York."

Correspondence

E-Mail to me of February 6, 2002 from Tina Skinner.

Letter to me of October 9, 2002 from Lois Rosebrooks, Church Council Secretary, Plymouth Church of the Pilgrims.

Letter to me of June 21, 2000 of Joyce Gold, *Joyce Gold History Tours of New York*.

Letter to me of December 29, 1994 of Quiche Lloyd-Kemble, Executive Director, American Renaissance Theatre quoting from their Dramatic Art's 1994 Haunted and Historic Walking Tour.

Telephone Conversations

With Robert Kohler, October 21, 2002.

With Joseph Esposito, Staff Member, Old Merchant's House Museum, October 16, 2002.

With Adam Weprin, Owner, Bridge Cafe, October 15, 2002.

With Shauna Lazarus, September, 2002.

With Jackie Plant, March 22, 2002.

With Louis Singer, January 9, 1995.

With Eugenie Martin.

Conversations

With Louisa Ruby, October 18, 2002.

With Fred Martinez, April, 2002.

With Laura Correa, March 27, 2002.

With Marie DaGrossa and Michael Meyer-Wakneen, March 21, 2002.

With Robert Diamond, October 2, 1999.

With Rob Warren, May, 1995.

Broadcast Media

New York One, March 15, 1997, "Loew's Paradise, Grand Concourse, the Bronx.

Good Morning America, ABC Television, interview with Johnny Mathis, October 1993.

Lecture

Alvarado, Carlos S., PhD. "Is the Merchant's House Museum Haunted?" April 25, 2001.

Index